Smart Contracting for
Local Government Services

Acknowledgments

This book was written while on a Harkness Fellowship in the U.S. in 1994/5. I was based at the School of Public Administration at the University of Southern California in Los Angeles. I am grateful to my then employers Price Waterhouse for giving me the time off from work in London to undertake the Fellowship. I am also grateful to the New York Commonwealth Fund for funding and organizing my Fellowship.

Countless individuals helped me during my year in the U.S. In particular, I would like to thank the following for their help and support:

Keith Kirby and Robert Kostrewza, formerly of the Commonwealth Fund of New York

Jim Ferris and Elisabeth Graddy of the University of Southern California

Howard Chambers of the City of Lakewood, California

Helene Heller of the City of New York

Ted Gaebler, the consultant and author

Connie Cushman, formerly of the City of New York

David Seader of Price Waterhouse

Dave Bunce of the Rural/Metro Corporation

Ann Kinney of the city of Milwaukee

Chris Brearley, Deputy Secretary of the Department of the Environment, London

Mike Garvey of the City of San Carlos, California

Selma Anderson of the County of Los Angeles

I would like to acknowledge the comments and assistance of Roger Woodgate (also a Harkness Fellow in 1994/5) in preparing Chapter 11 on the Rural/Metro Corporation.

Most of all I would like to thank my wife Cathy for putting up with me when I wrote the book and for accompanying me for the year in Los Angeles.

Contents

Library of Congress Cataloging-in-Publication Data

Lavery, Kevin.
    Smart contracting for local government services : processes and
experience / Kevin Lavery.
        p.   cm. — (Privatizing government, an interdisciplinary
series, ISSN 1087-5603)
    Includes bibliographical references and index.
    ISBN 0-275-96428-0 (alk. paper)
        1. Contracting out—United States.   2. Contracting out—Great
Britain.   3. Local government—United States.   4. Local government—
Great Britain.   5. Privatization—United States—States.
6. Privatization—Great Britain. I. Title. II. Series.
HD3861.U6L38   1999
352.5'38214'0973—dc21   98-33628

British Library Cataloguing in Publication Data is available.

Library of Congress Catalog Card Number: 98-33628

ISBN: 0–275–96428–0
ISSN: 1087-5603

First published in 1999

Praeger Publishers, 88 Post Road West, Westport, CT 06881
An imprint of Greenwood Publishing Group, Inc.
www.praeger.com

Printed in the United States of America

The paper used in this book complies with the
Permanent Paper Standard issued by the National
Information Standards Organization (Z39.48–1984).

10 9 8 7 6 5 4 3 2 1

Smart Contracting for Local Government Services

Processes and Experience

Kevin Lavery

Privatizing Government: An Interdisciplinary Series
Simon Hakim and Gary Bowman, Series Advisers

Westport, Connecticut
London

1

Setting the Scene

THE PUBLIC SECTOR CONTRACTING REVOLUTION

"Privatization" is grabbing the headlines throughout the local government world. Scottsdale, Arizona, contracts for fire protection with a for-profit company, the Rural/Metro Corporation. Baltimore contracted with a Minnesota firm to run nine of the city's schools. There are over 100 "contract cities" in California which have virtually all of their services provided by private firms and other governments. The city of Phoenix regularly gets its employees to compete with the private sector to provide city services. Indianapolis has contracted out its wastewater treatment plant and its airport. Chicago and Philadelphia have contracted for a range of services, from the janitors to the running of major recreational facilities (e.g., Chicago's Soldier Field Stadium). Even New York City, the bastion of the municipal unions, is talking about introducing its own version of managed competition, encouraging city workers to bid for city work in competition with private firms.

Elsewhere in the world things are no different. Indeed, in the U.K., New Zealand, and Australia, the public sector revolution has arguably gone further than in the U.S. In the U.K., for example, the government-owned utilities have been sold, and around one-third of rented public houses have been sold to the tenants. There is also a national system of school-based management and over 1,000 "grant maintained" schools, the equivalent of charter schools except that they are existing rather than new schools. The public bus system has also been deregulated outside London, which means that any firm can provide a bus service wherever it chooses. Finally, a system of mandated public/private competition for local government services has been established, the U.K. version of managed competition, covering a wide range of services from trash collection to legal advice and accounting.

WHAT IS CONTRACTING?

Most people understand the debate to be about "privatization." However, many use the word "privatization" carelessly, and as a result its meaning has become unclear and confused. It is sometimes used to mean voucher schemes for services, such as schooling and social services, and on other occasions asset sales, importing business techniques to the public sector (e.g., performance pay), franchises, public/private partnerships, and, of course, contracting. Genuine privatization is about selling public assets and relinquishing responsibility for services. Moreover, it is only a very small part of the public sector revolution, especially in the U.S. The bulk of the revolution is about contracting-out public services, usually but not exclusively to the private sector. Contracting has become the main alternative to direct service delivery by government employees. Every government entity contracts out something, but no two jurisdictions contract for the same set of services in the same way!

It is important to understand the different types of privatization. Savas (1987) identifies ten methods of service delivery, as set out in Table 1.1. These are ideal types; in practice, there is a wide range of hybrid methods, such as a franchised bus route that is also subsidized (a grant).

In essence, contracting involves one party exchanging a good or service for a reward, usually money. It therefore follows that contracting must involve separating the "provision" and "production" roles—that is, separating those who specify and buy a product or a service from those who perform the tasks. For organizations that were virtually self-sufficient, contracting presented a radical alternative approach. They began asking themselves whether they had to produce everything in-house. This is known as the "make or buy" decision.

Contracting also usually involves an agreement concerning what is needed. In the procurement jargon this is known as the "specification" (the statement of what is required) and the "contract" (the legal agreement). Contracting also usually involves the organization buying the product or service checking to ensure that they get what they asked for. This is called "monitoring" and "contract management." It is often assumed that contracting always involves competition, but in fact this is not the case. Many contracts are awarded without formal competition and, once awarded, tend to be renewed and extended. This approach of developing long-term contractual relationships is particularly popular in the private sector.

Another myth about government contracting is that it is something that only happens in conjunction with the private sector. It is true that most government contracting is with private firms. However, contracting with nonprofit organizations is becoming increasingly popular. There is also a significant amount of contracting with other governments and public agencies: this is referred to as

TABLE 1.1. Alternative Methods of Delivering Public Services

Method	Planning	Delivery	Payment	Example
Government service	Government	Government employees	Government	Municipal police department
Government vending	Another organization	Government employees	Another organization	City-paid-for crowd control
Intergovernmental agreement	Government	Employees of another government	Government	City buys patrol service from County Sheriff
Contract	Government	Another organization	Government	City pays a firm to collect trash
Franchise	Government or consumer	Another organization	Consumer	Resident pays firm to collect trash
Grant	Government and consumer	Private firm	Government and consumer	Subsidized theater
Vouchers	Consumer	Private firm	Consumer	Bus vouchers for the elderly
Market	Consumer	Private firm	Consumer	Individual buys a car
Voluntary service	Voluntary organization	Voluntary organization	N/A	Soup kitchen for homeless
Self-service	Consumer	Consumer	N/A	Residents install alarm in their residences

Source: Savas (1987).

"intergovernmental agreements." Finally, it is possible to have "internal contracting", where one part of a government contracts for a good/service with another part of the organization. This is now common in the U.K., New Zealand, and Australian public sectors and is being practiced by a few U.S. local governments, such as the State of Minnesota and the city of Milwaukee.

Contracting is therefore very different from pure privatization. The government remains responsible for the service—specifying, monitoring, and paying for it. In these circumstances the public will look to the government to ensure that a good service is provided at the right price.

"Smart Contracting"

Contracting can be a complex affair, especially where a service or elaborate capital project is involved. There are many options over what and how to contract. For example, which services are best contracted for, and which ones delivered in other ways? And how should the project or service be packaged for contract? Is it broken down into small discrete areas, the "pepperpot" approach, or bundled into one master contract, the "big bang?" Does the government retain ownership of equipment and other assets, or is this a responsibility of the contractor? Should governments favor public/private competition or simply contract with the private sector? Should the government specify the outputs of the service, or the inputs, or a combination of both?

The "how" questions throw up just as many issues. Is the contract awarded with or without open competition? Does the government want to encourage its employees to bid for the work, especially where they have been doing the work in the past? Does the government contract out the entire package or keep a proportion in-house? How is the contractor to be paid—with a fixed fee or depending on agreed variables—and should performance feature as a factor? Unfortunately, there are no straightforward "right" answers to these questions because they will depend on the service in question, the marketplace, and the government itself.

Unfortunately, much of the debate about contracting has been in the realm of politics. Politicians, ideologues, advocates, and opponents keen to advance or protect their respective positions have monopolized it. Ideologues see contracting as a panacea for everything that they think is bad in government—making government smaller, more efficient, and competitive. By contrast, unions and many managers see it as a threat to their jobs, pay, and conditions. Many elected officials also see it as a threat to their role and power base, while a few see it as an opportunity to make their mark. As a result the rhetoric is high on politics, philosophy, and emotion but ignores the practical issues of how to do contracting well. Moreover, the guidance that is available is drawn from the literature on public procurement. This is based on administration principles developed in the early part of this century to ensure the purchase of the right goods at the lowest cost. This approach is not always well suited to contracting for modern local government services as it takes little account of the conditions to ensure good purchasing of services—the systems, the personnel, and the environment. Meanwhile, the amount of contracting continues to increase.

This book represents an attempt to shift the debate away from the politics and the rhetoric to the practicalities and realities of contracting. The intended audience is the thinking practitioner—elected and appointed officials—as well as academics and students of public policy and administration.

What are the features of "smart contracting?" Which services can contracting be applied to? What are the best contracting strategies? What are the best techniques to use—competitive sealed bids, requests for proposals, or sole source negotiations? The book is also concerned with the strategic contracting issues. Who should the managers be? What skills do they need? What about the management systems? What sort of information is needed? Is the managerial environment one that helps or hinders smart contracting? What can be done to encourage contract managers to have a sense of personal ownership for their contract areas? Who should be held to account for the performance of the contractor, and how?

Underlying Assumptions

The field of public policy and management is not a science. It is never possible to demonstrate with certainty that a particular policy or management approach will have specified consequences. This is because we never have laboratory conditions with all variables except for one held constant. Careful research and analysis can reduce the problems of uncontrolled variables. Nevertheless, assumptions have to be made and subjective views and opinions play a role in analysis. It is therefore important to be clear on these assumptions and opinions from the outset.

Government has a crucial but not exclusive role in ensuring that collective social goods are provided—public safety, basic education, health care and welfare for those without work, and the provision and maintainenance of infrastructure. However, experience shows that government employees do not themselves have to deliver the service or create the facility. An open mind is needed about the means, ranging from direct government provision to private provision regulated by government. The market system is, on the whole, better at specifying goods and services, and producing them cost effectively. In relation to government services contracting out should be viewed as an option for a wide range of services, even those commonly regarded as core public services.

It is wise to be a little skeptical of some of the claims made about the productivity benefits of contracting. The private sector has some inherent advantages that make it a superior contractor—in particular, competition, the focus on profit, and the greater managerial flexibility it enjoys because it operates outside restrictive public sector rules on procurement, staffing, financial management, and management oversight. However, sometimes contract savings are simply the result of reduced pay, which is hardly a productivity improvement. Moreover, it is possible to eliminate and reduce some of the constraints on efficiency in the public sector, making government provision more effective. It is also possible to encourage public sector entrepreneurialism, getting government employees to operate more like businesses and even compete with the private sector and other agencies. Finally, many of the savings attributed to contracting are calculated before the contract is implemented or during its early months of operation; such savings are estimates, not actuals.

Contracting out is not a panacea. Some services will never be suitable for contracting, whereas for others the required conditions will not always be in place. It is also possible and indeed commonplace for governments to do contracting poorly. The government has to be clear and realistic on what it wants, and it must select the best contractors for the cost and then ensure that they meet their promises. Too often problems emerge on one or all of these fronts. Contracting can improve efficiency and effectiveness but only if certain conditions are met: first, the service must be suitable for contracting; second, there needs to be a market, or it must be possible to create one; third, the government's internal management arrangements and processes must be conducive to smart contracting; and, finally, the government needs skilled officials assigned to manage the contracting process. It is the last two of the four conditions that are most critical.

Contracting and attempts to reinvent government service delivery can improve but not transform government. In the U.S., thinkers on the Left and Right have been talking of reinventing and reengineering government (National Performance Review, 1993; Osborne & Gaebler, 1992). The Right has also begun pushing privatization and contracting again as a way of slimming down government (Gillespie & Schellhas, 1994). Expectations are high about government's ability to cut spending dramatically and improve services simultaneously through contracting, privatizing, and reinventing the management and delivery of government services. These expectations are often unrealistic and will only be realized where a reappraisal of the purpose of government and the nature and working of government accompany managerial reforms. The only sure way to slim down government dramatically is to stop and/or reduce services. Contracting does not do this.

What Are the Problems?

This book is concerned with four issues—the role of contracting in government, the appropriateness of different contracting strategies, the process of contracting, and who does the contracting.

1. *What Is the Role of Contracting?*

   Which services should local governments be responsible for, and, of these, which ones are suitable candidates for contracting?

2. *What Are the Most Effective Contracting Strategies?*

   What can the models tell us about contracting strategies to maximize value for money? For example, what is the advantage of outsourcing as opposed to public/private competition or of a partnership approach versus a competition-oriented strategy?

3. *Which Contracting Processes Are Most Appropriate?*

   Do the ideas and theories throw any light on the management information systems and decision-making processes that help or hinder smart contracting? This will cover, for example, accounting systems, performance management information, and rules on procurement and systems of reward and penalties.

4. *Who Does the Contracting?*

   What are the most effective organizational arrangements for smart contracting? Should, for example, cities centralize or devolve contract management? Who should evaluate and select contractors—elected or appointed officials? What role should purchasing professionals play compared with program managers?

Ideas on Contracting

There is a growing literature on contracting but no single, comprehensive, accepted approach. Some of these ideas have emerged in academia and are backed up with research. Others are practitioner oriented, while others were developed for advocacy purposes. All have something to say about contracting and, to a greater or lesser degree, throw some light on the issues.

Much has been written in political science, philosophy, and economics about the role of government. Traditional welfare economics, for example, explains the emergence of government in supplying social goods and services and regulation as a response to market failure. Several academics and political activists have developed ideas opposing this approach, explaining why, where, and how government fails and identifying some alternative approaches. These solutions entail increasing the role of the private sector and reducing that of government. The problems with government commonly cited relate to both the demand for and the supply of services. For example:

- *Overproduction.* Many argue that government has an inevitable tendency to grow because of the development of strong spending coalitions pressing for more and new programs and of the ability of government to spread the cost of growth thinly amongst taxpayers to reduce the risks of opposition, inertia, and "budget imperialism" of bureaucrats who use their specialist knowledge to maximize their spending as a way of increasing their power and prestige (see, for example, Niskanen, 1975).

- *Political management.* Electoral issues rather than efficiency usually motivate politicians. This encourages a range of inefficiencies, including: overemphasis on capital projects, often at the expense of basic maintenance; appointing staff for their political allegiances rather than their skills; and favoring a distribution of resources for political rather than efficiency grounds.

- *Monopoly.* Many government agencies are monopolies that are not responsive to their customers, failing to meet their needs and overcharging in the process. Savas (1987) cites the common example of police departments that use uniformed officers rather than lower-paid civilians for a wide range of tasks, such as computer maintenance and traffic-regulation enforcement.

- *Input rigidities.* Some criticize the civil service system for inefficiency (e.g., Savas & Ginsberg, 1973). It is, for example, difficult to fire poor performers, there are rarely systems in place to reward good performance, and there is a risk-averse culture. Moreover, there are often restrictive procurement, financial, and personnel regulations in place that make it difficult to manage a public service.

Contracting is one way of overcoming some problems of government failure. However, contracting only addresses supply-side problems. The government still defines the service requirement.

A new approach to understanding organizations has emerged in the last two decades with origins in neoclassical economics (see Moe, 1984). It tries to explain what the parameters of the firm are and why they develop with hierarchical structure rather than relying exclusively on markets. Why, for example, do firms choose to produce a service or good themselves rather than buy it? These theories were not developed to address contracting and privatization in the public sector. However, some of the ideas can help in an understanding of government contracting, especially "principal–agent theory" and the idea of "transaction costs."

How does a principal ensure that the agent does the task in question to his/her satisfaction at an acceptable price? (See, for example, Alchian & Demsetz, 1972; Arrow, 1985; Ross, 1973; Sappington, 1991.) This is the problem of agency. It recognizes the different interests and strengths of the principal and the agent. The principal wants to achieve the objective and minimize expenditure but may not know what is involved in completing the task. The agent, on the other hand, wants to maximize payment and minimize effort. He/she also is likely to be more expert than the principal in relation to the task (the economists call this "asymmetrical information"). These differences raise several issues. Can the principal specify what is needed and check to ensure that the good or service meets the requirement? How easy and costly is it to identify "shirking" by the agent? Are there alternative suppliers, and is the principal willing to use competition?

Williamson (1975, 1981) developed the transaction costs approach from work originally produced in the 1930s. The focus is on the exchange of goods and services within and between organizations. Principals incur transaction costs during exchanges to achieve their objective—for example, the effort and costs involved in writing a specification and monitoring performance of the contractor. The basic idea is that firms will decide to produce a good or service in-house where the transaction costs of using markets are high. This is likely to be the case where there is "uncertainty" and especially "asset specificity." The latter refers to investments that are specific to a particular transaction. These could be tangible things such as the physical buildings and facilities required for the production of a good or service. Alternatively, they could be the knowledge of the worker acquired while performing the tasks, especially where the knowledge is specific to the company. Williamson argues that where asset specificity is high, the buyer will favor in-house production to minimize the transaction costs. Otherwise the buyer will be subject to the "small numbers game," as the selected contractor will have a built-in advantage over other competitors.

Local governments have always contracted for goods and services, and a purchasing profession emerged in response to this need. Government purchasing has a distinctive set of values that departs from some aspects of practice in the private sector. In particular, the goals of government purchasing are more all-embracing. Governments are expected to meet equity and integrity objectives, achieve economy and effectiveness goals, as well as address other socioeconomic issues. The government is also expected to treat all bidders equally, showing no unfair preferences. In addition, there is a concern to avoid corruption by elected and appointed officials and to contract only with reputable firms. This results in an approach that emphasizes competition and has the following features:

- *Systematic advertising.* Using newspapers, market research, and direct approaches to potential contractors.

- *Detailed specifications.* Predefining the business solution by setting out in detail what is expected of the contractor.

- *Sealed bidding.* Having all bidders submit bids in the same format and timescale.

- *Formalized evaluations.* Identifying the criteria for selection in advance and formally scoring bids against the criteria.

- *The lowest responsible bidder.* Showing a strong preference—and, with the most common types of bid method, a legal imperative—to select the lowest bid.

- *Protest procedures.* Establishing appeal procedures for unsuccessful bidders who have a grievance. Modern purchasing practice is still based on the original principles of economy, integrity, equity, and competition, although some changes have been made to take account of the fact that local governments now contract for a much wider range of services. It is now common for governments to establish appeal procedures. The principles and practice of modern public sector procurement can be found in the American Bar Association's code (1979).

Several academics and practitioners have developed ideas on reforming the way that government manages service delivery. Osborne and Gaebler (1992) have popularized these ideas (see also Barzelay, 1992; Dilulio, 1994; Dilulio, Garvey, & Kettl, 1993; Thompson, 1993). A few writers in this tradition have written about government contracting, urging:

- *Deregulation.* The approach to contracting should be deregulated, allowing more discretion to officials managing contracts (Kelman, 1990).

- *Public/private competition.* Jensen (1987) argues in favor of allowing public sector employees to compete with the private sector, improving efficiency.

- *Intergovernmental competition.* Osborne and Gaebler (1992) argue that governments should look to provide services to each other and even suggest that they compete with each other.

- *Internal markets and support services.* Several writers have extolled the value of internal contracting for support services (Barzelay, 1992; Osborne & Gaebler, 1992).

The critics are largely drawn from public service unions and professions concerned about contracting and other forms of privatization. The most vocal critics are the American Federation of State, County and Municipal Employees (AFSCME) and the American Federation of Teachers (AFT). A few academic commentators have also critiqued privatization (see, for example, Kettl, 1993; Starr, 1987; Thayer, 1987) as have formal investigations (e.g., the Feerick Commission on New York City and the Little Hoover Commission on Los Angeles County).

The major criticisms of contracting are:

- *Real savings?* AFSCME argues that contracting costs more because, first, the extra costs of contracting, such as contract administration and monitoring, are often ignored; second, many cities and counties end up spending more on the contract than the figures contained in the contract price; and, third, contractors often reduce pay and benefits for their staff, passing some extra costs on to government, such as greater expenditure on welfare.

- *Poorer services.* AFSCME and AFT suggest that contractors often reduce the level and quality of services.

- *Poor management.* Most commentators have alleged poor management of public sector contracts (Kettl, 1993; New York State Commission on Government Integrity, 1989).

- *Corruption.* Some argue that contracting is prone to corruption, with politicians awarding contracts to friendly firms who repay favors with campaign donations. Indeed, some suggest that a new form of political patronage has emerged with the increase in contracting—*Governing Magazine* called this "pinstripe patronage" (Mahtesian, 1994).

A Model for Understanding Government Contracting

Academic theory provides guidance on where contracting is appropriate and how to assess the costs and benefits. It also helps identify appropriate contract strategies. However, there is little systematic thinking on the "how" question, especially concerning the features of effective contract managers and the conditions that encourage effective and efficient contracting. One explanation for this omission is an underlying assumption that management is not problematic and makes little difference in the long term. Management arrangements can affect value for money, quality, and service-delivery arrangements. Indeed, strong or weak management can transform a service-delivery situation—making contracting for an "easy-to-contract" service problematic or for a "difficult" service highly successful. The empirical work in this book supports the contention that the managerial difference is the critical ingredient.

The remainder of this section covers expectations in four areas: the historical and cultural context, where contracting works, the features of smart contracting, and the conditions conducive to smart contracting.

1. *The Historical and Cultural Context*

The following factors are expected to be important:

- *Local government system.* This would cover issues such as the range of functions, the funding systems, the degree of autonomy enjoyed by local governments, and the structure of local governments. Such issues will dictate how cost-sensitive governments are and their independence in deciding how to deliver services.

- *Form of government.* Of particular relevance are the extent to which decisions are made on political or managerial grounds and the extent to which decision-making power is centralized or dispersed. This will determine whether efficiency issues have high or low priority and how easy it is to change approach.

- *Starting point.* In particular, did government employees originally provide most local government services, or did a strong tradition of alternative service delivery exist. This history will influence how easy or difficult it is for a government to change service-delivery mode.

2. *Where Contracting Works*

There is a large measure of consensus on where contracting is most feasible. Contracting is the preferred mode of service delivery where:

—the service is tangible (that is, the requirements can be specified clearly)

—monitoring costs are not excessive

—a competitive market exists for the service.

Table 1.2 sets out some initial broad-based expectations of the contracting potential for selected service areas.

It is vital to include the transaction and productions costs in the make or buy decision. This means taking into account the costs of contract management and the costs of reestablishing an in-house service. It also means recognizing the risks of the "small numbers game" if a government contracts with a supplier in an area where there is high asset specificity.

There is also a fair measure of agreement on the appropriate contract strategies. First, there is an overriding preference for competitive contracting rather than simply contracting with the private sector and hoping that this will be

TABLE 1.2.   Contracting Potential for Local Services

Service Area	Specificity of Service	Monitoring	Extent of Competition	Overall Rating
Trash collection	1	1	1	1
Water supply	1	1	2.5	1.5
Fire service	3	3	5	3.5
Child welfare	3	3	5	3.5
Management of recreation facilities	3	3	3	3
Libraries	2	2	5	4
Personnel administration	2	3.5	3	3

Key: 1 = High contracting potential—tangible, easy to monitor, and with strong competition. 5 = Low contracting potential—service is difficult to specify and monitor and competition for it is weak.

superior to in-house production. Some challenge this position, arguing that, for services characterized by "asset specificity" and "uncertainty," long-term contracting partnerships are preferable to frequent, formal competition (Kelman, 1990). There is strength to Kelman's approach, but it will depend on the nature of the service and the costs of regular competition.

Second, most writers prefer small contract packages and partial contracting to large contracts with a single supplier (e.g., Kolderie, 1986; Savas, 1987). This is an extension of the competition argument, suggesting that governments should be wary of encouraging a private monopoly to develop. This can be tested, and the production savings associated with this approach need to be weighed against the transaction costs of greater contract management.

Third, there is a growing view of the appropriateness of different kinds of supplier for certain services. Most argue that contracting for "easy to contract" services should be with for-profits, whereas contracting with nonprofits and other public agencies should be favored for more difficult services. One area of disagreement is the appropriateness of support services to contracting. Should they be contracted out at all, or are they essential core services? If such services are to be contracted out, how should it be done—centrally within the government or by devolving the decision to the front-line departments (see Barzelay, 1992)?

A further subject receives little attention: whether government employees should participate in competitions for contracts—"public/private competition." Local governments can compete with the private sector if they can relax rigidities over, for example, job demarcation, staff numbers, salary levels, and conditions. However, where public sector managerial autonomy is tightly constrained, contracting out should be a more attractive option. However, it needs to be recognized that it is the elimination of input rigidities rather than competition that is the distinctive factor.

3. *The Features of Smart Contracting*

There are four features of smart contracting:

*   *A strategic approach.*   Is contracting part of a systematic service-delivery strategy? Are the details of contracting strategy carefully thought through? Is the market analyzed and exploited?

*   *Technical competence.*   Are the decision-makers competent in the basic techniques of service-delivery review, contract strategy, contractor selection, and monitoring?

*   *Information.*   Do the decision-makers have sufficient information? It is difficult to imagine, for example, a government making sensible decisions about contracting without knowing the cost and quality of in-house provision.

*   *Independence.*   Are the decision-makers and contract managers independent of contractors?

4. *The Conditions Conducive to Smart Contracting*

The major theories are silent on this issue, and little has been written on the contract management arrangements. Indeed, organizational economics has difficulty dealing with the fact that there are nearly always multiple principals in the public sector. The procurement professionals urge, not surprisingly, professional contract management but are agnostic on whether the function should be centralized or devolved. Others favor a degree of devolution and see contracting as an integral part of management rather than as a separate discipline (see Kelman, 1990; Kettl, 1993). Another issue on which there has been little discussion is the environment for contracting. Who is accountable for contracted services—the contractor, the contract manager, or the politicians? Who does the contract manager report to, and how is she/he held to account? Do certain governance structures help or hinder efficient and effective contracting?

Four factors help promote or constrain smart contracting:

*   *Politicization.*   The extent to which professional managers or politicians are in charge of contracting. The extent and power of the unions in relation to managerial autonomy over service-delivery methods is also relevant.

*   *Devolution.*   The extent to which managers are delegated responsibility for decisions and performance. This will affect both whether they "own" the preferred service-delivery mode and their enthusiasm to see it work. It will also influence the costs of decision making, with a more centralized structure having more personnel involved in monitoring.

- *Organizational culture.* In particular, the degree to which a government values good performance. This will be reflected in systems, processes, rewards, and penalties.

- *The influence of the media.* Especially the extent to which the media investigates and popularizes particular service-delivery modes and their strengths and weaknesses.

OVERVIEW OF THE BOOK

The remainder of the book explores the agenda set out above. Chapter 2 compares and contrasts the historical and cultural context of local government in the U.S. and the U.K. Chapter 3 examines the evidence on contracting. Where is it happening? Chapter 4 assesses the impact on expenditure. Are the theories right about the occurrence and potential of contracting? These chapters draw on existing research studies and data collected by the author from a wide range of case studies. Chapter 5 looks at the process of contracting. What methods are favored? What are the arrangements in place for managing contracts? Chapter 6 sets out a model of smart contracting and outlines a "health check" for governments to assess their own contractor capability. Chapters 7 through 12 contain summaries of some cases examined by the author. Chapter 13, which concludes the book, argues the case for reinventing government to improve service delivery. This includes an assessment of the case for mandated contracting, the use of public/private competition, and the need for reforming internal management systems.

2

Local Governments
in the U.S. and the U.K.

It is important first to understand the similarities and differences between local governments in the U.K. and the U.S. before attempting to compare, contrast, and learn from their respective approaches to contracting. There are strong similarities between the local government systems in the U.K. and U.S. Both have free-market economies and, compared to other Western countries, a *laissez faire* approach with less regulation of business and a smaller welfare state. Both have a common legal heritage, and home ownership is more extensive than in other major Western countries. Both countries have a two-tier system of local government. In this chapter, we look at the key differences and assess the implications for preferred modes of service delivery. The comparison between the systems of local government is divided into six areas—underlying attitudes, constitution, functions, structure, funding, and internal management.

UNDERLYING ATTITUDES TO GOVERNMENT

The distinctive American attitude to government has been the subject of much comment. Perhaps, the two best accounts are de Tocqueville's *Democracy in America* and Madison's *Federalist Papers*. These books highlight key features of the American ideology. Even if they are sometimes untrue, they have nevertheless shaped the U.S. Constitution and its institutions, including its local governments. Some of the key points include:

- *A fear of big government.* Many Americans see government as threatening freedom, a form of tyranny. This explains why there are so many checks and balances built into the U.S. system of government. It also helps to explain why there is such a strong emphasis on anticorruption measures, such as freedom of information.

- *An active civil society.*   This is what de Tocqueville described as the propensity of Americans to form groups and societies that in turn influence government. This helps explain the important place of volunteerism and the nonprofit sector in U.S. life. In addition, both volunteerism and the nonprofit sector play an important role in government. This feature also explains the predominant American attitude that people—not governments—solve problems.

- *Localism.*   There has always been a healthy debate in the U.S. about the respective powers of the states and the federal government. Nevertheless, the prevailing attitude has been that government works best when it is closest to the people. As a result, under the federal system, states have considerable autonomy to determine their own affairs. In turn, local governments have a degree of autonomy.

The U.K. and indeed European approach is rather different. There has always been a stronger faith in authority and government. As a result, government is not something that has been loathed. Moreover, government is often looked to as the best mechanism to solve a whole range of problems. Finally, there has been a technocratic approach to government, making it bigger, more efficient, and more centralized.

THE CONSTITUTIONAL BASIS FOR LOCAL GOVERNMENT

There is no local self-government in either the U.S. or the U.K.—local governments are not independent bodies. Local governments are creatures of states in the U.S. and of the national government in the U.K. However, this is where the similarities stop. In the vast majority of U.S. states, local governments have been granted a limited form of "home rule"—that is, a sphere of activities over which they have autonomy. This means that in broad terms local governments have more influence over what they do, how they do it, how they are organized, and how they are funded. The fact that local governments are the creation of states, coupled with the limited home rule that they are usually granted, makes for a diverse system. As a result, they vary enormously between and within states in terms of what they do, how they do it, funding, structure, organization, as well as electoral systems. This diversity is, of course, one of the underlying principles of the U.S. federal model. Indeed, it is difficult to speak of one system of local government.

U.S. county governments have much less autonomy than the cities. Citizens set up their own city governments by incorporating as cities and establishing special districts and joint power authorities. It is possible for cities to be established as or to become "general law" cities or "charter" cities. General law cities have less autonomy than their charter counterparts. In essence, they have police powers and public works powers. Charter cities are able to expand on the powers of the general law city, and the form of government or "internal management" is usually defined in the charter. State governments, by contrast, established counties, and much of their mission is to act as an agent of the state government. They also provide limited local services for those people living in "unincorporated" areas—that is, areas not part of cities. Most counties tend to be general law counties. Unlike their city counterparts, this means that their constitution is defined in state law. It is possible to have a charter county, and this is fairly common in western states such as California. Los Angeles County, the biggest county government in the U.S., is an example of a charter county.

The contrast with Britain could not be greater. Britain has a uniform, national system of local government. Moreover, the national government dominates. Local governments operate on the *ultra vires* doctrine—that is, they can only do what the national government expressly allows them to do. This is the very opposite of home rule. In the main, the national government establishes what local governments do, how they do it, the funding mechanisms, and the internal management arrangements. It is therefore possible to speak of local government in the singular to cover all local governments! The national government even creates and abolishes local governments. It is common for the national government to change the boundaries of a city or county, and it is not unheard of for the national government to change the entire structure, functions and funding of local government. Indeed, since the 1980s, among other changes, the Conservative national government:

—introduced a new uniform system of local funding

—abolished some local governments, modified others, and created new ones

—took functions away from local governments, such as responsibility for running public transport and further education, in addition to conferring new responsibilities, such as additional ones for human services.

This constitutional difference explains why U.K. local governments tend to be agents of the national government rather than independent city governments as in the U.S. However, it would be wrong to equate U.K. local governments too closely with U.S. counties. In general, U.K. local governments have much greater discretion than U.S. counties in carrying out their functions, whether these relate to social services, fire, police, or public works, because national laws rarely specify detailed standards and expenditure levels.

These diversity–uniformity and autonomy–agents distinctions explain virtually all of the differences outlined in this chapter.

WHAT DO LOCAL GOVERNMENTS DO?

Table 2.1 summarizes the main functions of local governments in the U.K. and the U.S. There is enormous diversity in what U.S. local governments do. A "typical" city will provide the following functions: waste management, street

TABLE 2.1. Local Government Responsibilities

Service Area	U.S. City	U.S. County	English Unitary	English County	English District
Trash collection	Yes	Limited	Yes	No	Yes
Waste disposal	Yes	Limited	Yes	Yes	No
Street repair	Yes	Limited	Yes	Yes	Limited
Bus transit	Around 35%	Around 25%	Very limited	Very limited	No
Water and wastewater	Most—80%	Around 40%	No	No	No
Electricity and gas	Around 30%	Just over 10%	No	No	No
Policing	Yes	Yes	A role[a]	A role[a]	No
Fire	Yes	Around 67%	Yesc	Yes	No
Emergency medical services	Most, over 80%	Most, around 70%	No	No	No
Social services	Very limited	Yes	Yes	Yes	No
Hospitals	A few large cities	Some—35%	No	No	No
Parks and recreation	Yes	Some	Yes	Limited	Yes
Culture/art	Most	Limited	Yes	Limited	Yes
Tax collection	Yes	Yes	Yes	No	Yes
Town planning	Yes	Limited	Yes	Limited	Yes
Rented housing	Some	Few	Yes	No	Yes
Schools	Very few	No	Yes	Yes	No
School support	Very few	Not usually	Yes	Yes	No
Direct education services[b]	Very few	No	Yes	Yes	No

Notes: Unitary local governments operate in the large urban areas of England. An English unitary is the only local government in a given area responsible for all local public services. In the remainder of the country a "two-tier" system exists, with counties providing some services and districts others.

[a]Outside London, unitary local governments and counties have representatives on police authorities which are separate local agencies part funded by local taxes and the national government.

[b]These cover services such as special education, careers guidance, and youth services.

[c]Sometimes this service is run by an intergovernmental agreement.

maintenance, parking regulation, water supply and wastewater treatment, police, fire, emergency medical services, environmental health, libraries, outdoor and indoor recreation, and town planning. Some cities are also responsible for health, public rented housing and social services, utilities such as gas and electricity, and public transport such as buses, transit systems, and airports. A typical county would provide prisons, social services, welfare, and crime prevention and suppression, such as the county sheriff and a prosecution service for the entire county. In addition, it would be responsible for basic local services for unincorporated areas, such as street maintenance, local policing, fire, and planning.

U.K. local governments are responsible for all of the basic local services, such as street maintenance, town planning, environmental health, libraries, waste management, and recreation. Private firms run all utilities such as gas, electricity, and water/wastewater. Many of these private utilities were operated by local governments in the past but were nationalized in the middle of this century and privatized in the 1980s. Some cities run airports (e.g., Manchester and Bristol), but public transport has been deregulated and most of the municipal bus companies have been sold to the private sector. Local governments do have major responsibilities for schools, social services, and rented housing. Indeed, the last three functions comprise the lion's share of the local government's budget. The social services responsibilities are significantly greater than U.S. counties because of the more elaborate welfare state in the U.K. and the smaller role of private provision.

The differences in functions make U.S. local governments more capital oriented and their British counterparts more people and service based.

THE STRUCTURE OF LOCAL GOVERNMENTS

Both countries have two-tier systems of local government, but the similarities are more apparent than real. In the U.S., the bulk of local services are provided by the cities, with counties providing local services outside the cities and countywide services on behalf of the state. In Britain, there is a unitary system of local government in the metropolitan areas and large cities of England as well as in all of Scotland and Wales. Unitary local government means a single tier with all local services being provided by the local government. In a few cases, such as fire protection in London, joint boards have been established to provide a service for a group of local governments. There is a two-tier system in most of the shires of England. Two-tier English "districts" (the most local form of local government) provide local services such as rented housing, planning, trash collection, recreation, and environmental health. The counties provide the big-spending services such as education, social services, highways, police, and fire. Northern Ireland has a system of districts. However, many traditional local government services there are run by the national government (e.g., education and social housing).

Significant difference exists between the U.S. and the U.K. relating to the degree to which local governments are consolidated or fragmented. The U.S. system is highly fragmented. In addition to the cities and counties, there are thousands of special districts and authorities. Special districts are single-purpose governments with elected leaders and tax-raising powers. The most common form of special districts are school and water districts; less common ones are business improvement districts, fire districts, library districts, and even mosquito-abatement districts! In most cases the boundaries of the special districts differ from those of the local governments. In California alone there are over 5,000 special districts but only 485 cities and 89 counties. In addition to the special districts, there is a vast array of public authorities and agencies. Unlike the special districts, these usually do not have separate elections and are often run indirectly by the parent local government (e.g., by the mayor appointing the board). These agencies might, for example, deal with public transport, airports and ports, and redevelopment projects. In the U.K. there has also been an increase in the number of nonelected public agencies known as QUANGOs (Quasi Autonomous NonGovernmental Agencies!) which are controlled by the national government. However, the number and power of these organizations is minuscule compared to agencies in the U.S.

A final difference between the local government structure is size. U.K. local governments are much larger than their U.S. counterparts in terms of resident population, expenditure, and employees. Most U.S. cities, for example, fall into the 25,000–50,000 range, whereas in England the average district will have a resident population of around 115,000. Large U.K. unitary cities and counties are huge organizations compared to U.S. local governments. An average-sized county or city in the U.K. will have an operating budget of around $1 billion and as many as 25,000 employees. The only local governments of this size or greater in the U.S. are the very large counties, such as Los Angeles and Orange, and the old large cities such as New York and Chicago.

THE FUNDING OF LOCAL GOVERNMENTS

In the U.S., local taxes provide the bulk of funding for local services. The most common taxes are property taxes on residents and businesses and sales taxes. Local income taxes are also fairly common. Local governments also get income through service fees and charges. Services such as water supply and wastewater are paid for through such charges, but this approach is spreading to other services such as trash collection. Special funding and grants from states and the federal government are common for infrastructure projects and for services such as social services and welfare.

Once again, the U.K. system is much more uniform than that of the U.S. The bulk of local government funding comes from the national government—around 80%. Most of this, approximately two-thirds, comes from national government taxes, while the remainder comes as a proportion of the local business tax. The rate is set nationally, collected locally, and distributed to local governments by the national government according to a need-assessment formula. Most of the national government grant comes in the form of a "block grant" that is not earmarked for any specific areas of expenditure. This explains why U.K. local governments enjoy flexibility over the use of resources. A small amount of national funding comes in the form of special grants, mainly capital grants for infrastructure projects.

In the U.K., the main source of local income is a property-based tax; this is designed nationally (including the valuations), but each local government is free to decide its own level of tax (except that there is a "capping" system to prevent local governments setting what the national government regards as too high a level of tax). Unlike their U.S. counterparts, there is not a strong tradition of levying charges to cover the entire cost of services or of having taxes reserved for a specific service. The only major area where this happens is public rented housing, where rents must cover the cost of the service. Local taxes and government grants cover the cost of other services such as trash collection. Nevertheless, there is a trend of increasing fees and charges for services such as recreation, but this only accounts for a small proportion of local funding.

INTERNAL MANAGEMENT SYSTEMS

The term "internal management" is used to describe the decision-making structures of the government. It is widely used in the U.K. What are the roles and powers of elected and appointed officials? How are they organized? How, if at all, are they paid? What role and powers do citizens have in local government, and, in particular, to what extent is the system representative or participative?

There is a national framework for the internal management of U.K. local governments. Councillors are elected on an area/district basis (known as wards) to sit on the council for a local government. The council delegates authority to a series of committees. These committees set policy and budgets, review performance, and confirm senior appointments. Normally, these committees reflect the local government's main service and functional areas. There is also usually a policy committee to establish the priorities and budget for the local government as a whole. A typical council will have around 60 councillors, and committees are usually between 10 and 20 councillors. The organization of the committees and the delegation schemes are matters determined by each local government. Councillors are part-time and unpaid, although they do receive an allowance to cover expenses. Until recently these allowances were nationally determined, but this rule was relaxed recently.

Council policies are implemented by appointed officials. These are permanent, career officials and not political appointments, even though elected officials make the senior appointments. Each local government is required to have a "Head of Paid Service," a "Monitoring Officer," a "Chief Financial Officer," and, where they are responsible for social services and education, a "Director of

Social Services" and a "Director of Education." With the exception of the chief financial officer there are no qualification requirements for these posts. It is possible to combine posts, except the roles of CFO and monitoring officer. Most local governments appoint a free-standing chief executive as the head of the paid service and a series of departmental heads for the main services as well as for finance, legal affairs, and personnel. The council, a committee, or a special panel of councillors normally appoints the chief executive, the departmental chiefs and usually senior officials within each department. Appointed officials report through the head of paid service to the council as a whole, not to the leader or a subgroup of the council.

Partisan systems are universal. Councillors are elected on a party ticket and are likely to belong to one of the three main national parties—the Conservatives, Labour, or the Liberal Democrats. Each party will have a manifesto, caucus meetings, and whip system to ensure that party policies are followed. By national law, the balance of the parties on the council must be reflected on committees.

It may seem strange to an American audience that the U.K. has a partisan system of local government supported by an impartial civil service. Nevertheless, this is the approach, and the politics–administration divide is also a feature of national government. However, it has become apparent in recent years that the impartiality of the local civil service is under threat because of the increasing politicization of local government, especially in the big cities. This has had three main impacts:

- *More political appointments* to the permanent civil service, despite the fact that, by law, senior local government officers are not permitted to be councillors. The increase in political appointments results in more mobility when administrations change.

- *The development of an informal cabinet system of government.* This is where the senior members of the majority party (such as the committee chairs) discuss and determine policy. This effectively bypasses the committee system and the freedom-of-information requirements.

- *More involvement in the details of policy and implementation*, especially by the party leaders and committee chairs.

There are enormous variations in internal management systems in the U.S. Nevertheless there are three main traditions:

- *The mayor–council model.* This is based on the federal model, with an elected chief executive (the president, or mayor) and an elected legislature (the Senate and Congress, and the council). There are variants on this model—the "strong" and "weak" mayor systems. The variations relate to the formal power accorded to the mayor and the council. In the strong mayor model, for example, the mayor will appoint agency heads and representatives to outside bodies, propose the budget, and have strong veto powers over council laws. In the weak mayor model, the council will consider all the mayor's recommendations for appointments and the mayor will not have the ability to veto council laws. New York, Boston, and Baltimore are examples of strong mayor cities, whereas Los Angeles, Chicago, and San Francisco are weak mayor cities.

- *The council–manager form of government.* This is based on the decision-making structure of a firm, with a board of directors (the council), an appointed, professional chief executive (a city or county manager), and shareholders (the voters). The council sets policy and appoints the city manager, which makes all other appointments and is responsible for all executive work. Phoenix, Dallas, and San Diego are examples of large council–manager cities.

- *The commission form of government.* This is where officials are elected to run specific areas and functions. A diluted form of commission government is common in county government, such as Los Angeles County and Maricopa County in Arizona. A county would typically have two sets of elected officials. First, a small number of "supervisors," elected on a district basis: they sit on a board and are responsible for the overall management of the county, and each individual commissioner tends to take responsibility for a function. Second, officials elected to specific areas, such as a sheriff, attorney, auditor, and treasurer. Underneath the board of supervisors there is a chief administrative officer or county manager, an appointed official.

There is a bewildering number of variations on the basic models, which makes for a complex and diverse system. For example, some strong mayor cities still have a number of elected officials, while an increasing number of council–manager cities have directly elected mayors (see Lavery, 1992, for further discussion of these models).

The fundamental difference between the U.S. systems is the extent to which management is delegated to professional managers or elected officials. In the council–manager model the professionals have greater executive power, with elected officials dominating in the mayor and commission models. Despite the differences, there are some common features of internal management systems in U.S. local governments which distinguish them from their counterparts in the U.K. These are:

- *Far fewer elected officials than in Britain.* A typical U.K. city will have around 60 elected officials compared to between 5 and 10 for a similar-sized U.S. city. The U.K. councils are much closer in size and operation to U.S. state legislatures.

- *More checks and balances on decision making.* In the U.K., decisions tend to be made by the relevant committee and then in some cases, as a formality, confirmed by the council. As a general rule, decisions are made in one place at one time. This is rare in the U.S., although more likely in a council–manager city. Power tends to be dispersed in the U.S. to promote pluralism and as a check on the potential tyranny of government. It is therefore always possible to challenge a decision by appealing/lobbying the mayor, council, another elected official, or the courts.

- *Freedom of information.* These requirements vary from state to state but are generally more extensive and onerous than the U.K.'s Access to Information Act for Local Government. For example, in California secret meetings of elected officials are outlawed—that is, it is not possible for elected officials to meet without declaring this in advance and publicizing it. Background briefings and information are also much more accessible.

- *Participatory democracy.* Many states, especially those in the West, have an initiative process. This allows citizens to decide issues by annual referenda. These referenda are held at state, county, and city levels. The government may place a proposition on the ballot, or citizen groups may place propositions if they obtain sufficient support. The precise rules for the initiative process vary from place to place. Referenda provide a further check on government and in recent decades have produced a number of decisions with a fundamental impact on local governments. For example, citizen initiatives have succeeded in limiting property-tax levels, stopping civic projects, and changing internal management systems.

- *Political management versus professional management.* There is a sharp contrast in the U.S. between the political management tradition of mayor and commission models with the professional management approach of council–manager governments. In the U.K., the management tradition has strong similarities with the council–manager plan, notwithstanding the politicization trend mentioned earlier. Officials report to the entire council, not to the dominant political group. Officials also tend to be appointed on the basis of their professional experience rather than their allegiance to a politician or party.

THE IMPLICATIONS FOR SERVICE DELIVERY

The variations in the local government systems in the two countries mean that the starting points for service delivery are inevitably different. These are examined under five headings—size of local governments, nature of services, internal management issues, cost sensitivity, and level of autonomy.

1. *Size of Local Governments*

One of the issues to explore is whether large government is likely to mean services delivered by government employees. There are certainly good grounds for expecting smaller governments to be more prepared to consider alternative approaches to direct provision in order to take advantage of economies of scale and specialist expertise. Consequently, more alternative service delivery in the smaller U.S. local governments is likely.

2. *Nature of Services*

U.S. local governments are much more focused on infrastructure than are their U.K. counterparts, where people services such as education and social services dominate. These differences lead to an expectation of more service contracting and other forms of privatization in U.S. local governments. This is for two reasons: first, infrastructure services are easier to specify and manage by contract than intangible people services; second, there is a stronger private sector for infrastructure-related works in both countries and therefore contracting is more feasible.

3. Internal Management Issues

The extent to which decisions on methods of service delivery are made on management or political grounds will have a decisive impact on whether the alternatives to direct provision are seriously entertained. The greater autonomy accorded to managers in council–manager governments would lead to an expectation of more experimentation than in politically led mayor, commission, and U.K. local governments.

4. Cost Sensitivity

U.S. local governments are more sensitive to costs than are their U.K. counterparts. First, most of their expenditure is funded locally. As a result there is a stronger ownership of costs, and poor control has a heavy impact on local taxes. Second, most local taxes are dependent on the level of economic activity, such as sales tax. As a result, governments have to work hard to attract and retain businesses, especially retailers, with low business taxes. Third, there is strong competition between local governments to attract and retain residents, and the level of taxes is clearly one of the major considerations here. U.K. local governments are less sensitive to costs, as they depend on central government for nearly all of their income. Moreover, with the system of spending controls, there is little distinction in local taxes and therefore less competition between governments for residents, businesses, and visitors. The greater sensitivity of U.S. local governments to costs is likely to lead them to look at alternatives to direct provision whereby they can save money.

5. Level of Autonomy

The national system of local government in place in the U.K., together with the national government's inclination to direct and regulate policies and methods, contrast sharply with the independence of U.S. local governments. There is also a major difference in orientation, with U.K. local governments more prepared to look to the central government for help, guidance, and solutions. As a result, more diversity in service delivery in the U.S. is likely.

3

How Are Services Provided?

How are local government services provided? Has the increased talk of privatization and contracting resulted in a real reduction in government provision and production? How much contracting is there with nonprofit organizations, and how much volunteering is used for services? This chapter examines these issues and draws extensively on the surveys conducted by the International City/County Management Association (ICMA) in 1988, and 1992. These surveys involved approaching all cities over 10,000 and counties over 25,000 and a sample of one in eight smaller local governments. The response rate for the 1992 survey was 31% and was similar in the earlier surveys (see ICMA, 1989; Miranda & Andersen, 1994).

OVERVIEW OF ALTERNATIVE SERVICE-DELIVERY METHODS

Using government employees remains the most common way of providing public services, but there has been a significant increase in alternative methods. Table 3.1 summarizes the results for selected services. Indeed, it shows that in-house provision is the dominant method of service delivery in virtually every service area. This includes those areas considered highly suitable for contracting such as trash collection, street repair, traffic sign and signal maintenance, and street sweeping. Provision by for-profits is dominant in only one area: legal services. The major spending areas where in-house provision does not dominate

TABLE 3.1. Service-Delivery Approaches by Local Governments (percentages)

Service	Entirely by Govt	Partially by Govt	Other Govt	For-Profit	Non-profit	Misc[a]
Residential trash collection	46.7	9.8	2.2	37.1	1.2	13.6
Street repair	42.6	52	4.9	29	0.5	0.7
Street cleaning	70	19.2	3	16.5	0.7	0.9
Traffic/parking enforcement	43.1	33.9	18.7	24.1	0.7	0.8
Water supply	74.6	8.7	15.6	4.9	0.8	1.0
Emergency medical services	42.7	19.1	20	13.7	8.3	14.3
Police	88.4	7.8	6.5	0.9	0.6	3.8
Fire	70.3	9.5	12.9	0.8	2.6	14.6
Animal control	59.2	12.7	20.5	5.4	8.9	1.9
Elderly programs	20.6	45.1	34.2	6.2	24.4	17.4
Child welfare	15.8	19.3	63.1	4.0	12.7	6.8
Management of recreational facilities	74.8	18.7	10.9	5.2	3.4	7.2
Landscape maintenance	73.8	19.8	8.3	9.5	1.7	3.7
Libraries	49.2	10.2	39.4	1.0	4.2	8.1
Cultural/arts programs	16.6	38.7	16.3	6.5	40.8	28.1
Building/grounds maintenance	65.4	32	1.6	19.8	1.6	1.8
Payroll	92.3	5.1	0.9	4.1	0.5	0
Data processing	80.2	14.9	5.7	8.3	0.9	0.2
Legal services	38.2	24.8	3.3	46.7	2.5	1.0
Building security	78.0	14.6	2.0	11.6	1.3	0.4

Source: Miranda & Andersen, 1994.

Note: Not all of the columns are mutually exclusive; figures have been rounded to the nearest decimal point.

[a]Covers franchises, grants, and the use of volunteers.

are the health and human services, where it is common for the services to be provided by employees of another government. Moreover, provision by another government is usually not organized on a contractual basis, although this is becoming more common. It is arguable that there is little difference between these sorts of intergovernmental agreements and in-house provision.

Table 3.2 shows service-delivery methods for selected services for some of the cities visited in gathering data for the book. This is not a representative sample of local governments. Indeed, local governments with a reputation for contracting are overrepresented. Nevertheless, it underlines the diversity of delivery methods and the overall dominance of in-house provision.

Contracting is by far the most popular alternative to in-house provision, and its use is increasing while that of others is waning. There is little "pure privatization"—few local governments are selling assets and discontinuing services, and the use of volunteers and franchises is declining.

Just over half of local governments use public employees to deliver services. However, there has been a small decrease in both the exclusive and the partial use of government employees for some services. Table 3.3 shows the changes for selected services. The use of government employees has increased in a number of areas, notably police and recreational services. The biggest decreases are in the human service areas, both the exclusive and the partial use of government employees. While the exclusive use of government employees has increased for data processing and payroll, it has decreased for most support services, such as tax bill assessing, processing, and collection (Miranda & Andersen, 1994). There has also been a general decline in the use of government employees in the public works area, such as street repair, street cleaning, and traffic sign and signal maintenance. Many of these areas have experienced an increase in partial provision by government employees.

Contracting is most popular for public works and social services and least common for fire and police and core administrative services. Nevertheless, a local government somewhere at some time has contracted out every service. Local governments are most likely to contract with for-profit firms for public works and professional services and with nonprofit firms or other governments for social services and policing.

Table 3.4 shows the main trends. Contracting with for-profits increased in the public works functions such as commercial waste collection, street repair, and cleaning. It also increased for certain support services (vehicle maintenance, payroll, and building security) but decreased for others (tax bill assessment, processing, and collection and data processing). Surprisingly, it increased for a range of human services, such as the operation of daycare facilities and the running of drug and alcohol programs.

Partial contracting remains popular, but there has been a noticeable increase in exclusive contracting with for-profits. Nevertheless, the case studies in this book show that even with exclusive for-profit contracting it is common to have con-

TABLE 3.2.   Service-Delivery Methods for Selected Services for Twelve Local Governments

Local government	Population	Trash collection	Fire	Data processing	Mgt. of recreation facilities	Libraries
Chicago	3,000,000	in-house	in-house	in-house	intergov./contract	in-house
Indianapolis	700,000	contract/ in-house	in-house	about to be contracted out	in-house/volunteers	in-house
Lakewood, CA	75,000	contract	intergov.	contract	mainly in-house	intergov
Los Angeles County	9,300,000	contract	in-house	in-house	N/A	in-house
Milwaukee	650,000	in-house	in-house	in-house, some contract	in-house	in-house
New York	7,000,000	in-house	in-house	in-house	in-house	in-house
Phoenix	1,000,000	contract/ in-house	in-house	in-house	in-house	in-house
San Carlos, CA	27,000	in-house	in-house	in-house	in-house	in-house
Santa Clarita, CA	170,000	contract	intergov.	in-house	in-house	intergov.
Scottsdale, AZ	170,000	contract	contract	in-house	in-house	in-house

Source: Visits to the local governments during 1994 and 1995.

TABLE 3.3.   Use of Government Employees, 1982 and 1992 (percentages)

Service	1982		1992	
	Exclusive	In-part	Exclusive	In-part
Residential trash collection	48	12	47	10
Street repair	65	33	43	52
Street cleaning	84	11	70	19
Traffic/parking enforcement	90	7	88	8
Water supply	—	—	75	9
Emergency medical services	39	27	43	19
Police	74	22	88	8
Fire	69	18	70	10
Animal control	61	16	59	13
Elderly programs	18	57	21	45
Child welfare	26	37	16	19
Mgt. of recreational facilities	58	35	75	19
Landscape maintenance	76	20	74	20
Libraries	48	20	49	10
Cultural/arts programs	11	46	17	39
Building/grounds maintenance	73	25	66	32
Payroll	86	11	92	5
Data processing	64	23	80	15
Legal services	41	29	38	25
Building security	85	11	78	15

Source: Miranda & Andersen, 1994.

tracts with more than one supplier. Multiple contracting is therefore replacing partial contracting in some local governments. For example, Indianapolis contracts with three for-profits as well as an in-house provider for trash collection.

Public/private competition has received much attention in recent years in large measure because of the well-publicized system at the city of Phoenix. Despite the extensive publicity, the 1992 ICMA survey found that only 20% of local governments introducing contracting allowed their employees to compete for the contract (Miranda & Andersen, 1994). Nevertheless, there is no doubt that this is an increase over recent years, but it is not possible to quantify the change as no comparative data exist for earlier years. There is also no data available on the success of in-house bids. Two cities practicing public/private competition, Indianapolis and Phoenix, were covered during the research for this book. In both cases, the public sector bids were competitive and their likelihood of success increased with experience of public/private competition.

Contracting with nonprofit organizations is popular for human and health services and for arts and culture programs and facilities. Contrary to conventional wisdom, contracting by local governments with nonprofits decreased significantly between 1982 and 1992. For example, contracting with nonprofits for the following functions decreased—elderly programs (28–24%), child welfare (22–13%), the operation of mental health facilities (38–29%), and public health programs (25–8%). The use of nonprofits increased for the running of animal shelters (17–23%). Some of the decreases may be a result of expenditure reductions, which in turn led to rationalization.

Intergovernmental agreements cover arrangements where one government pays another government to provide a service on its behalf. This category covers both intergovernmental contracting and provision by special districts and authorities, which are legally distinct bodies with specified functions and some-

TABLE 3.4. Use of Contracting and Intergovernmental Agreements, 1982 and 1992 (percentages)

Service	For-profit		Nonprofit		Other Gov'ts	
	1982	1992	1982	1992	1982	1992
Residential trash collection	34	37	0	1	8	2
Commercial trash collection	41	54	0	1	7	2
Street repair	26	29	1	1	5	5
Street cleaning	9	17	0	1	3	3
Police	—	1	—	1	5	7
Fire	—	1	—	3	8	13
Animal control	6	5	8	9	18	21
Daycare facility operation	33	54	34	35	15	18
Drug/alcohol programs	6	20	38	34	28	52
Elderly programs	4	6	28	24	21	34
Child welfare	5	4	22	13	26	63
Mgt. of recreational facilities	8	5	9	3	8	11
Landscape maintenance	9	10	2	2	5	8
Libraries	1	1	10	4	26	39
Cultural/arts programs	—	7	—	41	11	16
Building/grounds mtce	19	20	1	2	4	2
Payroll	—	4	—	1	2	1
Data processing	22	8	2	1	—	6
Legal services	48	47	2	3	6	3
Building security	7	12	1	1	3	2

Source: Miranda & Andersen, 1994.

times revenue raising powers. Unfortunately, the ICMA survey did not distinguish between the two types of intergovernmental agreement. It is likely that service provision using special districts and authorities is much more common than intergovernmental contracting.

An example of intergovernmental contracting is the contract between Lakewood and Los Angeles County for the provision of police services. An example of a special district is the Los Angeles Fire District, a separate local government that includes a large number of contract cities as members. The district contracts with Los Angeles County Fire Department to provide fire prevention and suppression services to its member cities.

Intergovernmental agreements are most common in the public works, transportation, and health and human services areas. Nearly half (49%) of bus transit services, two-fifths of libraries (39%), and one-third of wastewater programs are provided through intergovernmental agreements, for example. The use of intergovernmental agreements is increasing significantly in some human and health services, often replacing contracts with nonprofit organizations. For example, the use of intergovernmental agreements increased significantly for child welfare programs (26–63%), the operation of hospitals (21–39%), elderly programs (21–34%), and drug and alcohol treatment programs (28–52%). There has also been an increase in the use of intergovernmental agreements in the public safety area, including core services such as fire (8–13%). Relatively little use is made of other alternative methods of service delivery, and their popularity is declining. Franchises are fairly common for trash collection (13% for residential and 14% for commercial) and utilities (15% for electricity and 20% for gas). Subsidies are most common in the arts (e.g., 8% of arts/cultural programs) and human services (e.g., 8% of homeless shelters). However, the use of subsidies declined between 1982 and 1992 for virtually every area, and there were no cases of increased use. Volunteerism has a long and proud tradition in the U.S., especially in local government. It is most common for public safety (e.g., 14% for fire services), human services (e.g., 11% for elderly programs), and the arts (e.g., 17% for arts/culture programs). Once again, however, there has been a significant decline in the use of volunteers—with fire services falling from 17% to 14%, elderly programs from 18% to 11%, and arts/culture programs from 31% to 17% between 1982 and 1992.

There appears to be little genuine privatization in U.S. local governments. Few local governments are discontinuing services and shedding facilities despite financial constraints. One explanation for this is that many local services are mandated by federal or state law, especially county services. At city level, trash collection is one of the favorite candidates for shedding (e.g., in 1992, 12% of cities had ceased to be responsible for commercial collection). At county level, hospitals were the most popular area (e.g., in 1992, 9% of counties had ceased to be responsible for hospitals). Moreover, facilities such as airports, buses and subway systems, water supply, wastewater, and electricity and gas are often the responsibility of the local government. In an increasing number of other countries, such services/facilities have been privatized (e.g., the U.K., New Zealand and Australia—see Reason Foundation, 1994).

There are good grounds for believing that the use of alternative methods of service delivery has increased since 1992, but the evidence is impressionistic rather than systematic. The reasons are twofold—economic pressures and political initiatives. The recession of the early 1990s continued well into 1994, and this restricted local government income from a number of sources. Sales taxes declined, and state and federal grants for various programs failed to keep pace with increasing needs. At the same time, new mandates were passed by the federal government requiring extra spending by local governments. In essence, service requirements increased and revenues decreased. This has encouraged more local governments to experiment with contracting in an attempt to maintain services in the face of reduced revenues.

There has also been a major change in the national mood in relation to government. First, a movement emerged to "reinvent government." The publication of the book by Osborne and Gaebler (1992) captured the imagination of many interested in government and led to a number of initiatives at federal, state, and local level. In particular, the Clinton administration launched the National Performance Review, which led to an expansion of contracting and streamlining of procedures at the federal level. There has also been an increase in contracting at state level (Chi, 1994). This movement has affected local governments. There has also been a shift to the right, with the Republicans winning control of more and more governments. In 1993, New York and Los Angeles elected Republican mayors. The biggest change came on 8 November 1994, when the Republicans seized control of the Congress and Senate for the first time in 40 years. They were also swept to power at state level and now hold the governorships for 30 of the 50 states, including California, New York, and Texas. This shift to the right has added momentum to those pressing for more contracting and privatization.

There is anecdotal evidence to support the contention that contracting is on the increase. For example, the following mayor cities with a strong tradition of in-house provision are now developing major contracting programs:

—*Chicago:* Since 1989 Mayor Daley has contracted out 35 services, ranging from janitorial services to drug and alcohol treatment programs (Reason Foundation, 1994).

—*Philadelphia:* Since 1992 Mayor Rendell has contracted out 19 city services and has identified a further 30 services for competition (Reason Foundation, 1994).

—*Indianapolis:* This probably has the most extensive contracting program of any major U.S. city. Since 1992, under Mayor Goldsmith the city has contracted out 50 services.

—*Milwaukee:* Mayor Norquist introduced the Internal Service Improvement Project in 1992. This allows city departments to choose between in-house and private providers for 6 support services.

Indianapolis and Milwaukee are examined in more depth later in the book (see Chapters 8 and 10). Mayors in other large cities such as New York, Los Angeles, and Cleveland are currently examining the scope for contracting and privatizing city services, but little action had occurred at the time of writing.

Other Local Services—Education

One area where contracting has recently moved up the agenda is education. Action is taking place at local and state levels. Overall, government employees provide the vast majority of services, and the impact of contracting and privatization initiatives is at the margins. Nevertheless the main areas of change are:

- *Contracting for management.* A few school districts have contracted for management and support services. In 1991, Baltimore contracted with a Minnesota-based company, Education Alternatives Incorporated (EAI), to run nine of the city's schools. EAI, in partnership with Johnson Controls and KPMG Peat Marwick, provides school-based management. The same company was awarded a contract to provide school-based management for all of Hartford's (Connecticut) schools. The Hartford contract began in April 1995. EAI also has a school-based management contract with Dade County, Florida, for one school. Minneapolis has contracted with a consultancy company, Public Strategies Group, to perform the role of superintendent for the district's 79 schools. This is a limited contract, covering only the strategic management role, as the senior managers remain government employees. At the time of writing, the Hartford contract had been withdrawn and the financial position of EAI was in doubt.

- *Contracting for learning.* There has always been a significant number of private schools in the U.S. (around 7% of pupils). However, there has been a growth in contracting by school districts for instruction since the late 1980s. As a result the American Association of Educators in Private Practice was established in 1990. Baltimore has had a contract with Sylvan Learning since 1993 to provide remedial education to disadvantaged students in seven elementary schools. Berlitz International, the foreign language training company, has contracts in 13 states to provide language instruction. Ombudsman Educational Services from Illinois has contracts in 5 states to provide learning programs for around 2,000 pupils at risk of dropping out of school (Reason Foundation, 1994).

- *Contracting for school support services.* An increasing number of school districts are contracting out support services as resources are squeezed. School transport is overwhelmingly public in the U.S., with only 30% provided by private contractors (Reason Foundation, 1994). Moves are afoot to change this. Indiana, for example, adopted a law in 1993 to require school districts to consider contracting with the private sector for transport services. Fairfax County in Virginia contracted for school transport in the early 1990s with Johnson Controls but withdrew the contract after experiencing problems. Food services also tend to be provided by government employees. However, there has been an increase in contracting. The Reason Foundation (1994) estimates that the private sector share of school food services increased from 4% in 1987 to 11% in 1994.

- *Charter schools.*   This is where new schools are built to be run privately but with government financial support for capital and operations. Charter schools have been established in a number of states, including California, Michigan, and Massachusetts.

- *School choice schemes.*   A small number of voucher schemes have been established for public school pupils. For example, Wisconsin introduced a scheme in Milwaukee, providing vouchers for just under 800 pupils. There are also a few privately financed voucher schemes, such as the "Partners Advancing Values in Education" (PAVE), also in Milwaukee, which gives 50% towards the cost of tuition for around 5,000 pupils.

Privatization by the Back Door

A new form of privatization has emerged in the U.S. which involves supplementing government with private collective decision-making and service provision—a form of private government. This quiet revolution has been going on away from the gaze of the newspapers and accounts for a significant privatization of U.S. local government responsibilities (ACIR, 1989). Private government has emerged in residential areas (community associations) and city and town centers (business improvement districts).

Community associations (CAs) are residential developments where each owner is a member of a property organization and must comply with its rules and pay an assessment for the services provided. Some four-fifths of CAs are "private planned communities" (a sort of private new town based on a master plan prepared by a developer). In these communities, residents usually co-own the communal facilities such as roads and landscaped areas. Many of these communities are gated and are manned by security guards. Most of the remainder of CAs are condominiums (CAI, 1993).

Living in a CA is a part of the American way of life. One in eight of all Americans now live in CAs, some 32 million people. Over 50% of new house sales in the large metropolitan areas are in CAs. CAs can range in size from a three-unit condominium to a medium-sized planned city of 60,000 people (e.g., Columbia, Maryland). The average-sized CA is around 500 housing units (CAI, 1993).

CAs provide a range of services to their members. These often include security, leisure and recreation, refuse collection, water and sewerage systems, and grounds and roads maintenance. CAs also regulate different aspects of residential life. Typically regulations relate to the architectural appearance of housing units. Two-thirds of CAs use professional managers to provide the services, and of these two-thirds use a management company on contract.

Members pay an assessment, usually monthly, for the services. CAs are governed by boards of directors which are made up of elected volunteers drawn from CA residents. It is not far-fetched to describe a CA as a form of private local government with a government (board of directors), municipal services (security, libraries, and road maintenance), and a tax (the assessment).

Business Improvement Districts (BIDs) are permitted under legislation in some 43 states to improve and manage the city-center environment and provide services. Around 1,000 BIDs exist in North America (Bradley, 1995). As with the community associations, they are a form of private government with municipal-type responsibilities: they fund physical improvements and provide a range of services from street cleaning, trash collection, and security to economic development. Around 40% of the 1,000 BIDs in North America have significant service responsibilities. They levy taxes, usually in the form of a property tax based on capital value that is set for a five-year period when the BID is established. They also have a democratic structure for making decisions: a board of directors elected by the property owners in the designated areas. They do not operate on the basis of one-person one vote: usually the number of votes is based on the capital value of the property.

A number of the new-style municipal contractors for security, public safety, and facilities management count local governments and private governments among their clients.

Why Increased Interest in Contracting?

The 1992 ICMA survey identified lower costs as the driving force behind contracting. Around 70% of local governments had studied the feasibility of private service delivery (although the meaning of a feasibility study was not defined in the survey). Of these, around 90% cited it as an internal attempt to lower costs. Other significant factors were external financial pressures, politics, and the financial pressures resulting from state and federal mandates.

The Contrast with Local Government Contracting in the U.K.

There are some fundamental differences in local government contracting between the U.S. and U.K. Chapter 12 describes and analyses the U.K. situation in depth, but the key differences are:

- *Mandated competition.* Under U.K. law, local governments have to invite bids from the private sector for a wide range of services. This system is called "Compulsory Competitive Tendering" (CCT). This contrasts sharply with the freedom that most U.S. local governments have over service-delivery methods.

- *Complete contracting.* U.K. local governments tend to favor bigger contracts and often contract for an entire service with one firm.

- *Contracting in rather than out.* Public/private competition is the norm in the

U.K., and there is a well-developed system to ensure fairness for all bidders, public and private. Only one-fifth of U.S. local governments who contract for services practice public/private competition.

- *Emphasis on support services.* CCT began by requiring local governments to contract for manual services, such as trash collection, street sweeping, and vehicle maintenance. More recently, a range of professional support services was added to CCT. These include data processing, financial services, personnel, legal services, and the management of low-rent public housing. As a result, contracting in the U.K. tends to emphasize "white-collar" services as much as "blue-collar" services. By contrast, in the U.S., with the exception of legal services, government employees provide most white-collar functions.

Reality versus Expectations

How does contracting compare in practice with the expectations set out in Chapter 1?

- *Size.* We expected smaller local governments to favor contracting more than their larger counterparts. The ICMA data suggest that this is borne out in practice. However, larger governments, with the exception of governments with populations over 1,000,000, were much more likely to consider private sector delivery of services than were small governments (Moulder, 1994a).

- *Nature of the service.* Contracting is more likely for services that can be specified and monitored and where there is an established market. There is some correlation between the incidence of contracting and our expectations, but it is not strong. First, it is true that services that are "easy to contract" are among those most likely to be contracted out. These include trash collection, street sweeping, and street repair, for example. However, in-house provision for such services is still more common than contracting. Second, there is a range of "difficult-to-contract" services that are popular contracting candidates—for example, child welfare and services for the elderly. Most of this contracting is with other governments and nonprofit organizations rather than with for-profit firms. One reason for the popularity of contracting with nonprofits has been the encouragement by the federal government through the grant regime for human and health services.

- *Internal management.* We expected that local governments with council–manager plans would favor contracting more than local governments with mayor and commission plans. The reported results for the ICMA 1992 survey do not address this issue; however, analysis of the 1988 survey by Ferris and Graddy (1988) did support this expectation. Many of the more high-profile cases of contracting in recent years do, however, come from mayor cities.

- *Cost sensitivity.* The surveys confirmed that cost is indeed the driving motivation for contracting.

- *Level of autonomy.* The autonomy that U.S. local governments enjoy has resulted in considerable diversity in approaches to service delivery. Indeed, although every U.S. local government contracts out something, it appears that no two governments contract out the same set of services!

- *Input rigidities.* We speculated that direct provision would be favored where local governments could reduce internal rigidities to pursue more efficient and effective ways of delivering services. The survey did not address this issue, so the only available evidence is anecdotal. The evidence presented in this book suggests that U.S. local governments are reforming the civil service system and downsizing in-house provision. However, these reforms are largely piecemeal rather than a fundamental attempt to reinvent internally. This contrasts sharply with the revolution under way in countries such as New Zealand and the U.K. Many local governments in the U.K., for example, have broken away from national collective bargaining, introduced performance pay for all staff, and devolved budget and personnel powers to front-line managers. This piecemeal approach to civil service reform is also mirrored in state government (Chi, 1994).

4

What Difference
Does Contracting Make?

Does contracting result in savings? What happens to the government employees who lose their jobs? Does contracting lead to poorer services? This chapter focuses on the impacts of contracting. There is a large literature on the subject, comprising opinion surveys of public officials, before-and-after studies, and comparative research.

OPINION SURVEYS

Most people assume that the private sector is more efficient than government in providing services. It appears that many public officials share this view, at least for certain services! A number of surveys have been conducted in recent years that support this view. Here are some examples:

—Florestano and Gordon (1980) surveyed 89 cities with populations of fewer than 50,000. Around 60% of respondents said costs were the same or lower than in-house provision and nearly 80% felt that services were the same or better.

—A 1984 survey of 55 state and local highway officials by *Roads* magazine found that two-thirds of the officials planned, on cost grounds, to rely more heavily on contractors rather than on in-house providers (*Roads*, 1984).

—A 1986 survey of 247 New Jersey municipal and county officials found that around 90% were satisfied with contracted services (Eagleton Institute of Politics, 1986). Cost savings and in-house limitations were cited as the main reasons.

—A nationwide survey undertaken by Touche Ross in 1987 provided more support. Three-quarters of local governments contracting for services cited cost savings as a major reason. Of these, just under 40% reported savings of between 10–20%, and a little over 40% claimed savings in excess of 20%.

—The most recent national survey of local governments conducted by the International City/County Management Association again found that the main motivation for contracting was cutting service costs (Miranda & Andersen, 1994).

Unfortunately these surveys merely report the views of local officials. They do not provide any hard evidence that contracting does save money, nor is it clear where money is being saved, how much, and why. Are savings due to increased productivity or to reduced service quality? The only way to answer these questions is to examine the facts.

BEFORE-AND-AFTER STUDIES

Before-and-after studies involve examining the impact on program spending for a local government that used to deliver a service in-house and then contracted out part or all of the function. Care needs to be taken to ensure a fair comparison. For example, does the service level remain the same or change? Have all the relevant overheads for the in-house provider been included in the cost equation? In addition, do savings erode over time as contracts are extended or rebidded? Finally, what is meant by savings? Do program savings translate into overall reductions in expenditure, or are they diverted to other spending programs? Below are a number of examples of before-and-after studies. They are based on my visits (LA County, Phoenix, Indianapolis, Chicago) and published sources (Philadelphia, Massachusetts, the Federal Government).

* *County of Los Angeles.* Between 1980 and 1990, this county contracted out for services in some 22 areas, including building and landscape maintenance, parking, fleet maintenance, mental health clinics, child support administration, and dental services. The cumulative amount awarded was $731.1 million, with cumulative savings of $246.6 million. Annual expenditure on these contracted-out services is in the region of $250–270 million, with annual savings running at $50 million, a saving of around 20%. Nearly 5,000 positions were eliminated.

* *City of Phoenix.* Since 1979, Phoenix has subjected a wide range of services to competition. Unlike many other jurisdictions, Phoenix allows its employees to bid for the contract (public/private competition). A wide range of service areas have been subject to this process, including trash collection, janitorial work, street repair, public defender, housing management, and the ambulance service. Cumulative savings total $25.4 million. The city also identifies a number of service improvements. For example, since subjecting emergency transportation to public/private competition, the speed of response has improved dramatically. Prior to public/private competition, just under 50% of responses were within 10 minutes. Now, just over 95% of responses are within 10 minutes.

- *City of Indianapolis.* Since 1992, the city has contracted out over 50 services, including trash collection, wastewater treatment, and printing. Much of the contracting has been done using a public/private competition process similar to that in Phoenix. Annual savings amount to $28 million. Savings for most services are within the 20–40% range.

- *City of Philadelphia.* The Reason Foundation reports that Mayor Rendell has contracted out 19 services since 1992 resulting in annual savings of $21.5 million (Reason Foundation, 1994). Savings averaged between 40% and 50% of pre-contract budgets.

- *Commonwealth of Massachusetts.* Since 1991, Governor Weld has contracted out a wide range of services, from highway maintenance and mental health hospitals to prison health care. Cumulative savings total $275 million (Reason Foundation, 1994).

- *Office of Federal Procurement Policy.* The Office for Federal Procurement Policy examined 235 contracts awarded by one agency for support services such as data processing and food services. The study found that providing such services in-house was 28% more expensive (Office of Management and Budget, 1984).

The first issue to deal with is whether these savings real. Cities such as Phoenix and Indianapolis have calculated their savings carefully. Indianapolis has established a cost-accounting system that includes the relevant overheads in the cost of service activities, irrespective of whether they are provided in-house or contracted out. Phoenix has developed a systematic methodology for comparing contractor costs with the costs of in-house provision. The city's auditor makes an independent assessment of the full cost of in-house provision, including costs such as fringe benefits, internal support services (e.g., payroll), and capital. The additional cost of contract management is also added to the contractor's bid.

LA County also has a methodology for comparing the costs of in-house provision with contracting out, prepared by the auditor-controller. This involves calculating the "full" county costs, including direct service costs and relevant indirect costs such as departmental administration and countywide support costs. It also involves "leveling the playing field" to avoid comparing the costs of providing different levels of service.

There are some variations in accounting practices between the local governments. Phoenix, for example, includes an estimate of the extra management costs of contracting out. LA County and Indianapolis do not, and as a result they probably overstate the real level of savings being achieved by a small amount. Many cities, such as New York and Chicago, use traditional line budgeting, and cost-comparison calculations are decentralized without a clear citywide methodology. It is highly doubtful whether such cities can identify the real costs of in-house provision. There are also questions over the application of the methodologies. The Little Hoover Commission, for example, examined LA County's contracting program in 1983. It found that the methodology was not being applied consistently, although it did not challenge the county's estimate of the level of savings achieved through contracting. Phoenix and Indianapolis achieve consistency by centralizing the assessment process.

Another problem relates to employee displacement. Most local governments visited had progressive redeployment programs. If the local government decides to contract out a function, they freeze hiring and do all they can to redeploy those employees not hired by the new contractor. Phoenix, for example, allows a year for redeployment. This is a much more employee-friendly approach than is usual in the U.K. However, it has a cost, although none of the local governments was clear on the size of the cost, and such costs were not included in the cost–benefit equation.

When local governments talk about savings, they usually mean program savings rather than general reductions in expenditure. It is very difficult to establish what happens to program savings. The Milwaukee case study shows that the competition program for internal support services had little impact on the city's overall expenditure or that for support services. In Indianapolis, a significant portion of the savings from contracting were reinvested in other services, most notably community policing. Both LA County and Phoenix experienced rapid growth, and therefore savings were lost in overall budget growth.

Another issue relates to whether or not savings result from reduced service levels. Very little systematic data is available, but a casual examination of selected contracts suggests that supply-side factors are more important in explaining lower costs than changes in demand. In most cases service levels are maintained, and in a few cases they are improved. For example, in Indianapolis the service levels for the trash collection and wastewater treatment contracts remained broadly the same while producing substantial savings.

A final issue relates to whether savings last or whether they erode over time. Of the local governments with before and after data which I visited, only LA County and Phoenix have been contracting for sufficient time to make an assessment. In both cases, there was no evidence to suggest that savings eroded. Indeed, Phoenix found that savings improved steadily as competition increased, especially where the in-house providers developed strong bids. There are cases where contract prices increased and as a result the local government decided to bring production back in-house. This happened in Arlington, Virginia, where the county decided to bring street asphalt patching back in-house partially after experiencing a 44% increase in the contract price. The county estimated annual savings/cost avoidance of $100,000 as a result of this decision. One researcher found limited evidence of savings erosion (Rothenberg Pack, 1989). Rothenberg Pack revisited four years later a number of local governments that had contracted out services to see whether the savings had persisted over time. Although her sample was small, she found savings eroding in just under 50% of cases, mainly where there was a low level of competition. The general trend, however, appears to be in the opposite direction as more and more local governments contract for services and the level of competitiveness increases in most service areas.

COMPARATIVE RESEARCH

These studies compare local governments that contract for services with those that provide them in-house. The best comparative studies use samples of randomly chosen local governments. This section examines a selection of comparative studies in three categories—trash collection (the most studied local government function), other local services, and "macro" studies that look at the relationship between contracting, expenditure, and employment.

Trash Collection

Nine major surveys have been undertaken of residential trash collection in North America. Details of the studies are summarized in Table 4.1. Two of the studies challenge the view that private contracting is the most efficient method, but both contained methodological flaws. The first such study was that of Hirsch, whose sample was the smallest of the studies, and most significantly he failed to distinguish two types of private collection: collection by private firms under contract to the local government, and "open competition" where residents make their own arrangements with a private firm. He also expressed concerns about his data collection methods. The second, Collins and Downes, relied on published budget figures. Savas has shown that official budgets often underestimate substantially the true cost of service delivery to the local government (Savas, 1979). The other studies collected data on actual costs. The most thorough studies (Stevens & Savas, and Stevens) included the costs of contract administration.

There is a fair degree of consistency amongst the major studies:

—Collection using private firms on contract is the most efficient method, although there are significant variations in the level of difference.

—There is no difference in service quality between private contract, open competition, and municipal collection.

—Municipal collection is less costly than "open competition."

The reasons that private contracting is less costly than the municipal alternative can be found in Stevens and Savas and in Stevens. They found that private contractors:

—used smaller crews

—experienced lower absenteeism

TABLE 4.1. North American Comparative Studies of Public and Private Residential Trash Collection

Researcher	Area	Data Period	No. of Cities analyzed	Conclusions
Hirsch (1965)	St. Louis	1960	24	No difference between public and private collection
Kemper & Quigley (1976)	Connecticut	1972–74	101	Municipal collection 14–43% more costly than private contract collection
Stevens & Savas (1977)	U.S.	1974	439	Municipal collection 29–37% more costly than private contract collection. No difference in effectiveness
Kitchen (1976)	Canada	Reported in 1976	48	Municipal collection more costly than private contract collection
Collins & Downes (1977)	St. Louis County	Reported in 1977	53	No clear pattern
Petrovic & Jaffe (1977)	Midwestern U.S.	1974	83	Municipal collection 15% more costly than private contract collection
Bennett & Johnson (1981)	Fairfax County, VA	Reported in 1979	?	Municipal collection more costly than open competition
McDavid (1985)	Canada	1982	109	Municipal collection 40–50% more costly than private contract collection
Stevens (1984)	Los Angeles Region	1984	20	Municipal collection 42% more costly than private contract collectioncontract

—served more households per hour

—were more likely to use incentive systems

—used higher-capacity vehicles

—tended to use vehicles where the driver could double as a loader.

In short, productivity was raised by using fewer employees, working them harder, and taking advantage of technology (e.g., larger and better garbage-disposal trucks). Significantly, the improved productivity resulted from better management rather than economies of scale. Moreover, it is possible for local governments to erode the competitive advantage of private contractors by copying their approaches. A number of researchers have found this where city employees compete with private contractors (see Savas, 1987).

Other Local Services

No other local service has been examined in as much detail as trash collection, but there are still a number of studies. These are summarized below by service.

- *A range of local services—The Stevens Study.* Stevens examined 20 cities in the Los Angeles area to establish whether contracting provided the same service at lower cost for eight services (Stevens, 1984). These included 10 contract cities and 10 cities using in-house provision, and the services covered were: street cleaning, janitorial services, residential trash collection, payroll, traffic-signal maintenance, asphalt overlay construction, turf maintenance, and tree trimming. Stevens found that contracting was less costly for all but one service: payroll. Savings from contracting ranged from 37% (tree trimming) to 95% (asphalt overlay construction). Stevens included contract management in her cost–benefit equation and controlled for quality. She found no difference in service quality between private contracting and municipal delivery and no difference in wage levels and fringe benefits. The reasons for the cost advantage of private contracting were: using fewer employees and getting them to work more productively; using the least-qualified personnel for a job; more part-time employees; and devolved management responsibility to front-line supervisors (e.g., responsibility for hiring and firing and equipment maintenance).

- *Buses.* There have been a number of studies of urban bus systems. Morlok and Viton (1985) conducted an international study that included the U.S. (in addition to Australia and the U.K.). They found that local governments saved around 50–60% by contracting with private operators. There is also evidence to show how private delivery works best. Perry and Babitsky (1986) found that private delivery was more efficient where the buses were privately operated and owned but not where the local government or agency owned the buses and contracted out only the operation. Others have found that competition is also a key issue. Both Morlok and Moseley (1986) and Savas (1993) show that competitive bidding for contracts results in lower costs. Savas, for example, cites savings of 45% in San Diego and 51% in Los Angeles as a result of competitive bidding.

- *Water and wastewater.* Crain and Zardkoohi (1978) found that water supply by public agencies was around 33% more expensive than private supply. However, the weight of evidence suggests that there is no significant difference between public and private delivery (see Byrners, Grosskopf, & Hayes, 1986; Feigenbaum & Teeples, 1982; Feigenbaum, Teeples, & Glyer, 1986; Teeples & Glyer, 1987). There are no major studies of wastewater systems. However, Indianapolis did contract for the operation of its wastewater plant in 1994. Indianapolis saved $65 million over five years, and contracting was 44% less costly than in-house provision. The in-house employees submitted an unsuccessful bid that was 10% less than the cost of the operation before the competition. The main reason for the saving was reduced staffing—the new company used around 200 employees compared to 330 under the in-house operation. The city's specification requires that water-quality standards be maintained.

- *Fire suppression and prevention.* Chapter 11 examines the Rural/Metro Corporation, the largest private fire company in the U.S., and shows that private contracting for Scottsdale is considerably more efficient than a municipal operation. The two studies of the Scottsdale set-up cite savings of 53% (Ahlbrandt, 1973) and 43% (University City Science Center, 1989). Chapter 11 identifies some concerns with regard to these conclusions, challenging the size of the savings, but accepts that the operation is significantly more efficient than municipal delivery. The reasons for the superior efficiency are threefold: first, an innovative fire-prevention system requiring sprinklers in all new buildings; second, the use of fewer employees, working longer hours; and, finally, active management that stresses devolved responsibility to front-line supervisors and considerable emphasis on team building. Intergovernmental contracting for fire protection is much more common than contracting with private firms, and the practice is growing. Chapter 7 examines the LA County Fire District and shows a significant cost advantage over direct provision by local governments. A good example can be found in 1994 when the city of Pomona eliminated its fire department and joined the LA County Fire District. A conservative estimate suggests that Pomona saved at least $1.3 million annually, representing a saving of 10%. The saving was possible because of economies of scale—LA County was able to deploy fewer firefighters and reduce management staff without affecting service levels, largely because they could draw on firefighters in neighboring jurisdictions.

- *Policing.* There has been a growth in the use of private security firms by governments and homeowner associations. Local governments, for example, use such firms for specialized purposes such as protection of civic buildings and patrolling shopping malls and city-owned public-housing estates. Homeowner associations often use private security firms for general patrol duties, although they do not have enforcement powers. For example, in Leisure World in Orange County, civilian security officers were employed to patrol and guard the gates for a gated community of around 19,000. Major local governments do not contract with security firms for basic policing. However, some local governments contract with other governments for police patrols. Such a practice is common in Southern California, especially LA County. Only one piece of research was found on the comparative costs of direct provision versus intergovernmental contracting (Mehay & Gonzalez, 1985). This work suggested that small local governments were able to achieve economies of scale and that there was a competitive pressure on the county sheriff to keep costs low because cities could always set up their own police department. The study of intergovernmental contracting in LA County, reported in Chapter 7, also suggested a cost advantage for intergovernmental contracting. Indeed, there is some evidence to show that the competitive pressure on county sheriff's departments is increasing. The city of Whittier, for example, replaced LA County as the provider of police services in the city of Sante Fe Springs. In nearby Orange County, the city of Brea supplies police services to neighboring Diamond Bar. Some cities have begun to issue requests for proposals (RFPs) and seek competitive proposals for police services rather than rely on the traditional intergovernmental contract.

- *Education.* There is little contracting for education services, other than for support services such as janitors, buses, and food. There are a few examples— Baltimore's contract with EAI and Sylvan Learning and Minneapolis School District's contract for the superintendent role with Public Sector Strategies. It was clear in both cases that the contracts had no impact on expenditure, and this was not seen as an objective of contracting. It was also difficult to assess the impact on schooling—the evidence in Baltimore, for example, showed a deterioration in the examination performance of pupils in the contracted schools, but it is not clear whether this was due to the contract, the disruption in changing systems, or other factors.

- *Public housing.* There appears to be only one study of public versus private management of public housing. A 1983 federal government study of 19 public-housing authorities using contract management found no cost advantage over authorities that managed their stock in-house (Department of Housing and Urban Development, 1983).

- *Human services.* There are very few studies of the impact of human services contracting, despite the fact that contracting is common. Contracts tend to be with nonprofit organizations or other governments rather than with for-profit firms. One of the few researchers to examine this area was De Hoog (1984), who examined contracting in Michigan's Departments of Social Services and Labor. She did not examine and compare actual service costs. Nevertheless, the picture that emerged was mixed. Cost considerations rarely had high priority, and the government agencies encountered problems in managing contracts. Noncompetitive contracting was the norm for the social services department, while the labor department did use a RFP process. In both cases, however, the market was weak.

Macro Studies

A small number of researchers have examined the impact of contracting on total local government spending, employment levels, and wages (Deacon, 1979; Ferris, 1988; Miranda & Lerner, 1995; Stein, 1990). Is contracting associated with lower overall expenditure—are program savings translated into lower taxes? How are savings achieved—fewer staff positions, or lower wages, or a combination of both? Four of the five studies use the data from the 1982 ICMA survey and are able to draw statistically significant findings (Deacon is the exception).

There is some disagreement between Stein (1990) and Miranda and Lerner (1995) over the respective merits of complete and joint contracting. The latter refers to local governments who retain some in-house capacity while contracting out part of a function. Stein shows that joint contracting does not lead to lower expenditure, whereas Miranda and Lerner argue the opposite. Despite this disagreement, all of the researchers found that:

—contracting is associated with lower expenditure by local governments

—the relationship between contracting and expenditure is not strong, supporting suggestions that some of the savings are used for expenditure elsewhere in the government

—contracting is also related to lower employment

—contracting does not affect wage levels, and indeed there is some evidence, albeit not statistically significant, to suggest that it is related to higher wages

These studies confirm the service-specific studies referred to earlier because they suggest that the causes of savings are reduced personnel levels rather than wage reductions. However, the studies could not establish whether productivity or reduced service levels led to reduced personnel levels.

DISCUSSION OF RESEARCH

The weight of research shows that for most services contracting saves money. However, the levels of saving vary significantly. This is because they are highly situational, depending on:

—the efficiency of the local government operation in the first place

—the marketplace—the number of suppliers and the degree of competition

—the function—the ease of specifying and monitoring performance

—the local governments contract management arrangements—the strategy, information systems and quality of monitoring.

This is well illustrated by comparing trash collection with the provision of human services. In the case of trash collection, there is a competitive marketplace, and contracts are often awarded solely on price using a competitive sealed-bid process; specification and monitoring is reasonably straightforward. Such conditions are often not present in human services, in which the marketplace is weak, contracts are often awarded on a noncompetitive basis, decision making is often highly political, cost considerations rarely have high priority, and contract management arrangements are inadequate, with poor information on the service requirement and little or no monitoring (see De Hoog, 1984). It is ironic that a great deal of contracting takes place in an area where these features are not always present—human services. Contracting in this area was encouraged through federal and sometimes state policies and grant regimes rather than a cost–benefit analysis of the available service-delivery methods.

Most of the evidence suggests that competition is a key factor in producing savings. The case studies in this book support this view. Indianapolis and Phoenix, for example, achieved impressive savings as a result of strategies designed to maximize competition, including encouraging their own employees to respond to RFPs and competitive sealed bids. There is some evidence to suggest that noncompetitive contracting can work to the advantage of the local government in certain circumstances. Scottsdale's private fire operation is effectively a monopoly, yet it has resulted in a low-cost/high-quality service. The same argument can be advanced for intergovernmental contracting in Southern California, especially for police and fire services. However, even with a monopoly supplier there is a degree of competition—local governments can always replace a private contract with a municipal operation, and there will always be vocal politicians and employees who will press such arguments. Such pressures keep monopoly suppliers on their guard, but the contract management strategies in place are also a critical ingredient. Scottsdale achieved impressive results, in part, because of its far-sighted prevention strategy. Baltimore, by contrast, appeared to have little idea of what it wanted from its contract with EAI for school management services.

The studies also seem to agree that the main reason for savings relate to management, not to reduced wages, poorer services, or indeed economies of scale. In practice, contractors employ fewer staff and get them to work harder. Only in a few areas did economies of scale appear to be significant—in particular, policing and fire services in urban areas.

What happens to displaced employees? Most of the cities and counties visited by the author laid off few employees. Indeed, they made every effort to redeploy displaced employees. Typically when a major contracting program is under way, the local government freezes hiring, has first right of refusal for jobs with the contractor for displaced employees, invites voluntary redundancies on generous terms for those with long service, and allows a long period for absorbing the remainder of displaced employees elsewhere in the organization. Phoenix, for example, allows up to 12 months for redeployment. This is a progressive approach, but it does have a cost. Such costs are never taken into account in the costs and benefits of contracting.

If improved productivity results primarily from staff reductions and higher output, it ought to be possible to replicate this within the public sector. The Phoenix and Indianapolis examples show that this can be done using their systems of public/private competition. However, the main trend is against public/private competition. Politicians often avoid the issue of internal reinvention because it can be more painful than contracting out. Contracting is therefore often used as an alternative to vigorous management of an in-house service.

The economic case for contracting for a range of local government services is powerful. Yet in-house provision remains the most common way of delivering services, even for those services that are easy to contract for. This is because economic considerations do not dominate the make or buy decision. Many elected and appointed officials want to retain detailed control over service delivery, and there are always major obstacles to contracting out a service. Moreover, an analysis of the case studies in this book suggests that extraordinary circumstances have to be present for a local government to change its service-delivery methods radically. This is shown below:

- *California contract cities:*   The contracting model was adopted to avoid annexation by neighboring cities.

- *LA County:*   An ambitious contracting program was developed in the 1980s following the election of a conservative-orientated board of supervisors keen to downsize county hall.

- *Indianapolis:*   The contracting program was the product of a new mayor and financial pressures due to ambitious capital projects by previous administrations.

- *Baltimore:*   The city's education system was in crisis, with high levels of illiteracy, poor examination results, and high dropout rates.

- *Chicago:*   Contracting was a response to financial pressures and a new mayor.

- *Milwaukee:*   Contracting was promoted by a highly regarded appointed official close to the mayor.

- *Phoenix:*   Contracting was a response to financial pressures and a charismatic appointed official, the public works director, who promoted public/private competition.

- *Scottsdale:*   A private operation was established before the city had established a municipal department—contracting was therefore the easiest way forward.

Only in Milwaukee was there an absence of major change. Significantly, the Milwaukee scheme is one of the more modest programs among the case studies.

CONCLUSIONS

Contracting saves money where there is competition and it is easy to specify and monitor performance by a contractor. However, levels of savings are highly situational, and the management arrangements appear to be the critical factor affecting the success or failure of contracting. Which areas are selected for competition? What is the strategy for contracting? Is the specification clear, realistic, and understood by the contractor? Does the local government monitor performance? These are the "inside the black box" issues to which we now turn.

5

The Make or Buy Decision
and Contract Management

The make or buy decision is rarely straightforward, as it often includes a series of decision points. The first decision concerns the level and nature of the service required. The second concerns the preferred service-delivery methods. Where in-house activities have been identified as candidates for contracting, decisions are needed on how to contract. How are the activities to be packaged? What contract conditions are appropriate? What procurement methods should be used? Having decided how to contract, a final and highly political decision is needed—who is to be the contractor?

This chapter examines the make or buy decision and contract management. The chapter is divided into five sections, the first of which examines the legal framework. The bulk of the chapter comprises a comparison between the theory of the make or buy decision and the practice—the initial decision, feasibility studies, contract packaging, the contracting methods, contract length, pricing, and service specifications. The approaches to contract monitoring are then examined. Next is an analysis of who makes the critical decisions. The final section discusses the main lessons for practice.

THE LEGAL FRAMEWORK

Compared to their U.K. counterparts, U.S. local governments enjoy considerable freedom over what and how they provide services. There is no U.S. equivalent of compulsory competitive tendering. Nevertheless, there are a number of laws that affect contracting. These are now explored.

Federal Laws

The Sherman Anti-Trust Act prohibits "anticompetitive" practices such as bid rigging, unfair exclusion of certain contractors, and corruption. This law affects local government contracting, unless there is a clear state law to the contrary. This view was confirmed in 1982 with the *City of Boulder v Community Communication Company* ruling. The U.S. Supreme Court ruled that Boulder, despite being a home-rule local government, must comply with antitrust law because there was no explicit state law to exempt the city from the law.

The federal government also regulates contracting where it funds projects and services. Here are three examples:

- *The Brooks Act.* This applies to infrastructure work largely funded by the federal government. It sets out, for example, detailed requirements for the selection of firms for architects/engineering contracts—the selection criteria, the evaluation process, the basis for selection, and the negotiation process.

- *Funding for human services.* During the 1960s and 1970s, the federal and state governments encouraged contracting with nonprofit organizations for the provision of human services. This helps explain why the nonprofit sector is so important today for the delivery of human services.

- *Privatization of utilities.* Utilities owned by local governments, such as a wastewater facility or an airport, are typically built with considerable funding support from the federal government. Cities have encountered legal problems in trying to dispose of such assets because of the federal connection. This happened with Indianapolis in relation to wastewater and the airport. The city eventually decided to contract out the running of both facilities rather than sell the facilities to a private concern.

State Laws

State laws vary enormously from state to state. Illinois, for example, has a Municipal Purchasing Act that regulates the contracting process for cities in the state with populations in excess of 500,000. The law applies to any purchase order or public works contract over $10,000 and only affects Chicago. Clearly, it was an attempt to discourage corruption. California introduced a law in the mid-1980s to regulate intergovernmental contracts provided by counties with populations in excess of 6 million. This was a successful attempt by contract cities to stop LA County including general county government overheads in the charges for intergovernmental contracts for sheriff's services and public works. New York State established the Wicks Law, which applies to construction projects with a value in excess of $50,000. The law requires multiple contracts for construction projects. In practice, this means separate contracts for electrical work, plumbing and gas fitting, and heating and ventilation work.

Despite the diversity, there are two common areas of state law:

- *The "lowest responsible bidder" principle.*   Virtually every state has a similar law governing the evaluation of bids and award of contracts using the competitive sealed-bid process, as distinct from RFPs or RFQs (requests for qualifications). These laws require that local governments contract with the lowest responsible bidder—in other words, the bidder with the lowest price who can meet the specification. Local governments need to have very clear reasons for rejecting the lowest bid, and they do run the risk of litigation from the unsuccessful lowest bidder. Local governments can, however, choose not to adopt the competitive sealed-bid approach.

- *Sunshine laws.*   Most states have adopted open-government provisions that affect local governments. The details of these laws vary from state to state, but most require decisions to be made in public and any financial or personal interests to be open to scrutiny. This affects contracting—public officials, for example, have to declare any financial contributions received from a city contractor for electoral campaigns.

Local Government Laws and Policies

Once again there is great variety in local ordinances and policies which affect contracting. There are three common ways such laws and policies impact on local contracting.

- *Laws restricting contracting and privatization.*   Laws making it difficult to contract out or privatize civil service positions are fairly common in unionized states and especially the older, larger cities. Two examples illustrate this. The city council in New York established a law to require a public hearing wherever the mayor proposes contracting out civil service positions. This delays the contracting process and provides another opportunity for opponents to make their case. The Los Angeles County Charter used to include a prohibition on contracting out civil service positions—this was amended in the late 1970s.

- *Collective bargaining agreements.*   These sometimes restrict or eliminate contracting. In New York City, for example, the unions negotiated the right to put in a counter-proposal after a private contractor has been selected for a city service but before the contract has been awarded.

- *Affirmative-action and preference programs.*   Many cities and counties have price and policy preferences for contracting for goods and services. The author found preference programs in operation in the larger and older local governments—New York, Chicago, Baltimore, and Los Angeles County. The smaller rural and suburban governments tended not to have preference programs. Table 5.1 summarizes the results of a 1993 survey by the National Institute for Governmental Purchasing (NIGP, 1993). The survey does not constitute a representative sample of local governments but does give a feel for the extent and nature of preference programs.

TABLE 5.1. Preference Programs (percentages)

Preference	Cities	Counties	School Districts	Special Districts
Local—buying from a locally based vendor	25	19	16	33
Buy-American	13	15	20	29
Small- or disadvantaged business	13	6	14	29
Minority-business enterprise	21	13	16	14
Woman-owned business	21	12	14	31
Recycled-products	43	49	41	58

Note: The survey included 136 cities, 78 counties, 44 school districts, and 52 special districts. No information was available on the sample or the response rate.

The NIGP data also show the following:

—There has been a significant decline in local preference buying in recent years.

—Preference programs for small businesses, minority-owned businesses, and woman-owned businesses are overwhelmingly based on goals rather than set-asides. In other words, they involve targets but do not reserve a set proportion of business for the group in question.

—Most local governments believed that preferences for small and minority- and woman-owned businesses are effective—they increased the number of bidders and improved the competitiveness of the target group. Few local governments rated the local preferences as effective.

MAKING OR BUYING

In an ideal world, a local government would approach the make or buy decision as follows. First, it would establish how much it costs to provide a service in-house. Then, it would review all the alternatives to in-house provision. Having decided to contract for certain services, it would then determine the most appropriate contract strategy (the packaging and the terms and conditions of the contract) and the service specification to ensure the highest level of service at the lowest cost. Unfortunately, the make or buy decision is rarely like this in the real world of local government. Indeed, Table 5.2 shows that few of the local governments visited by the author undertook all four steps, and this sample includes local governments renowned for their innovative approaches to contracting. The four steps of the make or buy decision in practice are now examined.

TABLE 5.2.   The Make or Buy Decision in Practice

Issue	Ind	Ph	Ch	NY	LA	Mi	Bal	Lkd	Ro	SC
Knowledge of the costs of in-house provision?	Y	IP	N	N	IP	IP	N	Y	Y	Y
Systematically reviews service-delivery options?	Y	N	N	N	N	N	N	IP	IP	IP
Strategic approach to contracting?	Y	N	N	N	N	N	N	IP	IP	IP
Carefully considers service requirement?	Y	Y	N	N	N	N	N	Y	Y	Y

Key: Y = yes; N = no; IP = in part; Ind = Indianapolis; Ph = Phoenix; Ch = Chicago; NY = New York; LA = LA County; Mi = Milwaukee; Bal = Baltimore; Lkd = Lakewood, California; Ro = Rosemead, California; SC = Santa Clarita, California.

The Preconditions to the Make or Buy Decision

Few local governments know the full costs of in-house service provision. Traditional government budgeting and accounting focuses on inputs such as salaries, equipment, and goods. It does not focus on activities. As a result, the full costs of in-house service delivery are often not known. Moreover, many costs are excluded from the traditional line-item budget. For example, the traditional trash-collection budget would exclude the costs of capital equipment, overheads such as payroll and support services, and other indirect costs such as fringe benefits and pensions.

Modern budget practice has led to the development of "program budgets" that collect costs on the basis of a program. Even here, however, capital and overhead costs are usually excluded from the budget. In the late 1970s, Savas surveyed local governments to compare budgeted and actual costs—he found that budgets consistently understated the true costs of in-house provision (Savas, 1979). This finding still holds true today, although the gap that Savas found—of around 30%—is probably significantly smaller.

One way to overcome the deficiency in budget information is to calculate separately the costs of in-house provision and contracting. Most local governments do this. However, practice varies widely between and within local governments. Few local governments have a standard approach that is consistently applied.

How do the case-study local governments fare on the quality of their financial information?

• *Indianapolis:* gets highest marks. In 1992, the city implemented an "activity-based costing" system called ABC, using a firm of consultants. This determines the full costs of city services, including capital and fixed costs such as building costs. It also compares service costs to outputs, allowing management to compare efficiency within the city organization. However, the city does not have a standard methodology for comparing the costs of in-house provision to contracting. A standard methodology does not mean that the comparison will be similar in each case, but merely that the same principles are applied. There are sound reasons for expecting differences—the cost of contract management, for example, will vary from service to service. The city hires outside consultants to make the comparison. This is fine, but there is a risk of inconsistent approaches being adopted.

- *Phoenix:* does not have an activity-based cost-accounting system in place but does have a well-developed and comprehensive methodology for comparing public and private costs. Moreover, the cost comparison is the responsibility of the city auditor, which ensures a consistent approach.

- *Los Angeles County:* has an activity-based cost-accounting system and a methodology for comparing public and private costs of service delivery. However, there are some shortcomings with both tools. The cost-accounting system allocates relevant overhead costs to cost centers but does not include costs such as capital equipment. The methodology for public/private comparisons assumes no contract management costs when a service is contracted out on the grounds that such management effort is required whether a service is provided in-house or contracted out. This may be an effective strategy to contain contract management costs, but it does not provide an accurate picture as contracting nearly always involves some extra management effort, although the extent will vary from service to service. Two external investigations in the 1980s also found that the methodology was not followed consistently by all departments.

- *Baltimore, Chicago, and New York:* all have traditional line-item budgets. At the time of writing, only New York had developed a methodology for comparing in-house costs with contracting.

- *Lakewood, Santa Clarita, and Rosemead:* as most of their services are contracted out or provided by other governments, the issues are less critical. Nevertheless, all three cities have cost-accounting systems in place for the small volume of services delivered in-house.

Systematic Feasibility Studies

Only a few of the local governments visited genuinely examined all of the options for delivering services. Indianapolis was the best example. Mayor Goldsmith established the Service, Efficiency, and Lower Taxes for Indianapolis Commission (SELTIC) in February 1992, shortly after his election. SELTIC comprised nine local entrepreneurs, who were supported by over 100 volunteers. The commission surveyed city assets and services and made proposals to the mayor for change. Many of these involved contracting out services, and most were implemented by the mayor. SELTIC was the decision-making process for service-delivery methods.

The other example of a comprehensive approach is that of the California contract cities. Unlike Indianapolis, these cities never had a tradition of in-house provision. They began life contracting out all services with the parent county following incorporation as cities. Over time, however, these cities typically examine all of their services and decide whether to continue intergovernmental agreements with the county, to contract with other providers (including for- and nonprofit firms as well as other governments), or set up their own in-house service. All of the contract cities visited had a much more diversified pattern of service delivery today than they had at the date of incorporation. There were numerous examples of contract cities examining the feasibility of providing police services in-house or contracting with a neighboring city rather than continuing to use LA County. There were also examples of full-service cities which had invited LA County to undertake feasibility studies involving replacing in-house fire and police services with intergovernmental agreements and contracts.

Few of the other local governments adopted a systematic approach to reviewing service-delivery methods. Chicago and Baltimore, for example, were highly opportunistic in their approach. There was no comprehensive review of activities and possibilities. In Chicago what typically happened was an official in the mayor's office or in the office of budget and management or even an outsider making a proposal that would be considered on its merits. If the mayor favored the idea, a contracting process would follow. In Baltimore, major contracting exercises involving education were undertaken without any detailed feasibility studies. The mayor was clearly impatient to introduce change.

Contract Packaging

Packaging is in many ways the key to successful contracting. Does the local government contract out an entire service or part of a service? Does the local government retain responsibility for equipment and facilities or not?

A wide variety of approaches to contract packaging were found, as described below:

- *Contracting for peaks.* A number of local governments staff-up for a basic workload and contract for peaks. A good example is Chicago's Department of Transportation. Prior to Mayor Daley's administration, the bulk of design and construction management work was done in-house, even though the workload varied according to the size of the capital program and the level of funding available. In practice, the function was overstaffed during certain times because it was staffed to cope with peak workloads. Over the past six years, the Daley administration downsized a substantial part of the in-house function and contracted for more work.

- *Contracting for competition.* A number of local governments, although fewer than anticipated, structured their contracts to encourage competition to reduce the risks of private monopoly. They did it in a variety of ways. Phoenix and

Indianapolis, for example, developed public/private competition where public employees were encouraged to compete against the private sector for city contracts. Another approach was to retain some work in-house and contract out for the remainder—partial contracting. Phoenix always kept a minimum of one-third of its trash collection workload in-house, while Lakewood, a contract city, kept some of the tree-trimming work in-house. Yet another approach was to contract with more than one provider—multiple contracting. Indianapolis, for example, divided the city into ten trash-collection districts but prohibited a contractor from winning more than three areas.

- *Complete contracting.* This is where a local government contracts for an entire service with one provider. There appeared to be relatively few examples of this kind. The Scottsdale contract with the Rural/Metro clearly falls into this category, as do the Indianapolis contracts for wastewater, the airport, and data processing. These contracts tend to be long term—Scottsdale's fire contract is for five years, and the Indianapolis contracts are for seven to ten years.

- *Total contracting.* This is where contracting has become a way of life for the local government. The make or buy decision is an integral part of strategic management—the local government regularly asks how it should ensure that its services are delivered. Indianapolis and the California contract cities were engaged in total contracting. Few functions were viewed as sacrosanct, and all service-delivery options would be considered. This was in sharp contrast to all the other local governments visited, even Phoenix, which has achieved an international reputation on the basis of its system of public/private competition. While Phoenix had applied public/private competition mainly to public works functions, the dominant philosophy in the city government was to improve in-house service provision with a quality-management system—there was a whole range of services that were not going to be subject to public/private competition.

- *Noncompetitive contracting.* A surprising amount of contracting was noncompetitive. Contracting in cities such as Indianapolis and Phoenix was strongly based on the competition ethic—contracts were designed to maximize the number of bidders, and a formal competition would normally be held when the term of a contract expired. However, this approach was not the norm in most of the local governments visited. Contracts for public works, technical services, and professional work would be the subject of formal competition at some point. However, where a government was happy with a contractor, it was common to extend the contract without going through competition. This is well illustrated in Chapter 7, where contract cities routinely extend contracts for many years. The city of Rosemead, for example, contracts with a professional engineering and planning firm to provide engineering, traffic engineering, and building official functions. The contract is an open agreement that Rosemead can terminate with 30 days' notice. The fee structure is agreed annually. The contract was awarded in 1978 following a competitive RFP process but has not been subject to competition since. Lakewood has an annual contract with a firm to collect residential trash which has been extended for 28 years. Noncompetitive contracting is even more common with nonprofits and other governments. New York was fairly typical in awarding human service contracts to nonprofits on a noncompetitive basis—this is now changing, as is described in Chapter 9. Intergovernmental contracting for sheriff's services in Southern California is also usually noncompetitive.

• *Devolved contracting.*   This is where the responsibility for determining the level and nature of a service is devolved within an organization. Devolved contracting was not common in the local governments visited, except for Milwaukee, where the responsibility for a range of support services had been transferred from the support services to user departments. Using their newfound freedom, some user departments chose to contract out some of their support services. Devolved contracting is much more common in the U.K. because of the emphasis on devolution.

• *Contracting for management.*   This is the least common form of contract. The Minneapolis School District's contract for the superintendent's function with a public sector consultancy was an example of this.

• *Contracting for support services.*   This is less common in the U.S. compared to the U.K. In the U.K. it is now mandatory for local governments to invite private sector firms to provide what many would regard as core administrative services such as financial services, data processing, and personnel advice. This area is beginning to grow in the U.S., however. At the time of writing, for example, Indianapolis was negotiating to contract out its data-processing function. Baltimore's schools contract with EAI covers management and support services, but the teachers remain employees of the city.

• *Contracting for direct services.*   This is the norm in the U.S., especially for public works and human services.

The above strategies demonstrate the variety of potential approaches, both in theory and in practice. The particular strategy adopted should depend on a number of factors, notably:

   —the nature of the function: how easy is it to specify and monitor?

   —the marketplace: how many providers are there?

   —management factors: what are the costs of contract management?

   —quality of contract management: how smart are officials in examining the options and selecting the one that maximizes value for money?

In practice, decisions about contract strategy often do not take into account the above considerations. Decisions tend to be made primarily on political grounds and be event-driven, rather than the result of rational analysis.

In most the local governments visited, the push for contracting came from a new administration. New mayors in New York, Chicago, and Indianapolis put contracting on the agenda, as did the election of a more conservative board of supervisors in LA County in the early 1980s. In Baltimore, the mayor was the prime mover behind the contracting initiatives. Only in Phoenix and Milwaukee did the initiative come from appointed officials.

Many of these initiatives were political responses to crises of one kind or another. Financial problems loomed in most of the large cities, such as New York with a huge $2 billion deficit and Indianapolis with a $20 million deficit. In Baltimore, contracting was part of a political response to a growing crisis in the school system—high levels of illiteracy, poor educational performance, and so on. In LA County, contracting was part of a political campaign to make government smaller. The California contract cities adopted contracting for pragmatic rather than ideological reasons—contracting allowed them to incorporate without imposing new and higher taxes on their residents and businesses. This is because they were able to avoid set-up costs and achieve economies of scale. Scottsdale's contract with the Rural/Metro had unusual origins—the private company existed before a municipal department could be established. As a result, establishing a contract with the company was an easy and obvious solution for a new and growing city.

The political influence can be illustrated through what is included in and excluded from consideration. The city of Santa Clarita, for example, has three trash-collection districts supplied by private collectors on a franchise basis. These franchises were in practice a continuation of the situation prior to incorporation, and under California law the city would have to give five years' notice to change the arrangement. It was clear during the author's visit that appointed officials recognized the inefficiency of the existing arrangement—substantial savings of perhaps 20% would be possible by reducing the number of districts to one and subjecting them to vigorous competition. This had been raised in the past but rejected by the elected politicians who had developed a close relationship with the contractors. Continuing the existing approach of multiple, noncompetitive contracting was politically expedient.

Few local governments appeared to take a strategic approach to contracting. Chicago, for example, had no obvious strategy for contracting. Decisions appeared to be highly opportunisitic, and there were significant variations between departments in their aggressiveness towards contracting. No survey had been undertaken to identify the best candidates for contracting, and there was no formal plan for the future. Baltimore's contract with EAI for running nine of its schools also lacked a clear strategy. The mayor responded to a growing crisis in the city's education system with the contract with EAI. He clearly wanted to be seen to be doing something highly visible. However, no feasibility study of the options had been undertaken, there was no contract specification to speak of, there was no competition for the contract, and the whole contract was rushed through in just three months, with a letter of intent in June of 1991, a contract in July, and the start of the contract in September.

New York City had a puzzling pattern of service delivery. Most of the service contracting was for difficult-to-contract services in the human service area, and virtually all of the easy-to-contract areas were provided in-house—trash collection and public transit, for example. The main reasons for this pattern were political—encouragement by the federal and state government to contract for health and human services and resistance by in-house unions to contracting for trash, transit, and other public works functions. The city had, however, established a committee to review all services to identify candidates for contracting and privatization.

The clearest example of a strategic approach was Indianapolis. The city began by establishing business systems such as activity-based costing. It also surveyed all services to identify promising candidates for contracting and privatization. Then it reviewed strategic options for specific areas such as trash collection, wastewater, data processing, and the airport, often using outside consultants.

The California contract cities provided an example of a mature approach to contracting which evolved over nearly 40 years. Over a long period, cities had experimented with a variety of providers—private firms, the county, or an in-house function—eventually settling for a pattern that was both cost-effective and politically acceptable.

CONTRACTING METHODS

Procurement Techniques

There are three main contracting methods used—competitive sealed bids, requests for proposals (sometimes called negotiated contracts), and sole-source negotiations.

Sealed competitive bidding is the most common method used (the invitation for bids: IFB). It involves a comprehensive and precise description of what is required—the service specification. The contract is also awarded to the "lowest responsible bidder." In other words, cost is the decisive factor in deciding who gets the contract. No modifications or negotiations are possible once the bid has been submitted.

Requests for proposals are the second most common method. They are the preferred approach for professional service contracts. Like competitive bidding the process involves a sealed bid. However, a comprehensive service specification is not always a feature of an RFP. This is because prospective contractors are often encouraged to develop their own approaches. RFPs also use multiple criteria in evaluation and selection. Cost is only one factor and rarely the most important.

Despite the difference, there are a number of similarities between IFBs and RFPs. Both techniques are designed to encourage competition. As a result, IFBs and RFPs are usually advertised in trade journals and newspapers. Another common method is to approach potential contractors directly or to commission consultants to undertake market research to identify suitable contractors. Both techniques use formalized evaluation processes, and both usually include protest procedures to enable unsuccessful bidders to complain if they feel that they have been treated unfairly.

A small number of contracts are awarded on a sole-source basis—that is, without going through a competitive process. Sole sourcing has to be fully justified when, for example, there is a patent or copyright issue or there is only one supplier.

The procurement literature stresses the different purposes of the techniques—IFBs where you can specify the service or product clearly, RFPs where specification is more difficult and you want to encourage innovation, and sole sourcing where there is only one supplier. Are these the grounds that local governments operate on in practice?

- Seven IFBs—three for custodial service contracts, three for trash collection contracts, and one for personal care attendants—were examined. The only one where there are grounds for using an RFP approach rather than an IFB was the last one, personal care attendants.

- Of the eleven RFP contracts examined—one for education services, two for architectural/engineering services, two for social services, two for legal services, one for information technology services, one for the running of an airport, one for operating a wastewater facility, and one for youth services—there were questions in relation to seven of them. The social services and youth services RFPs were very detailed and highly prescriptive, which left the author wondering why an RFP rather than an IFB was used. The legal services and architectural/engineering contracts, on the other hand, were thin on inputs, outputs, and processes—there was no specification in place—and as a result there were strong similarities to in-house provision.

- Only two of the contracts examined were procured on a sole-source basis—the Baltimore schools contract and the Scottsdale emergency services contract. In both cases there are few suppliers in the marketplace. However, it would have been possible in both cases to adopt an RFP process, negotiating with the small number of firms that do exist. However, a large number of contracts are renewed and extended without going through a competitive process, a form of sole sourcing by the back door. This practice was especially common among the California contract cities. Trash collection contracts and franchises and professional services contracts (e.g., for city engineer and building-official functions) are regularly extended without going through a competition, although most of the contracts/franchises were originally awarded following competition. In addition, the vast majority of intergovernmental contracts were awarded on a sole-source basis.

There is clearly a strong attraction to noncompetitive contracting, despite the appearance of open competition. The large number of extensions and renewals demonstrates this. It is also supported by the preference for RFPs over IFBs for services, especially where it is possible to specify the outputs, inputs, tasks, and workload volumes. Many of the public officials interviewed stressed that they wanted to be able to select their contractor without being wedded solely to price.

Entering into contracts without a real specification is fairly common. This was true of many of the professional service contracts and the intergovernmental contracts. There is nothing wrong or inappropriate here, except that it does demand more attention during the contract management phase to ensure that the local government knows what it wants and checks to make sure it gets it.

Contract Length

Table 5.3 shows the contract lengths and termination clauses for some of the contracts examined. There are three broad types of contract length:

- *Short contracts for a period of one or two years.* These are normally used for straightforward contracts such as trash collection and custodial services.

- *Long contracts for three to ten years.* Most of these are for large, complex packages of services, such as school-based management, emergency services, or law enforcement. There are exceptions such as the Arlington County trash collection contract with a minimum period of four years.

- *Open contracts that are for an indefinite period but notice can be given at any time.* There is a surprising number of open contracts in Southern California for a wide range of services. This underlines the wish of many local governments to minimize formal competition.

Many of the short and long contracts include the option of extending the contract for a specified period. Most of the contracts give the local government the ability to terminate the contract for default or convenience with a relatively short notice period and in some cases no notice at all.

Pricing

There are four types of contract fee arrangements (see Harney, 1994). The first is the fixed-price contract. This is where the fee is fixed in advance and the contractor bears the risk for any unforeseen costs. Normally, such a contract would be adjusted periodically, usually annually, to recognize inflation. Some fixed-price contracts include incentives for "good" performance. Many of the larger, long-term contracts were fixed fees, such as the Scottsdale emergency contract, Baltimore's school contract, and the LA County law enforcement contract.

The second type is the cost plus fixed fee contract. Here the contractor is reimbursed for costs incurred as well as fixed fee. This type of contract is common for professional services. Few examples of this kind were encountered except for the Rosemead contract for city engineering and building official duties. The contract fee involved a monthly retainer but was primarily based on the volume of work and a percentage of fees.

TABLE 5.3. Contract Length

Local Government	Contract Length
Arlington County—custodial services	Up to two years; ability to terminate for default or convenience with 15 days' notice.
Arlington County—trash collection	Four years, with 3 one-year renewal options; ability to terminate for default or convenience with 15 days' notice.
Baltimore County—meals for the elderly	One year, with an option to renew for a further year; 60 days' notice required to terminate for unsatisfactory performance.
Baltimore School Board	Five years, with the ability to extend one year at a time for an indefinite period; 90 days' notice required to terminate for convenience or default.
Chesterfield County—architectural/engineering services	Two years, with the option of renewing it for a further two years.
Howard County—custodial services	One year, with the option to renew for two further one-year periods; ability to terminate for default or convenience.
Howard County—legal services	One year, with the option to renew for two further one-year periods; ability to terminate for default or convenience.
Indianapolis—operation of the airport	Ten years.
Indianapolis—information technology services	Ten years.
Indianapolis—trash collection	Three years.
Indianapolis—operation of wastewater facility	Seven years.
Lakewood—street maintenance contract with LA County	Five years, renewable for successive five-year periods; 60 days' notice required for termination.
LA County—law enforcement contract	Five years, renewable for successive five-year periods; 60 days' notice required for termination.
Minneapolis School District—superintendent	Three years, with the ability to terminate with 30 days' notice.
New York—home attendant services	Either: two years, with two separate renewal options each for two years; or three years with the option to renew for a further three-year period.
Phoenix—custodial services	One year, with the option to extend up to three years in one-year increments; ability to terminate contract immediately for default.
Phoenix—trash collection	Two and a half years, with the option to extend for a further two years in one-year increments.
Rosemead—city engineering and building official duties	Open contract with ability to terminate without cause and without notice at any time.
Scottsdale—emergency services	Five years, with the option to extend for a further 15 years in five-year increments.

Sources: Contracts supplied by the NGIP and visits to some of the local governments.

The third type of contract is the time and materials contract, with the cost dependent on the amount of labor and materials used.

The final type is the percentage of revenue contract. This type is often used where contractors have a concession and receive revenues. Lakewood had a contract for catering that fell into this category.

The one thing that surprised the author was the number of time and materials contracts. These were fairly common for professional services such as legal and architectural/engineering services. These are often the same contracts without a specification. Once again this points to the critical nature of the contract management arrangements for such contracts.

The Service Specification

The quality of a specification is a critical ingredient of smart contracting. It determines the kind of relationship between the government and the contractor. Is it clear what is required? The detail and nature of specifications vary from area to area and depend on the ease of specifying the activity, the extent to which the activity is routine or nonroutine, and the type of contracting method used—an invitation for bid, an RFP, sole sourcing, or intergovernmental contracting.

Some of the key issues to look for in a specification are set out below. They all relate to the clarity of what the local government wants.

• *Inputs.* Does the local government specify the resource inputs needed—the personnel, equipment, and facilities? This can help the bidder understand the volume of work to be done, but it can also eliminate innovation.

• *Processes and tasks.* Does the local government identify the tasks to be performed? Again, the level of detail and prescription is of interest here.

• *Outputs and performance.* Are any particular results expected? Is "good" and "bad" performance spelled out? Is any attention devoted to quality?

A sample of over 20 specifications and contracts were examined, comparing them to the questions identified above. These were drawn from the cities and counties visited and supplemented by a sample of well-thought-of specifications supplied by the National Institute for Governmental Purchasing. They cover a wide variety of services, from trash collection to human services and fire protection.

1. *Easy-to-Specify Services*

Table 5.4 summarizes the author's analysis of specifications for trash collection and custodial services. All of the specifications were for competitive sealed bids, and all were good examples of their kind—clear and comprehensive speci-

TABLE 5.4.   Specifications for Trash Collection and Custodial Services

Specification	Comments
Trash collection	
1. Phoenix, AZ—for the emptying of dumpsters from city-owned buildings	Specifies locations and size of contractor-supplied containers as well as the frequency of collection. Gives the city the right to terminate the contractor where it feels that the work is unsatisfactory, but this is not defined.
2. Arlington County, VA—residential trash collection	Specifies properties to be served and excluded, collection routes, handling of refuse, the schedule, supervision, and the need for public education. Also specifies the equipment and various requirements of contractor personnel—behavior, uniforms, safety. Mentions inspections and the need for the contractor to have "sufficient" personnel but does not spell out what is meant by these terms.
3. Loudoun County, VA—collection of trash from county buildings	Specifies locations, size of containers, and frequency of pick-up.
Custodial services	
1. Phoenix, AZ—custodial services for police facilities	Specifies areas to be cleaned, frequency of cleaning, standards, equipment, and product requirements. Also requires employees to be able to read. Describes monitoring requirements. Includes a 5% price preference for MBEs and WBEs.
2. Arlington County, VA—custodial services for the county courts/police building	Specifies areas, frequencies, tasks, and hours. Does not specify equipment and product standards. Various employee requirements—uniforms, security, supervision, etc. Involves a "double-envelope" approach.
3. Howard County, MD—custodial services for a detention center and an animal control facility	Specifies areas, frequency, tasks, and hours. Requires a "sufficient" number of employees (but does not specify), as well as supervision. Contractor must also comply with federal minimum-wage requirements and have at least 10% minority representation on the workforce.

Sources: 1994 City of Phoenix IFB No 94-417 for Refuse Collection—Requirements Contract; 1994 Arlington County IFB No 6-95 Residential Refuse Collection Amendment No 1; 1993 County of Loudoun IFB for Refuse Collection Services, issued 5-10-93; 1994 City of Phoenix IFB No 94-263 for Custodial Services—Requirements Contract (Police Facilities); 1994 Arlington County IFB No 453-94 Amendment No 1; 1994 Howard County IFB No 95-037 for Custodial Services.

fications. In every case, the inputs and tasks were spelled out in detail. In the case of trash collection, for example, this involved the number, nature, and frequency of pick-ups; for custodial services, the areas to be cleaned, the hours, the frequency, and the products to be used. The custodial specifications were also the most output-based of the group that I examined. The Phoenix custodial specification gave the most attention to this, with specifications for equipment and products to be used and, most significantly, a clear description of cleanliness standards. For example:

—*Dusting.*   "A proper dusted surface is free of all dirt and dust, streaks, lint and cobwebs."

—*Sweeping/vacuuming.*   "A properly swept floor is free of all dirt, grit, lint and debris, except embedded dirt and grit."

—*Glass cleaning.*   "Glass is clean when all glass surfaces are without streaks, film, deposits and stains, and have a uniformly bright appearance and adjacent surfaces have been wiped clean."

Arlington County's custodial service specification adopted a "double-envelope" approach to emphasize quality issues. Bidders were first screened to establish whether they meet the technical aspects of the specification. Then the lowest-price bid of the technically sound bids was selected.

2.   *Difficult-to-Specify Services*

Many services are more difficult to specify than trash collection and custodial services. The following is an analysis of specifications and agreements for a wide range of services from fire protection to social services:

* *City of Scottsdale's contract with the Rural/Metro Corporation for emergency services.*   This is a good example of a service agreement. Inputs, processes, and tasks are specified in detail. For example, detailed requirements are made covering staffing levels and training and equipment responsibility and levels. The contract includes a requirement that wages for Rural/Metro staff remain roughly comparable with similar staff in neighboring jurisdictions. There is also an attempt to identify performance and output measures. Target responses to incidents are included. There are also requirements for prevention work such as those relating to the number of inspections undertaken of fire hydrants and sprinklers in homes and businesses.

* *Baltimore School Board's contract with EAI for school-based management and support services.*   This spells out inputs, tasks, and processes such as responsibilities for minor maintenance, employees, equipment (e.g., computers), and use of premises and facilities. It also agrees to the adoption of EAI's approach to education, which is called Tesseract. This involves a multicultural curriculum and personal education plans for each pupil. The contract is sketchy on performance

standards—it specifies some areas for evaluation standards but has no targets. Here is the relevant excerpt from the contract:

> The Department (the School Board) and EAI agree to meet and agree on evaluation and performance criteria for the 1992–1993 School Year as soon as possible, and to meet 30 days prior to each succeeding school year to agree on evaluation and performance criteria to be utilized for that school year. The criteria should be weighted and site specific to meet the individual needs of each school and targeted to measure specific relevant achievements at each school. The criteria may include, but are not limited to: 1. Standardized Tests; 2. Criterion-referenced Tests; 3. Attendance; 4. Retention; 5. Q.S.I.; 6. P.E.P.; 7. Private Alternatives Returning (e.g., special education; other priorities; etc.).

At the time of my visit to Baltimore (December 1994), no evaluation criteria had been set. However, one internal evaluation report for 1992–93 had been completed, and outside investigators from the University of Maryland had been commissioned. The former evaluated Tesseract schools against comparator schools in relation to a number of factors such as material resources, instructional technology, parental involvement, student outcomes, and teacher outcomes.

• *Minneapolis School District's contract with The Public Strategies Group Inc. for the superintendent's role.* This is an unusual agreement. It does not include any input requirements but does identify a number of "accomplishments" required, together with financial rewards for each one. The accomplishments, however, relate more to process rather than results. It is, nevertheless, an interesting attempt to specify what is needed in a professional services contract. It also illustrates the difficulty of setting performance measures when the local government lacks a performance management system. For example:

D. Review and Develop a Plan To Increase Attendance

$4,000   1. Complete a baseline review to determine the percentage of time that students are not in constructive educational settings because of truancy, expulsions, suspensions, referrals to behavior rooms, or dropping out.

$2,000   2. Develop a plan for increasing the percentage of time students spend in constructive educational settings for implementation in the 1994–95 school year.

$2,000   3. Complete a baseline review to determine the level of staff attendance.

$2,000   4. Develop a plan for increasing staff attendance for implementation in the 1994–95 school year.

• *Agreement for Building Official and City Engineering Services between the City of Rosemead and Willdan Associates.* This contract is fairly typical of a professional service contract for contract cities. It sets out the general tasks to be done. For most of the contract, the volume of work is not specified, and it is paid for either on an hourly basis or as a proportion of city fees.

- *Baltimore County Council RFP for Meals for the Elderly.*   Although an RFP, it specifies in considerable detail the responsibilities of the contractor and the county. For example, it specifies the meals, menu requirements, food require- ments, locations, frequencies, volumes, and delivery arrangements. It also sets out requirements for quality assurance and accounting.

- *Howard County RFP for Legal Services, representing economically disadvan- taged residents.*   This sets out the activities in a general way and provides sketchy information on work volumes. The contractor is paid on the basis of the case workload.

- *LA County Law Enforcement Agreement with Contract Cities.*   This is a general contract used for all of the sheriff service contracts with cities in LA County. The contract is largely input orientated, with no output measures. It sets out the general services and the volume of service—number of and staffing of squad cars, hours of work, and numbers of parking control officers, crossing guards, detectives, and community relations officers.

- *Street Maintenance Agreement between LA County and Lakewood.*   This is a standard agreement between the county and one of its cities. This is a very general agreement for the county public works department to "construct, reconstruct, maintain and repair all public streets within the city with the same power with reference theretoas if said streets were within the unincorporated area of county, the City Council of City exercising the same authority with reference to said work on said streets as the Board of Supervisors would exercise if said streets were in the unincorporated territory of the county." Work is divided into "ordinary maintenance" and other work. County workers perform ordinary maintenance on a routine basis in order to keep streets in a similar condition to that of county highways. Other work has to be specifically commissioned by the city. Payment is made on the basis of hours worked.

- *LA County General Services Agreement for Cities.*   This is a master contract to provide a wide range of miscellaneous services (e.g., animal control and street maintenance) on an "as-needed" basis. Payment is made on the time worked, at agreed rates.

- *New York City RFP for the Provision of Home Attendant Services to Medicaid recipients.*   Although an RFP, it sets out detailed requirements in relation to inputs, tasks, and processes. It also sets out the maximum charge rates. It requires proposals to assume a preset ratio of posts and of posts to clients. It even sets out the maximum salaries for specified posts such as program directors, nurses, clerks, and so on. It includes price preferences for minority- and woman-owned businesses.

- *Warren County IFB for Personal Care Attendants for Disabled People.*   This is an IFB rather than an RFP, yet the specification only describes activities in a general way. Contractors are selected on the basis of variable charge rates, and the work is determined on an "as-needed" basis.

    It is clear from the analysis of contracts that the quality is highly variable, as follows:

—Most RFPs, IFBs, and contracts specify the tasks to be done. Some are very detailed (e.g., Baltimore County, New York) while others are fairly general (e.g., LA County).

—Few contracts include meaningful output or performance measures.

—Some contracts say little about either inputs or outputs. In practice such contracts leave it to the contract manager to agree work as required and ensure that it is satisfactory (e.g., the Rosemead contract, the LA County General Services Agreement, and the Warren County contract).

There can be no one rule on the level of specificity of a contract. The potential for being specific varies from area to area, and the advisability of specificity will vary depending on a range of factors such as the relationship with the contractor, the nature of the work, etc. However, what is a little strange is that some RFPs, as opposed to contracts, set out very detailed requirements on staffing levels, pay, organization, and service-delivery methods (e.g., New York and Baltimore County RFPs for social services). This constrains the RFP process enormously, severely limiting the ability of the bidder to come up with innovative solutions. It also means that the purchaser is managing the service in considerable detail and leaves open the question about why it is being contracted out at all.

CONTRACT MANAGEMENT

The overwhelming impression was of the absence of formal contract management. Moreover, few people engaged in contract management had any formal training in procurement. Some of the key features of contract management relate to the following:

—the nature of the specification/contract

—the volume of monitoring and oversight

—the extent of customer involvement

—the influence of the political process

—the degree of centralization

—the nature of monitoring

—the role of procurement professionals.

These issues are examined in turn.

1. *The Nature of the Specification and Contract*

The specification and contract determines the approach to monitoring. As shown earlier, most contracts specified inputs, not outputs, and many were fairly loose on requirements generally. This constrains contract management, meaning that it is difficult for local governments to monitor outputs and outcomes.

2. *The Volume of Monitoring and Oversight*

It was striking how many of the larger local governments adopted a "minimalist" approach to contract monitoring. It is no exaggeration to say that they devoted great energy to selecting the right contractor and then appeared to assume that everything would run smoothly thereafter! New York City, for example, had elaborate oversight arrangements for contract award but little in terms of contract management.

Baltimore's contract with EAI was also a good example of light monitoring. One official was responsible for financial monitoring. This involved scrutinizing bills and payments and participating in annual funding negotiations for schools with the contractor. No dedicated official was responsible for assessing the quality of the contractor's performance, and no reports on the quality and nature of the service were required of EAI. There were, however, general performance data—enrollment rates, examination results, test scores—available for all Baltimore schools, including the nine schools that were part of the contract. These are all general measures that are difficult to relate to specific school actions. There were no surveys of pupils and parents and no monitoring of actions required as part of the contract. The school board did, however, commission the University of Maryland to review the contract halfway through its five-year term.

The smaller local governments tended to assign contract management responsibilities to specific individuals, but invariably this was one of a number of duties. In the case of Lakewood, for example, one of the assistant city managers was responsible for monitoring the contract with the LA County sheriff, which represented the largest slice of expenditure in Lakewood.

Some of the smaller governments adopted a "hands-on" approach to monitoring. For example, Rosemead had a very loose contract with Willdan Associates for professional engineering services, but every small scheme had to have approval before proceeding. In these cases, the contract managers were performing a line-management role in relation to the contractor.

In Scottsdale, there was one official responsible for monitoring the fire and emergency services contract with the Rural/Metro Corporation. Again, this seemed very light given the high profile of the service and the scale of expenditure.

3. *The Extent of Customer Involvement*

Most local governments do not involve citizens actively in monitoring contracted services. This is reasonable where services do not have an interface with the public (e.g., legal advice and computing). However, it does seem sensible to involve the public in assessing the performance of direct services. There were a few notable exceptions:

—Lakewood used a well-publicized telephone hotline to encourage complaints and comments on contractor performance. This also enabled the city to analyze the performance over time.

—Lakewood and other LA cities have introduced a system of "block watch captains": members of the public who help increase community awareness of crime and crime prevention. These civilians also act as the city manager's "eyes and ears" on crime and provide useful input to the monitoring of the law enforcement contract with the county.

—The LA County sheriff's department organizes regular community meetings involving the police, local council members, and the public.

—Officials in New York interviewed a sample of clients of the homecare schemes to monitor quality.

4. *The Influence of the Political Process*

In the main, the politicians were far more interested in contract award, and contract management was rarely high on their agenda, except where there were clear problems with a contractor. However, politicians and pressure groups did get involved in monitoring contracts that were viewed as controversial. This was the case in Baltimore and Scottsdale, in both of which internal and external opposition to the administration resulted in external consultants and academics being asked to review the performance of the contractor.

5. *The Degree of Centralization*

Contract award in many governments is fairly centralized, but monitoring is highly decentralized.

6. *The Nature of Monitoring*

Most local governments relied heavily on self-reporting by contractors. Very little reporting was automated, and most of the monitoring related to costs. The approach to monitoring appeared very informal. The author found little evidence of formal observation reports, scheduled random monitoring, or regular formal review meetings with the contractor, regular contract status reports provided by the contractor to the government or by the official to the council.

7. *The Role of Procurement Professionals*

The role of procurement professionals was variable. On the whole they had an even smaller involvement in contract management than in contract award. Their role was peripheral. Moreover, the majority of officials monitoring contracts had little or no training in procurement skills and techniques. A few governments were making efforts to professionalize contracting, especially New York and Scottsdale. New York had decentralized procurement into the agencies, established a major training program for procurement staff. Scottsdale was also introducing an accreditation program for procurement staff.

Conclusions on Contract Management

It was difficult to avoid the impression that the purchasing side was weak in most local governments in terms of numbers of staff, expertise in purchasing and contracting, the status of the function, and knowledge of the service, systems, and data. This underlines fears that contractors will have the upper hand in negotiations with officials.

WHO DOES WHAT?

There are three issues to examine in relation to who does what:

—What are the respective roles of elected and appointed officials?

—Does the local government centralize or devolve decision making?

—What roles do the various professional groups play in the process, such as the service chiefs, finance professionals, and purchasing officers?

The main conclusions in relation to these questions are as follows. First, contracting decisions are much more politicized in mayor cities compared to manager cities and counties. The decisions on which area to contract, how, and with whom were subject to strong political influence. This relates in part to the system of partisan politics, but also to the form of government and the strong tradition of political management. In both New York and Chicago, the mayoral staff—the senior appointments to which are largely political appointees—can veto a proposal at any stage in the process and often make proposals over the head of the agency chief. The city council and other elected officials also get involved in decision making. This is clearly demonstrated in Chapter 9 in relation to New York's council, borough presidents, city comptroller, and procurement policy board.

Decision making in manager cities is much less politicized. Decisions on which areas to subject to contracting, the strategy, and the evaluation are by and large left to the professionals. However, politicians usually make the final formal decision of who gets the contract. This is not strictly consistent with the council–manager model of government—in a full-service city, the manager is responsible for staffing issues, so one would expect the selection of contractors to fall into this category, but this is not the case. There are also sometimes tricky political areas. In the California contract cities, for example, the whole issue of trash collection was very often political—trash collectors were high-profile in the local community and often contributed toward the campaign funds of the local politicians. This makes the politicians sensitive to any changes, such as subjecting a trash collection franchise or contract to open competition.

Decision making generally was much more centralized in U.S. local governments compared to the U.K. Notwithstanding this, centralization appeared stronger in the larger local governments, a rather puzzling finding. This reflected the difficulties of managing a large organization as a single body. Chicago had a centralized procurement function that handled all contracting with a dollar value above $10,000. In New York the procurement function was devolved, but there were ten central oversight agencies concerned with contracting decisions. In practice, major decisions required mayoral approval. All the large cities had a single procurement framework to regulate purchasing activity. Arms-length city agencies, such as a transit authority, usually did not follow such requirements.

The smaller cities also had a centralist approach. Typically the city manager would play the key role in deciding for what to contract. A staff member would then follow that through, keeping the manager informed and comfortable with the direction taken. However, because of the small size of the organization, the formal processes and amount of oversight were not needed.

The influence of procurement professionals varied considerably. They played a significant role in New York, Chicago, and Arlington County. In Chicago procurement was centralized, whereas in New York and Arlington it was devolved, but this meant different things. In New York the procurement professionals were located in the agencies, whereas in Arlington the procurement professionals were at the center of the local government but decision making had been devolved. In the other cities visited, procurement professionals were less influential. In Phoenix, the key contracting decisions were handled by service staff and the city auditor's department. In the California contract cities, there were few procurement professionals and most concentrated on traditional purchasing issues such as goods and construction. The key personnel were city manager staff and the service professionals. In Indianapolis, it was a similar combination of mayoral staff and service professionals.

Implications

The way local governments make contracting decisions has a critical impact on the success of contracting—selecting the right functions for contracting, packaging activities in a sensible way, insisting on appropriate terms and conditions, and choosing the successful bidder in a fair way that maximizes value for money. This model is often far from the reality. The obstacles that sometimes get in the way of smart decision making are now examined.

1. *Overt Political Management*

Traditional public administration assumes a clear divide between politics and administration—politicians decide policy, and administrators execute the decisions. The distinction is blurred in practice—administrators often have an important influence on policy because of their specialist knowledge, and politicians often get involved in implementation because they recognize the potential to effect change in line with their priorities. Contracting is one of those issues that straddles the policy/administration divide. Many politicians see the decision to make or buy as a key policy issue. It certainly is a political issue, especially as it impacts on the municipal workforce and the local businesses.

There were significant variations among local governments in the degree to which contracting was seen as a matter for politics or administration. In general, the local governments with a mayor form of government, a partisan system, and strong tradition of unionization tended to have a politicized approach to contracting, with politicians having a major say over where contracting is to apply, how it is to happen, over what timescale, and who gets the work. In council—manager governments, the politicians would be involved in decisions over where contracting is to apply and the final decision on who gets the contract, but the details would be left to administrators to sort out.

The politicized approach can produce a dramatic shift in an organization, transforming a bureaucracy. This clearly is happening in Indianapolis. Generally, politicization carries high risks. In particular, it explains why:

—so many local government activities that are highly suitable for contracting are kept in-house

—little attention is devoted to the details of contract strategy—packaging, terms, and conditions and the length of the contract

—contracting is done at great speed without the proper groundwork.

Such contracting has a cost. First, it means that many local governments incur higher costs in delivery services than they need to because they rely too heavily on in-house provision. Second, those local governments that do resort to contracting do not always get all of the benefits.

2. *The Control Culture*

In the larger jurisdictions, there is a plethora of rules and regulations governing the contracting process. These rules and regulations are often accompanied by large numbers of people in oversight agencies checking to make sure that probity prevails in contracting. Local government employees are seen by some as untrustworthy and prone to corruption and by others as incompetent and incapable of managing contracting in a business-like way. They need detailed guidance and rules on what they can and cannot do. This approach is less strong in the smaller local governments in the West of the U.S.

The designers of the rules and the people staffing the oversight agencies are undoubtedly well-intentioned. However, this approach has high costs. It often removes a sense of ownership from the front-line managers, the people who really understand the service. The centralization and regulation discourages them from seeing the contracting process as theirs, as a series of decisions in which they have a stake and can make a difference. It also results in high expenditure on contracting. The oversight activity costs money. The rules and oversight usually extend the timescale for contracting. The bureaucracy and lengthiness of contracting can discourage firms from bidding, which in turn reduces competition and the submission of value-for-money bids and proposals. This was clearly the case in New York City, where City Hall was viewed as a customer of last resort by many members of the business community.

Decisions on contracting may not include the concerns and expertise of front-line managers and as a result may not always exploit the opportunities in the marketplace. This is because centralization means that decisions are made by people far removed from the day-to-day realities of the service. A good example of this is human services contracting in New York City. The excessive regulations coupled with a fear of making mistakes results in specifications that attempt to specify everything—how the service will be delivered, the number of employees needed, the staffing structures for the contractor, and even the maximum salaries for the staff! Such an approach assumes that the contractor, too, is a numskull and effectively removes the ability to develop an imaginative approach to the specification.

3. *Pepperpot Contracting*

The typical approach to public policy and administration in the U.S. can be described as experimental, piecemeal, incremental, gradual, and evolutionary rather than based on revolutionary change and long-term planning. This approach was dominant in the local governments visited. There were few examples of "big bang" contracting—Indianapolis, Baltimore, and Scottsdale were very much the exceptions rather than the norm. Contracting tended to follow the essential features of U.S. public policy and administration. Local governments would contract for a service in one small area. If it proved successful, they would gradually expand the amount of contracting.

The end result is an organization with a highly diversified pattern of service delivery. To a European such an approach appears fragmented. The author calls it "pepperpot" contracting—doing a little bit here and a little bit there, without a grand design. There are strengths to this approach: it is less risky, it is also less disruptive. Finally, contracting is only used if it delivers benefits, but there can also be problems:

- The nonstrategic approach can result in the exclusion of suitable areas and inappropriate packaging because of the preference for small-scale contracting.

- The pepperpot approach ignores the organizational issues. The organizational structure and arrangements remain unchanged. This is not a major problem if the local government only does a small amount of contracting. Conflicts of interest can arise where there is a great deal of contracting. This is most pronounced where a government engages in public/private competition but is present in more common contracting out. This is because the departmental head is responsible for provision and production. Too often the departmental head adopts a production rather than a provision view—that is, he or she thinks more about who does the work and has a preference for in-house provision.

- The pepperpot often relies on the existing management processes, but these are deficient from a contracting perspective. In consequence, the local government starts to contract out without having good information on costs or performance. As a result, the make or buy decision may be wrong. It also makes monitoring more difficult.

- Pepperpot contracting can result in heavy contract management costs with many contract managers, many contracts, and high processing costs for small dollar values.

4.   *Cozy Contracting*

It has already been demonstrated that a surprising amount of contracting is noncompetitive, some due to sole sourcing but mainly because of extensions and renewals. In addition, cost and materials pricing is fairly common, as is having a contract without a specification. These practices can encourage "cozy contracting," where the contract manager effectively loses control of the contract.

There are sometimes sound reasons for cozy contracting. Often it is important to establish a partnership with a contractor rather than maintain an arm's-length relationship. This is especially true of professional services and core services such as police and fire and key support services such as information services. It is less applicable for arm's-length services such as street sweeping and trash collection, yet there is much evidence to indicate cozy contracting in these areas.

Cozy contracting can lead to all of the problems of in-house provision and the worst aspects of principal–agent relationships. The principal effectively abdicates his or her responsibilities, and the agent takes over. This is not surprising, as there is little threat of replacement and the agent knows much more about the technical details of the contract. This can also lead to higher-than-necessary costs and poor work.

CONCLUSIONS

This chapter has demonstrated the crucial impact that the make or buy decision and contract management can have on the success of contracting. A strategic approach can ensure the right selection of areas as well as appropriate packaging and terms and conditions. A deregulated procurement framework and devolved contract management arrangements can promote competition and ownership of the contracting process by the contract managers. Most significantly, an intelligent contract-management function within government can ensure value for money and quality during the selection and running of a contract.

6

Smart Contracting for Public Services

INTRODUCTION

Research shows that contracting saves money, but the full potential of contracting is frequently not exploited. Despite the strong financial case for service contracting, most governments prefer in-house provision, even for those services well suited to contracting. Even where contracting is used, there can be problems. My work suggests that savings from contracting vary widely depending on market conditions, the efficiency of the government function in the first place, the nature of the service, and the quality of contract management. It is the last factor that is most significant, but the quality of contract management function varies widely.

Some of the common problems include:

—lack of hard information on service costs and performance

—ill-thought-out contract strategies

—bureaucratic and cumbersome processes

—corruption

—noncompetitive contracting

—excessive, inappropriate, and costly micromanagement

—poor and nonexistent contract monitoring.

Poor contracting reduces competition and results in higher-than-necessary costs. The reason tends to be because political rather than managerial values dominate.

Decisions on what to contract for, how, and with whom are often made on electoral grounds or to satisfy interest groups rather than for sound service-delivery reasons. The assumption that officials cannot be trusted to do their job honestly or well dominates. Therefore their behavior needs to be guided, regulated, and controlled. Such an approach has huge implications, both financially and managerially. More generally, reward and penalty systems within the government and the diffusion of accountability and responsibility provide little incentive for good performance.

This chapter sets out the features of smart contracting. It also outlines a methodology for undertaking a health check for a government and identifying improvement opportunities.

THE FEATURES OF SMART CONTRACTING

Contracting is not a panacea for local government. Where it is well executed, it offers many advantages over in-house provision, but it is not always the most appropriate solution. Some of the benefits of contracting can be achieved with in-house provision, but only where civil service systems are reformed and a genuine managerial approach and culture developed. Unfortunately, the features of government decision making and tradition make this difficult, especially in mayor and commission local governments. This is why governments often prefer to contract out the management of public services rather than reinvent internally.

In other cases, pure privatization or greater use of nonprofits offers a better combination of value for money and quality of service than contracting. Real privatization has greatest application where there is a clear customer–supplier relationship and few issues of redistribution. This would certainly include utility services, such as water supply, electricity, and gas. Even trash collection could be privatized. Contracting will remain an option as well as in-house provision. Which approach offers the best combination of value for money, service quality, and long-term security will depend upon the flexibility of the workforce, the skills of the government in managing services, and the competitiveness of the market. These factors will also change over time. Nevertheless, there are good grounds for believing that even for those services well suited to privatization, in-house provision and contracting will continue to be the most common methods of service delivery. Privatization provokes the greatest opposition from unions and consumer groups. It also takes longer to do than contracting, which can make it unattractive in a world where short-term political horizons dominate. Negotiations between parties are time consuming because more is at stake and often the government has to establish new bodies and laws to regulate the new operator. Privatization is also more risky. Unlike contracting, it is a permanent decision that is difficult to reverse. In addition, because of the long-term nature of the arrangement, this makes setting up the regulatory environment more risky than drawing up a contract. As a result, local politicians will always approach privatization warily.

Using nonprofits has become increasingly popular in certain areas—human services and the arts. The former has been encouraged by governments on grounds of ideology and cost. The scope for extending use of nonprofits into mainstream services such as police, fire, tax collection, and support services is limited, however. Moreover, contracting is increasingly being used as a tool by governments to regulate their relationships with nonprofits. Contracting with nonprofits tends to be noncompetitive, but there have been a number of initiatives to encourage competition for such contracts.

In reality, therefore, contracting remains the main alternative to in-house provision. Given the potential and the problems of contracting, we need to focus on how to do it well. What are the features of doing it well, or smart contracting? Which services can contracting be applied to? What are the best strategies? Should we, for example, favor public/private competition, or should we simply contract with the private sector? In packaging contracts, is it best to break activities down into a large number of small contracts—the "pepperpot" approach—or do we lump activities together into one or two large contracts—the "big bang" approach? What are the best techniques to use? Who should the managers be? What about the management systems? What sort of information is needed? What sort of environment encourages smart contracting? Who should be held to account for the performance of the contractor, and how?

The following are suggested as features of smart government contracting, the eight Cs:

- challenges the status quo
- A comprehensive, corporate, and systematic approach
- careful preparation
- thinking creatively
- cuts red tape
- clean and independent
- competent in service contracting
- customer-friendly approach.

These features are now examined in turn.

1. Challenges the Status Quo—Reengineering the Decision-Making Environment

The case studies show that those governments that depoliticize service-delivery strategy and management are more likely to make the right decisions about how to deliver services and do it efficiently. In particular, a system of decision making which embodies three separate but related principles—clarity, professionalism, and devolution—seems to be most successful. Clarity is about knowing who is responsible for the service. Many government systems confuse this. For example, politicians are supposedly in charge of strategy, with appointed officials being responsible for implementation; however, in practice, this is not always followed. Moreover, in many governments it is unclear who is responsible for the management of a service—the functional head, director, officials from the mayor's or city manager's office, or elected officials. Professionalism is about making sure that experienced managers run services. In most cases this applies, but where governments have elected executives there is sometimes a trend of having senior managers in post with little real experience of running large public sector agencies. Devolution is the third principle. Devolving responsibility to the functional managers has a number of advantages. Most importantly, it encourages a sense of personal ownership and provides a strong incentive to achieve good performance. It also ensures that decisions more closely reflect local circumstances.

The case studies also show that the council–manager form of government is more likely to embody clarity, professionalism, and devolution than mayor and commission forms of government, but this is not a universal rule. Indianapolis, for example, with a mayor form of government, outperformed many of the council–manager cities visited on all three principles. Examples of manager cities where there was heavy interference by elected officials, a highly centralized approach, and a lack of professionalism among senior managers were also found. Nevertheless, the manager form of government is more likely to promote the three principles, because it:

- formally attempts to separate politics and management by placing more power in the hands of an appointed, career official—the city manager

- reduces the risk of the "political manager" emerging by having a system of part-time elected officials

- minimizes the risk of conflict within the government by having one decision-making vehicle, the council. Mayor forms of government have at least two power bases (the mayor and the council and often other elected officials), whereas commission forms of government tend to be weak relying on cooperation between powerful commissioners, elected officials, and a chief administrative officer with few executive powers.

The manager governments tend not to be as highly unionized (because they are newer, located in the West and South and tend to be smaller governments running fewer sensitive services such as human services and education). This also helps to depoliticize decision making considerably.

2. Comprehensive, Corporate, and Systematic Approach—Reviewing All the Options for All Services

By reviewing all options for services, the government develops a vision of where it wants to go and the role of competition in that vision. This book shows that those governments that review service-delivery options in a comprehensive, corporate, and systematic way are most likely to achieve quality and value for money. In practice, this involves three features:

- *Reviewing the options for all services*—in-house provision, contracting, franchising, privatization, use of nonprofits, etc. Few governments visited did this in a systematic way. Indeed, of the twelve governments visited, only two— Indianapolis and Lakewood—appeared to adopt a systematic approach. It is no coincidence that both cities could demonstrate significant improvements in value for money as a result of their contracting regimes. Indianapolis had the most explicit review of services. One of the first things that the mayor did following his election was to establish an external group of entrepreneurs with extensive support to review the city's service provision. This resulted in proposals to improve efficiency. It also resulted in an extensive contracting program that involved inviting bids for the running of the airport, wastewater treatment facility, and the city's information systems. Lakewood did not have a formal review process in the same way, but the city had examined every service in detail since its incorporation, including how public protection services were to be delivered. Even the much-praised city of Phoenix did not systematically review the options for service delivery. Despite achieving substantial savings from contracting in the public works area, the city appeared reluctant to test other services in a similar way. By ignoring the market test option for much of its services, Phoenix and other governments are foregoing substantial potential savings.

- *Having a strategy, rather than "muddling through."* The piecemeal approach adopted by the majority of U.S. governments was striking. This is probably due to the author's European perspective, where there is a stronger tradition of long-term planning. Nevertheless, few governments had a comprehensive plan for service levels and standards, and few had explicitly considered the potential role of contracting in relation to each service. The typical approach appeared to be pragmatic and experimental—contracting out a problem service or responding to an opportunity. For example, the city of Chicago had contracted out a wide range of services, yet there was no publicly available overview of why this particular set of services were chosen, what the expectations were, or what the future plans were. Once again, Indianapolis was the exception, and again Indianapolis appeared to be achieving the greatest savings.

- *Carefully selecting the contract approach and conditions.* Few governments undertook market surveys to establish the best way to package contracts. Indianapolis did, and the California contract cities had gained extensive experience of the marketplace over a 40-year period. Most governments tended to package a service on the basis of how it had been structured internally. They also tended to opt for the pepperpot approach of small packages of contracts. The impression was that this approach was not based on an assessment of the market opportunities and risks, but rather represented a cautious approach. U.K. local governments are more likely to undertake market research to assess the packaging options. They are also more likely to adopt the "big bang" approach of contracting out a large package of services.

3. *Careful Preparation—Developing the Systems, Skills, and Culture in Advance of Contracting*

Smart contracting depends on careful preparation and having the right infrastructure in place. Unfortunately, in the U.K. and the U.S. the majority of governments rushed into contracting with inadequate preparation. As a result, the information was not available or inaccurate and their staff often ill-prepared. Too often governments would make decisions about what to contract out and how to do it in the absence of professional advice. They would decide a contract strategy as they were establishing the contract management function. This was clearly the case in Baltimore with its decision to contract out the running of nine of its schools.

Many other governments lacked the necessary information systems to make intelligent decisions about service delivery. The three basic requirements are a good understanding of activity costs (including the allocation of relevant overhead costs and capital costs), service standards, and actual performance. Indianapolis had a system of activity-based costing, whereas LA County and Phoenix had well-developed methodologies for comparing the cost of in-house provision with the contract option. Many governments did not, however. As a result they would have to make informed guesses as to how to allocate overhead costs to services when making the make or buy decision. In the U.K., there are national requirements about how to compare costs of in-house bids against outside those firms.

Of all the governments visited, Milwaukee stood out as the strongest on preparation. The internal market that it has developed was done in a phased way. It also allowed city agencies, both purchasers and providers, to develop their contracting skills in a measured way and enabled them to build up a clear picture of service costs, standards, and performance.

4. *Thinking Creatively—Developing a Strategic Approach to Contracting Which Takes Nothing for Granted*

Another factor that promotes value for money is imagination. Contracting is not a straightforward matter of replacing in-house provision with an outsourced arrangement. There are many variations to the basic approach, including:

- *Public/private competition:* as used in Indianapolis, Phoenix, and U.K. local governments. This is where the city employees bid against the private sector. This is obviously good for staff morale, and it can result in similar levels of savings to using private firms. The performance of in-house bidders has been impressive in both cities. It also forces the city government to adopt a rather more sophisticated approach to costing services. After all, they have to be absolutely clear that awarding the bid to the in-house or out-house bidder will save the city money. Public/private competition is a serious option where there is enthusiasm among staff and managers. It can also help stimulate competition where there are few competitors.

- *Internal markets:*   such as the initiatives in Milwaukee and the state of Minnesota. This involves establishing an internal purchaser and an internal provider. The purchaser also has the freedom to buy the service externally. As a result, an internal market can lead to straightforward outsourcing, public/private competition, or in-house provision. The internal market approach has a number of advantages: it allows the purchasers to develop their contracting skills; it helps to train the in-house providers, developing a more business-like approach; and it can produce savings and services that better meet service needs. One of the dangers, however, is a bureaucratic approach. This is most apparent where there is no ability of purchasing functions to test the market.

- *Intergovernmental agreements:*   such as the contracts between LA County and Lakewood and the LA Fire Protection and Libraries Districts. These are especially useful where there are no private sector alternatives. They enable small governments to achieve economies of scale and provide high flexibility compared to in-house provision.

- *Shared services:*   this is a variation on intergovernmental agreements. It involves governments joining together to establish organizations to provide or organize service provision. In California, these are called Joint Powers Authorities (JPAs). In San Mateo County in Northern California, for example, nine cities have formed a JPA to organize trash collection. The JPA, in turn, has eleven contracts for trash collection in the nine cities. There also JPAs for cable TV, fire protection, and planning. JPAs can achieve economies of scale where they are service providers or economies of expertise where they are contracting organizations. Either way, JPAs, like intergovernmental agreements, are about achieving the benefits of big government within a small-government system.

- *Franchising:*   a slight variation on contracting, which involves users paying the provider directly. The advantage is that it makes a direct link between the cost of the service and the charge, and the local government does not have to get involved in the payment function. However, most research tends to show that franchising is often a more expensive option compared to straightforward contracting.

- *Community empowerment:*   such as business improvement districts and resident associations. These effectively supplement local services with private provision of services such as street cleaning, road maintenance, and security. This approach reduces the need for public expenditure and can allow the local government to concentrate scarce resources where they are most needed.

Which contracting option is selected should depend on a range of factors, such as the competitiveness of the market, the quality and efficiency of in-house providers, and the management capability of the local government. It is clear, however, that an imaginative approach can produce large returns. Few can argue that public/private competition in Indianapolis and Phoenix has produced tangible benefits above straightforward outsourcing. Similarly, it is difficult to show that intergovernmental agreements and JPAs in California have not significantly improved value for money.

An important aspect of many of the approaches is competition. Public/private competition as practiced in Indianapolis and Phoenix promotes competition among potential providers. Other strategies can also encourage competition, such as partial and multiple contracting. Phoenix, the California contract cities, and Indianapolis all adopted variations on this theme. Phoenix tended to keep at least one-third of a function in-house. The reasons were twofold—to retain an emergency capability and to provide the in-house option should problems emerge with a contractor or bidding situation. Multiple contracting is where the city awards a contract involving more than one firm. For example, California contract cities sometimes award legal and engineering contracts to more than one firm and then select firms on a project-by-project basis. Competitive contracting is where the bidding process is explicitly designed to maximize competition. Indianapolis, for example, divided the city into ten areas for trash collection and decided to award more than three areas to one contractor. All of these methods are ways of minimizing the threat of monopoly.

Few local governments in practice encouraged competition. Indeed, noncompetitive contracting was commonplace. This can reproduce the complacency problems of in-house provision. The starkest examples of this were the trash collection contracts in some California contract cities that had been renewed on an annual basis for many years and, in some cases, decades. In these circumstances it was difficult to separate contracting from in-house provision.

There are many situations where a partnership approach to contracting is more appropriate than the traditional arm's-length relationship. This usually applies where a long-term relationship is required, either because capital facilities have to be established, the contractors develop a set of skills and knowledge which is particular to the contract, or the costs of regular rebidding are too great. An example of the former includes the intergovernmental contracts between the contract cities and LA County and the Scottsdale Fire Prevention contract. The outsourcing of IT would be an example of the development of contract-specific knowledge and high rebidding costs. This is why many firms and governments outsourcing IT increasingly favor a negotiated approach (which narrows the selection down to one or two providers) and long-term contracts. However, many of the long-term contracting relationships covered services that could easily be subjected to regular competition, such as trash collection.

5. *Cuts Red Tape—Eliminating Excessive Micromanagement and Streamlining the Contracting Process*

Smart contracting requires a businesslike approach to the process of decision making—a streamlined process that empowers individual managers and promotes a sense of personal ownership. Many governments create an environment that is quite different, however.

Cities like Chicago and New York City provided the clearest examples of heavy micromanagement and bureaucracy. This had a number of damaging consequences:

—making the contracting process time-consuming

—reducing the incentive on the part of officials to get it right first time, because they knew that someone further up the decision chain was likely to undo what they had done

—discouraging competition for city contracts, because of the time-consuming, political, and bureaucratic nature of the process

—making contracting more costly than it needed to be, because of the extra administration, lack of ownership, and reduced competition.

While New York had serious problems, it recognized that its management arrangements had a major impact on contracting. It had introduced a range of initiatives to develop links with local businesses, devolve decision making, reduce oversight, and streamline processes. Many governments have failed to examine their contracting arrangements and processes.

Some strategies to reduce red tape involve:

- *Clarifying the roles of elected officials.*   Elected officials should be encouraged to focus on setting service levels and monitoring/reviewing performance, leaving matters of service-delivery strategy and management to professionals.

- *Devolving responsibility to relevant managers.*   Managers on the ground should be given the discretion to adjust the approach to meet local circumstances. This means keeping rules to a minimum.

- *Challenging the need for oversight agencies.*   Many governments respond to a scandal or problem by establishing a new set of rules or an oversight agency—the cost and impact of such an approach towards competition needs to be carefully considered.

- *Monitoring results, not procedures.*   Many local governments have detailed rules about how to undertake contracting and monitor compliance carefully. A review process that focuses more on value for money and performance against contract would encourage a less bureaucratic approach.

- *Simple and user-friendly approach.*   Language should be kept simple, and briefings should be provided to the business community. This is something that New York City has promoted through its department of business services.

6. *Clean and Independent—The Contract Managers Are Genuinely Independent of Vested Interests, Both External and Internal*

Most U.S. cities did have contract managers who were independent of the contractors, but there were strong pressures on officials to lose their objectivity. Manual services are subject to an objective competitive bidding process. However, once contracts were awarded there was strong pressure from elected and appointed officials to avoid a rebidding exercise. Elected officials were cultivated by contractors with donations and support for election campaigns, while appointed officials sometimes wanted to avoid the work and the uncertainty of a rebidding exercise. This situation was even more likely to occur for professional services where a request-for-proposal approach was adopted. This is because it is easier to select contractors on subjective and qualitative grounds.

However, the most serious problem occurs when governments provide services in-house. In the worst cases, governments insist on in-house provision without properly examining the alternatives. The reasons tend to relate to:

—union and staff opposition keen to protect their jobs and power bases

—opposition from elected officials, who in turn often rely on staff and unions for support during election campaigns and fear losing detailed control over contracted services

—ignorance of the opportunity costs because of the absence of accurate information on costs, standards, and performance and comparisons with other organizations adopting different service-delivery approaches

—managers more concerned to retain and expand their power base than to provide quality and value for money.

The issue of managerial independence is highlighted where public/private competition is adopted. In the U.K., the national government has regulated competitive bidding by local authorities to ensure a "level playing field" between external firms and the in-house team. In particular, local governments must include the full costs of the in-house bid in the comparison, the process must be transparent, and there has to be a "Chinese Wall" between the internal client or purchaser and the in-house provider. Public/private competition is new in the U.S., but it was clear in the examples examined—Milwaukee, Phoenix, and Indianapolis—that the issue of independence had not been approached with the same rigor as in the U.K. examples. This is an issue that will need to be developed if public/private competition is extended in the U.S.

7. Competent in Service Contracting—Specifying the Requirement, Analyzing the Market, Deciding the Strategy, Comparing Bids, and Monitoring Performance

Competent service contracting is clearly a prerequisite for outsourcing. However, many local government officials are not experienced in this area, and the skill levels are sometimes below what they should be. In practice, officials are usually able to specify the requirement, although there is too often a willingness to replicate the current pattern and standard of service or to go for a much higher standard without properly considering the cost implications. They also are usually able to compare the bids in a systematic way, but again there is sometimes a tendency to underestimate in-house costs. The areas in which they encounter most problems, however, are analyzing the market, deciding the contract strategy, and monitoring performance. It is rare to find officials doing careful market surveys and consciously examining the options for contract strategies. In part this is because officials do not possess the basic procurement skills, but more fundamentally it reflects the absence of strategic thinking. Monitoring also tends to be a weakness. In part this is due to unimaginative contracts that focus on deadlines and inputs rather than on outputs and outcomes. Most of the contract specifications were unimaginative in this way. In addition, many local governments do not invest in monitoring contractor performance. This will be a serious issue for the future as local governments fail to develop an intelligent purchaser side to review and improve service delivery.

8. Customer-Friendly Approach—Considering the Impact on Quality and Involving Citizens in Specifying Services and Monitoring Performance

In the U.K., a sea change of approach has been evident in recent years. Initially, contracting had an efficiency and internal focus. The emphasis was on savings and internal assessment of the contractor. Things have now begun to change, however. Increasingly, local governments publish their service standards for the public and provide complaint systems and telephone hotlines to encourage public comment. This is a new form of monitoring. There is also an increase in encouraging public involvement in the setting of service standards, which in turn influences service contracts. The best example is the case of contracting for the management of public housing.

Local governments now consult on the basic service standards, and some, such as Westminster, have surveyed residents on the service and cost options before settling the contract specification.

Only a few examples of customer contracts and customer monitoring were found in the U.S. One of the best, however, was Lakewood's customer hotline and monitoring system. Lakewood uses a dedicated hotline system to encourage public comment on the performance of contractors. Complaints and queries are then logged and passed on to the contractor or relevant department for action.

UNDERTAKING A HEALTH CHECK OF YOUR LOCAL GOVERNMENT

Having identified the features of smart contracting, we now turn to how to compare a government to the model—what questions should be asked of a government, and what evidence is needed to determine the answers? In this section a number of questions are suggested under the headings of strategy, people, structure, process, technology, and impacts. Some indicators that can help provide the answers are also identified.

The Key Questions

1. *Strategy*

- *Is a comprehensive approach to service delivery in place?* Does the local government have a clear vision of where it wants to be in the medium term and of how competition can contribute to that? Has the government considered the people, structure, process, and technology implications of competition? The contention here is that those governments that secure the largest benefits of competition (in terms of savings and quality improvements) are those that adopt a comprehensive approach.

- *Is a genuine contract strategy in place?* Has your government a clear contract strategy? Has it examined the marketplace and considered which of the many contracting options are most appropriate? Even if there is no explicit strategy, has it adopted the right approach? Should it, for example, favor public/private competition or simply contract with the private sector? In packaging contracts, should it break activities down into a large number of small contracts—the pepperpot approach—or lump activities together into one or two large contracts—the "big bang" approach? Has the contract strategy encouraged or discouraged competition?

2. *People*

- *Who makes the decisions?* Does your government have the right balance of roles and responsibilities between elected and appointed officials and between oversight and staff officials and those dealing with service delivery? Good practice would include a fair degree of devolution to officers in relation to contract strategy, packaging, specification, and managing the tendering process. Politicians should be involved at the outset in setting service levels. The issues to look out for here are bureaucracy and politicization that discourage competition and good management resulting in increased costs.

- *Who manages the contracts?* Are the right people managing the contract process? Again, good practice would involve devolution, but elected officials ought to receive information on performance. The issues to look out for here would be over-involvement of elected officials and a hierarchical approach.

- *Quality of relationships with contractors.* Good practice would involve adopting an arm's-length approach to all contractors/bidders during the tendering process but once the contract has been awarded developing a partnership with the contractor. Many local governments adopt an adversarial approach to contractors that can damage the relationship unnecessarily, with service quality suffering.

- *Skills of the contract management function.* Does your government have a competent contract management function? Officials need an understanding of the service plus a combination of strategic and operational contracting skills—ability to research the market, formulate a contract strategy, produce a specification, monitor performance, negotiate with the contractor, etc. The main area to look out for here is that of strategic skills, as these are often lacking. Another issue is appointing staff with little experience of contract management and then failing to provide training.

3. *Structure*

- *The purchaser/provider split.* Is your contract management function genuinely independent of external contractors and in-house providers who may or may not be contractors? Where your government operates public/private competition, a hard purchaser/provider split can encourage genuine independence, but it is not the only way forward. The issue to examine here is whether the structure results in the contract management function being in-house-contractor-dominated favouring in-house bids or, more significantly, being unable to subject in-house providers to competition where there is a compelling case to do so. Good examples of this might be in-house services for trash collection, grounds maintenance, legal services for small local governments, and professional engineering services that are not properly costed and have not been subject to competition.

- *Size, cost, and quality of the contract management function.* Is the government getting good value for money for contract management? Good practice would involve a slim but high-powered contract management function. International research has identified clientside costs of between 2% and 7% depending on the service (Savas, 1987). The real issue is quality, however, as the costs will always be small compared to the contract cost. Typical problems to look for here would be low status attached to the contract management function and lots of ineffectual officers.

4. *Process*

- *The processing of contracts.* How smooth is the contracting process? Is it done in a speedy fashion? Is it understandable to potential bidders? In examining the process, it is important to look at the entire process—the preparatory work, the stages of the tendering process, and the time between award and the start of the contract—not just the visible component. In timescales, for routine service contracts such as trash collection and legal and engineering services the entire contracting process should take between nine and twelve months. More complex contracts for, say, IT services may take longer. Perhaps the biggest issue is how the government's approach is viewed by potential bidders. How does the local chamber of commerce view the local government's approach?

- *Quality of monitoring data.* Is the local government monitoring the right things or is monitoring merely what is most easily quantified? In particular, are they making use of customer monitoring, output measures, and quality indicators and processes?

- *Activity costing.* Does the government have a good grasp of how much services cost? In particular, are costs attached to activities and are overheads properly allocated to services? Without basic information on service costs, governments will be making decisions in the dark about service-delivery methods.

- *Accuracy and independence of monitoring.* Most government contracts rely on the contractor to do the vast majority of monitoring. Do they have the right checks built in to reduce the risk of inaccurate data? Alternatively, are they going way over the top in terms of checking and gathering data direct rather than relying on the contractor?

5. *Technology*

- *Is quality information available on quality and cost in a timely fashion?* Can the government provide comprehensive data quickly on the impacts? The point here is that governments that are managing competition well will have a thorough grasp of the impacts.

- *Is a quality technology in place?* To what extent does the government rely on manual or high-technology approaches? Technology has a major role to play in streamlining the contracting process and providing the ability to interrogate data and undertake further analysis, especially in the long term as governments contract out more and more.

- *To what extent can systems talk to one another?* Are the IT systems for the contracting process fragmented or integrated? The future will be about full integration so that data need only be added once and can be easily transferred from one system to another. By contrast, a highly fragmented approach could be costly and time-consuming.

6. *Impacts*

- *Costs.* What difference has contracting made to service costs? Is the government above or below average in terms of spending, and are there good reasons to expect a variation from the norm (e.g., the quality of the local marketplace, the efficiency of the authority, the quality of the contract management function, and the specification—were changes in service required?)? Evidence shows that, internationally, governments do make significant savings from contracting.

- *Service Levels.* Did service standards change? Was this conscious or not? If so, what was the rationale? One of the problems with contracting is assuming that current service levels are satisfactory rather than using competition as an opportunity to review requirements and adjust them to meet future needs. Another issue to look for is developing very high service specifications that involve significant but hidden growth.

- *Performance.* Did performance change? Were higher or changed standards met? Is there any evidence of slippage in performance based on monitoring reports, defaults, terminations, and failure of in-house contractors to meet required rates of return?

- *Customer satisfaction.* What does your government know of customer views? Has the government surveyed and tracked customer satisfaction with front-line services? If so, what has been the impact of contracting?

ASSEMBLING THE EVIDENCE—SOME KEY INDICATORS

Table 6.1 identifies a number of issues that can shed light on how well a government handles service contracting.

STRATEGIES TO IMPROVE SERVICE DELIVERY

There are, of course, many ways to improve the use of contracting within local governments. Eight "breakthrough" strategies to improve service-delivery methods are set out below.

1. *Establishing a stronger purchaser/provider split.* In large governments, care should be taken to separate the purchaser and provider functions to ensure an objective management view of the best service-delivery approach.

2. *Developing a clear cost picture.* A proper cost-accounting system should be in place to capture the full costs of service delivery, irrespective of whether it is provided in-house or contracted out. Activity-based costing (ABC) is a common way of doing this.

3. *Creating a performance culture.* Clear service standards should be set and monitoring systems established to check performance against the standards. This will highlight any concerns about service, especially when combined with accurate cost information provided by ABC.

4. *Developing a strong purchasing function and introducing a purchaser/provider split.* Many local governments devoted considerable energy to improving the competitiveness of their in-house providers but forgot about the purchasing function. It is vital to nurture the contract management employees—give them status, train them, and establish the function in advance of competition so that they can play a full part in shaping the strategy. Most significantly, this can involve separating in-house purchasers from in-house providers. Significantly, in-house purchasers should not be equated with procurement specialists. They are the staff who determine service strategy and manage performance in addition to looking after the procurement process.

TABLE 6.1. Undertaking a Health Check

Indicator	Strategy	People	Struc-ture	Pro-cesses	Tech-nology	Impacts
1. Level of competition—number of bids submitted from reputable firms	✓	✓	✓			✓
2. Establishment of the clientside in advance of competition	✓	✓	✓			
3. Information available on savings and service quality	✓			✓	✓	✓
4. Savings achieved	✓	✓	✓	✓		✓
5. Contract problems with contractors (defaults, terminations, etc.)	✓					✓
6. Has systematically reviewed service-delivery options	✓					✓
7. Existence of an explicit contract strategy	✓	✓				
8. Evidence that a review of the market had been undertaken	✓					
9. Speed of contract processing				✓	✓	
10. Evidence of active contract management		✓		✓		
11. Clarity of responsibilities for strategy, monitoring, and management		✓	✓			
12. Evidence of customer involvement	✓			✓		
13. Quality of relationship with contractor	✓	✓				✓
14. Strength of in-house bids	✓		✓			✓
15. Decision-making levels—how much devolution is there?		✓	✓	✓		
16. Evidence of reengineering the organization	✓		✓			
17. Evidence of reengineering systems—ABC, performance management	✓		✓		✓	✓

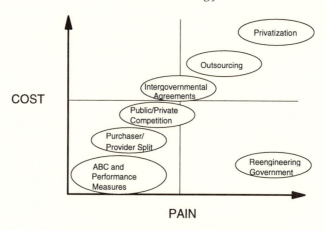

Figure 6.1.   Analysis of Breakthrough Strategies

5. *Encouraging public/private competition.*   This involves exposing in-house providers to competition. To have the greatest impact, in-house contractors need to gain freedom to operate in a commercial manner. In-house providers cannot always be competitive when they have to meet government financial, personnel, and procurement regulations. Where possible, these should be relaxed—increasing the threshold for purchases without formal competition, allowing the manager greater freedom to transfer moneys from one budget head to another, and allowing agreements on performance pay and bonus systems. Most importantly, bid teams should be able to rethink their staffing needs and ways of working during the bid process.

6. *Introducing intergovernmental agreements.*   These can be low-risk ways of retaining service standards while securing economies of scale and specialist expertise. It is possible to develop intergovernmental agreements with one government or invite one or more governments to compete for a contract, even with private firms.

7. *Reengineering the government system to promote a more business-like approach to running services.* This would involve reducing the role of elected politicians in management decisions with more autonomy for professional managers. It also involves reforming the system of government to reduce conflict and the level of politicization. There are a number of ways of doing this. One radical approach would be to introduce a council–manager form of government, with fewer elected politicians, without executive powers, one decision-making point (rather than two or three, which is the norm in mayor and commission forms of government), and nonpartisan elections. Another approach would be to introduce more limited reforms moving in the direction of focusing the elected politicians role on policy and community representation.

8. *Outsourcing and privatizing activities, where there is a compelling case.* Obvious candidates include trash collection, grounds maintenance, engineering services, legal advice, computing, and facilities management. Many organizations in the public and private sector have successfully outsourced these activities and achieved significant improvements in value for money.

Figure 6.1 plots each strategy on a risk–pain matrix. This helps identify the quick wins (areas that have low risk and can be achieved quickly at low cost) and the longer term "must do's" as well as options that should be avoided. The analysis suggests that developing a performance culture, introducing cost transparency through ABC, and introducing a strong purchasing function are the first three strategies to pursue. Public/private competition is the easiest of the alternative service-delivery methods to pursue, because it has the insurance option of retaining the current arrangements as it includes a bid from the existing workforce.

CONCLUSIONS

Contracting is no panacea for local governments. However, where it is well executed it can improve value for money significantly. The most important feature of best practice is to adopt a strategic approach to service delivery. This means reviewing all of the options to deliver services, including in-house provision and contracting. Another feature of best practice is to reengineer the decision-making process to devolve the operational management of the contracting process (including the selection of areas for contracting) to professional managers rather than elected officials. Other essential features include developing good information on costs, standards, and performance. Finally, local governments should examine carefully the possibility of introducing public/private competition for services rather than outright outsourcing. Public/private competition can achieve similar levels of savings without the disruption and damage to employee morale that often accompanies outsourcing.

7

Only in Los Angeles— Contract Cities and LA County

"Inside every fat and bloated local authority there is a slim one struggling to get out." —Ridley (1988)

The late Nicholas Ridley served as Mrs. Thatcher's minister responsible for local government in the 1980s. Clearly he did not have a high opinion of British local governments. He sometimes compared them unfavorably with local governments in California. In particular, he wrote about the U.S. local governments, with few employees, where the council members met once a year to review the contracts. These local governments employed few staff and contracted out for all of their services. He was writing long before the U.K. legislation on Compulsory Competitive Tendering (CCT) materialized. At the time, many in the U.K. found such ideas far-fetched and hard to believe. In fact, such councils do exist and have a long history: they are the California contract cities. So what are "contract cities"? How did they emerge? Are they a superior form of local government? Is the Ridley image accurate?

Contract cities were not unusual in contracting for services. U.S. local governments had been contracting for well over 100 years. Their uniqueness lies in providing an alternative model of local government, based on contracting as "a way of life." They tend to be small cities (a typical contract city has a population of around 50,000), employ few staff, and arrange for other bodies to deliver virtually all of their services. These include "easy to contract for" services such as street maintenance and refuse collection but also services that would be regarded as sacrosanct public services in the U.K.—policing, fire, libraries, and a wide range of support services. These contracts and agreements are with a wide range of suppliers drawn from the private and public sectors. Los Angeles County might, for example, provide police and public works services with private for-profit firms collecting the trash, sweeping the streets, and providing information systems and legal services. In addition, nonprofit organizations might help run arts and recreational facilities.

The remainder of this chapter is divided into four parts, the first two of which examine the origins and evolution of the contract cities. These are followed by an analysis of how the contract city model works in Los Angeles County today. Next is an examination of a number of issues relating to the contract city model, including whether it offers a superior model of local government, the strengths and weaknesses of intergovernmental contracting, and the lessons for service contracting in local government generally.

THE ORIGINS OF THE CONTRACT CITIES

The first contract city was born in 1954 when Lakewood was incorporated as a city government. At the time, Lakewood was a new and growing suburban community of 70,000, some 20 miles south of Los Angeles and adjacent to Long Beach. Lakewood was an "unincorporated" area—that is, there was no city government. Local services such as policing, fire, and road maintenance were provided by Los Angeles County. Local taxes were low, and residents wanted it to stay that way. City governments traditionally provide a higher and wider range of local services than counties (e.g., recreation, landscaping, and arts and cultural programs) and levy higher taxes.

The local community had spent years fighting the attempts of the city of Long Beach to expand its boundaries and take over Lakewood. They did not want to be swallowed by "Big Brother Long Beach" but at the same time could not afford to set up their own local government. The county of Los Angeles was also unusual in the U.S. context. Most counties administer statewide services such as prisons, courts, and the welfare system as well as providing limited local services to small numbers of residents living in unincorporated areas most of which are in rural areas. Los Angeles, however, provided local services to a very large unincorporated urban population and provided, by county standards, a high level of services. Moreover, both the political leaders and workers of Los Angeles County wanted the county to retain this role as a major urban government (Miller, 1981). After all, there were jobs and political careers at stake! Miller (1981) talks about the crucial role played by the county firefighters in incorporation. They actively campaigned for the Lakewood Plan, providing information and campaigning on the streets.

The idea of creating a contract city in Lakewood was a novel marriage between the county interests and the local residents (Miller, 1981). Lakewood would become a fully fledged city but would contract with the county for its services. In particular, Lakewood contracted with the county for police, public works, recreation, and general services. Special districts were established to provide fire and library services, with county workers supplying the services. As a result, Lakewood was able to establish its own government but did not have the high setting-up costs that normally accompany incorporation. Indeed, in the early years Lakewood only employed three staff—an attorney, a city manager, and a secretary! Other unincorporated areas threatened with annexation soon followed the Lakewood lead. In 1957, the California Contract Cities Association (CCCA) was formed.

Los Angeles County was able to retain its service-delivery role and leadership of the metropolitan region. The losers were, of course, Long Beach and other "full-service cities" such as Los Angeles and Pasadena, as their expansionist plans were halted. The full-service cities, through the Independent Cities Association, continued to oppose the Lakewood Plan. There have been a number of battles over the years, some ending up in the courts, others in the State Legislature. Most of these battles related to one of two issues:

—*Incorporation*: The question was whether it should be made easier or more difficult for areas to incorporate as contract cities.

—*Subsidies*: The full-service cities were concerned that local taxes that their residents paid for countywide services were helping to pay for services to contract cities.

The key subsidy issue was the level of county overheads that could or should be included in the cost of an intergovernmental contract. At first, it was the independent cities that campaigned for the full overheads to be included in the contracts. Later, LA County itself would press for all relevant overheads to be included. This change in position was a direct consequence of financial pressures—county supervisors had helped to establish the contract cities with a "sweetheart deal" to retain its regional dominance but saw little point in continuing to subsidize the cities. They were happy to provide services to them, provided that all costs were covered. The debate was about what was included in the "full costs."

Some of the key points in the development of the contract cities include:

- *1956—the Bradley Burns sales tax.* This allowed newly incorporated cities to tap into a new source of revenue without increasing property tax rates. This, along with the Lakewood plan, fueled the incorporation model.

- *1962—LA County Grand Jury.* The Grand Jury drafted a formula to determine the annual cost of a patrol car to the contract cities. The formula was based on the assumption that the county should charge only for the marginal costs of providing the service. The Grand Jury reviewed the formula each year without proposing any change until 1969.

- *1969—Booz, Allen and Hamilton report.* LA County hired consultants KPMG to review the pricing methods for the city contracts. The consultants concluded that overheads were being excluded and recommended a major increase in the contract prices. The CCCA responded by hiring its own consultants, Booz, Allen and Hamilton. However, the Booz, Allen and Hamilton report was also unfavorable to the CCCA, arguing that full overheads should be included in contract prices.

- *1973—Gonsalvez Amendment.* In its second attempt, the CCCA succeeded in legislating the amount of overheads that could be charged in city contracts. Congressman Gonsalvez sponsored the Bill, and Governor Reagan signed it in 1973. The Bill had been bitterly opposed by the county supervisors and the ICA but supported by the county sheriff and the CCCA. The Act provided that for contract services a county with a population in excess of 6 million must include only overheads directly attributable to the services. This prevented LA County from including overheads of general county government, such as some of the costs of the CAO's office and those of the county supervisors.

- *1981—Amendment of Gonsalvez Act.* The Act was amended so that the principle that overheads included in the cost of an intergovernmental contract must be directly attributable to the service should apply to all counties in California, not just LA County.

THE EVOLUTION OF THE CONTRACT CITY

Lakewood did not invent contracting in Southern California. LA County had been contracting for services since the last century. Moreover, when Lakewood was incorporated, the county had over 400 service agreements with 45 cities (LA County, 1977). What was significant about Lakewood was:

—it was based on contracting as a way of life for a local government

—it was the first incorporation in 15 years

—it led to a flood of incorporations, all but one based on the contract model

—it supported LA County's position as the lead local government within the LA region.

By 1970, there were 32 contract cities. Today, according to the CCCA, 116 of California's cities (there are just under 500 cities in California) are contract cities. A new form of local government had been created, and it became known as the "Lakewood Plan." The CCCA itself now has 74 members, of which 52 are cities in LA County.

As times have changed, so has the Lakewood Plan. Contract cities no longer contract exclusively with the county. They contract with a variety of suppliers, from the private and voluntary sectors as well as the county. Some contract cities have also set up in-house service providers. Lakewood, for example, uses city staffs for tree trimming, parking control, town planning, and financial and personnel services. Lakewood, with a resident population of 80,000, now employs around 160 staff.

At the same time, the full-service cities have changed too. An increasing number have experimented with contracting as a way of cutting costs. This is a direct response to the reduction in local tax income as a result of Proposition 13 (a limitation on the property tax rate) and the decline in sales tax as a consequence of the recession. For example, it is becoming increasingly common for full-service cities to contract, at least in part, for refuse collection.

HOW THE CONTRACT CITY MODEL WORKS

This section draws on fieldwork done with four local governments—LA County, Lakewood, Rosemead, and Santa Clarita—and a range of contractors. It is divided into six sub-sections, the first of which outlines the case studies. The second section describes the operating framework and is followed by an analysis of the service providers. Next, the approaches to contracting are examined and the impact on value for money. Finally, the decision-making environment is addressed.

The Case Studies

- *Los Angeles County.*   With a population of 9.23 million and a land area of over 4,000 square miles, this is by far the largest county government in the U.S. The county is governed by a five-member board of full-time, paid supervisors who are elected on a district basis. It also has an elected sheriff, attorney, and assessor. The supervisors also serve as the boards for special districts, such as the Consolidated Fire District and the Libraries District. The county has a nonpartisan system of government. LA County has been a charter county since 1913. It provides a range of countywide services, such as health, prisons, tax collection, property assessment, the courts, and social services. It also provides a comprehensive range of municipal services (e.g., public works, law enforcement, libraries, and fire) to residents who live in unincorporated areas. The unincorporated population of the county is a little under 1 million (960,000). In addition, the county provides a range of municipal services (e.g., law enforcement and public works) on contract to the 88 cities within its boundaries. Finally, the county provides a range of services—e.g., fire and libraries—to residents who live in cities that are part of special districts. The county has an operational budget of $11.1 billion and employs around 88,000 staff. Combining the municipal service provision for the unincorporated population together with the contract cities, LA County is one of the biggest municipal governments in the U.S. alongside Chicago, LA City, and, of course, New York City.

- *City of Lakewood.*   This is the original contract city, incorporated in 1954. It has a council manager form of government. The five-member council selects a mayor from its own ranks and appoints a city administrator and an attorney. The city administrator makes all other appointments. The attorney function is contracted out to John Todd Associates. John Todd was the lawyer who invented the Lakewood Plan, led the incorporation of the city, and has served as its attorney, on contract, ever since. Lakewood's operational budget in fiscal year 1995/96 was $27.5 million (this excludes expenditure on fire and libraries that are included in the county's budget). Around $14.1 million is spent on contract services, of which 32% represents law enforcement and 23% trash collection. The city employs around 160 staff.

- *City of Rosemead.* This is situated 9 miles east of LA. The city has a population of 54, 000. It was incorporated in 1957 and adopted the same constitution as Lakewood. The city had an operational budget in fiscal year 1994/95 of $14.4 million. Most of the expenditure is on contracted services, with only 14.6% spent on city employees.

- *City of Santa Clarita.* With a population of 147,000, it is the largest contract city in LA County. Santa Clarita lies 35 miles north of Los Angeles and was just 15 miles north of the epicenter of the 1994 Northridge earthquake. It is also one of the newest contract cities, having been incorporated in 1987. The city has a similar constitution to Lakewood—the council appoints a city manager who, in turn, makes all other appointments.

- *Willdan Associates.* This is a civil engineering and planning firm with in excess of 300 employees. William Stookey and Dan Heil established Willdan in 1964 as a partnership with only 12 staff. Both partners had worked as engineers for the city of Fullerton. Today, Willdan is a private limited company providing a range of engineering, building safety, and engineering services to government clients in California, Nevada, and Arizona. At the time of writing, the company has over 400 clients, the most important services for which are as city engineer for 19 cities, traffic engineer for 12 cities, building official for 12 cities, public works plan checking for 26 cities, building inspection for 13 cities, and building plan checking for 149 cities. The company does most of its business in Southern California and Nevada.

The Operating Framework

- *Private contracting.* Under California law, general law cities have to provide fire, police, and public works services, but there are few requirements over how such services are provided. There is no compulsory competitive tendering in California, and few charter cities in Southern California are precluded from contracting out functions provided by government employees—this is, however, the case in both LA County and LA City. Cities can contract for any service, including police, fire, social services, and even the city manager! There are some requirements over the contracting process. Where a sealed competitive-bid process is used, the city must award the contract to the lowest responsible bidder, and the usual federal laws on antitrust and federal programs apply. Large local governments such as LA County, the Metropolitan Transit Authority, and LA City have preference programs, but the smaller cities generally do not.

- *Intergovernmental contracting.* The California Government Code permits a county to contract with any city within its boundaries to provide municipal services. Contract terms cannot exceed five years, but they can be renewed for successive five-year periods. Either party can dissolve the agreement. Under state law, a county cannot make a "profit" on contracted service. Charter counties may also set additional requirements for intergovernmental contracting, as is the case in LA County. The county decided to engage in intergovernmental contracting provided that: it does not interfere with the county's main mission; the contracted services are self-financing; the service levels required by the city are at least equal to the level provided by the county in the unincorporated areas; liability is shared with the contractee; and the city must request the service by a formal resolution of the council. LA County also uses standard boilerplate contracts for most of its contracts. These are for five-year periods and can be terminated with six months' notice. Most of the specifications are also standardized. Table 7.1 shows the extent of intergovernmental contracting in LA County.

- *Special districts.* These cover services provided by special purpose local governments. The two major special districts for the contract cities in LA County are the fire and libraries districts. Other districts exist for sanitation, street lighting, flood control, and even mosquito abatement. Boards comprising the county supervisors govern these special districts, and county employees deliver the services. Financing arrangements vary, with the Consolidated Fire District receiving a fixed proportion of the property tax while the Libraries District relies on moneys from the county's General Fund and a part of the property taxes. Unlike the intergovernmental contracting, there is no clear purchaser–provider relationship here between the county and the cities. Residents in contract cities pay for these services through their county taxes and elect the county supervisors to oversee the operation of the districts. However, cities can decide to opt out of the special districts and set up their own municipal service or contract with another organization.

- *Joint powers authorities.* These are a more flexible form of the special district concept but are not separate local governments. The JPAs are formed by the local governments and are accountable to them for their performance. The governing committee/board is usually nominated by the local governments rather than elected by the people. The funding comes from the member local governments rather than through a separate, independent source. Generally, JPAs appear to be more common in Northern California, especially for basic service provision such as waste management.

The Service Providers

Table 7.2 outlines the practical—as opposed to theoretical—service-delivery options available to a city in LA County. In practice, there are four issues for a contract city to determine:

—whether to contract with the county or another government for law enforcement

TABLE 7.1. **Intergovernmental Contracts and Agreements between Cities and LA County for Selected Services**

Function	Number of Contracts
General law enforcement	42
Traffic law enforcement	40
Detective services	40
Helicopter programs	19
Members of the Consolidated Fire District	51
Members of the Library District	52
General Services Agreement	87
Street maintenance	10
Sewer maintenance	5
Traffic signals	60
Industrial waste	45
Building inspection	24
City prosecution services	68
Animal control	35
Animal shelter services	40
Lifeguard services	7
Beach maintenance	4
Facility maintenance	3
Roadside tree service	1
Recreation service	3
Real estate services	9

Source: LA County, July 1991.

—whether to remain in the special districts for fire and libraries

—the extent to which it wants to contract with for-profit firms for professional services

—the extent to which it wants to contract with for-profit firms for manual services.

These four choices are now explored.

1. *Law Enforcement*

The principal choice here is whether to set up a municipal police department or contract with the county sheriff. The pattern of service delivery has been

TABLE 7.2.   **The Service-Delivery Options for Cities in LA County**

Service	Direct Provision	Intergov'tal Contract	Special District	JPA	For-Profit Contract	Nonprofit Contract
Trash collection	Y	N	N	N	Y	N
Street repair	Y	Y	N	N	Y	N
City/traffic engineer	Y	Y	N	N	Y	N
Planning/zoning	Y	N	N	N	N	N
Building control	Y	Y	N	N	Y	N
Street cleaning	Y	Y?	N	N	Y	N
Traffic/parking enforcement	Y	N	N	N	Y	N
Water supply	Y	Y	Y	Y	Y	N
Police	Y	Y	N	N	N	N
Fire	Y	N	Y	N	N	N
Animal control	Y	Y	N	N	N	Y
Management of recreational facilities	Y	N	N	N	Y	Y
Landscape maintenance	Y	Y	N	N	Y	N
Libraries	Y	N	Y	Y	N	N
Cultural/arts programs	Y	N	N	N	N	Y
Building/grounds maintenance	Y	Y	N	N	Y	N
Payroll	Y	N	N	N	Y	N
Data processing	Y	Y	N	Y	Y	N
Legal services	Y	N	N	N	Y	N
Building security	Y	N	N	N	Y	N

relatively stable over the past two decades, with most contract cities opting for a contract with the sheriff and full-service cities operating an in-house service. However, in recent years a few other options have emerged. A few contract cities have terminated their contracts with the county sheriff and contracted with a neighboring city. For example, the city of Sante Fe Springs recently gave notice to terminate its contract with the sheriff in favor of a contract with the adjacent city of Whittier to begin in October 1995. There are also some counter-examples of full-service cities contracting with the sheriff to provide specialized policing or as a supplement to their basic policing. The city of Long Beach, for example, contracted with the sheriff to provide a law enforcement service in the northern part of the city for two years in the early 1990s. The city of Hawaiian Gardens recently terminated its contract with the sheriff in favor of setting up its own municipal department, while a number of full-service cities have examined the possibility of dismantling their in-house forces and contracting with the sheriff. Full-service cities requesting formal feasibility studies in recent years include Long Beach (in 1991), Bell Gardens (in 1991), and Hermosa Beach (in 1991). In 1995, 41 governments contracted with the sheriff for law enforcement services, while the vast majority of the remainder operated a municipal police service.

2.   *Fire and Libraries Districts*

There are two options for providing a fire service—establish a municipal fire department or become a member of the Fire District. There is no significant intergovernmental contracting for fire services within LA County and no city contracts with one of the private fire companies. Fifty-one local governments are members of the Fire District, covering a little under 3 million people and 2,500 square miles. As with law enforcement, the pattern of service delivery has been stable for the past two decades, but there has been a small amount of change at the margins. The city of Pomona, a full-service city, joined the Fire District in 1995, while Signal Hill left the district in the 1980s only to rejoin some years later. The city of Hawthorne recently commissioned a feasibility study to dismantle its fire department and join the Fire District.

Fifty-two cities are in the LA Library District, covering around 3 million of the county's residents. The district's annual expenditure is around $60 million, and it employs around 800 full-time equivalent positions. Once again, the pattern of service delivery is stable. There has been the occasional withdrawal from the district. Cerritos, for example, withdrew in the mid-1970s and set up its own library service. Palmdale was the last city to leave the district in 1977. At the time of writing, because of funding cuts by the county, a number of cities were considering withdrawing from the district. These included Claremount, Diamond Bar, and San Dimos.

3.   *Professional Services*

Table 7.3 shows the level of competition for selected professional and manual services in Southern California. Few cities contract out planning and zoning or budgeting and accounting, nor do they contract for routine personnel administration, although this is a minor function for most cities given the small size of their workforce. Cities do contract on a project basis for nonroutine activities such as planning studies and executive selection. Another area that is usually kept in-house is the management of recreation facilities. However, it is common to award concessions to catering companies and contract for the janitorial services for recreational facilities.

Legal services are nearly always contracted out, usually to small and medium-sized companies that specialize in providing city attorney services. City engi-

TABLE 7.3.   The Level of Competition for Professional and Manual Local Government Services in Southern California

Activity	Number of Providers
Professional services	
Labor negotiations	4
Computer services	13
Computer maintenance	13
Auditing services	10
Legal services	8
City engineering services	7
Building inspection	6
Plan checking	7
Manual services	
Sewer maintenance	3
Street sweeping	6
Landscape maintenance	10
Traffic signal maintenance	5
Median strip maintenance	12
Tree trimming	10
Refuse collection[a]	20
Janitorial services	6
Parking enforcement	4

Source: California Contract Cities Association survey conducted in 1989; 63 questionnaires were sent out and 32 responses received. As a result, the findings probably understate by a small amount the number of providers.

[a]Thirteen of the providers do both residential and commercial trash collections; seven do only residential collections.

neering, traffic management, and building and safety work are also contracted out. Many cities, such as Rosemead, contract with private firms such as Willdan or BSI. There are around seven firms in Southern California who provide professional planning, engineering, and building services. Others contract with LA County. Some of the larger and older cities have set up their own in-house operation.

Most cities operate in-house data-processing operations, but this is beginning to change. Lakewood, for example, owns the computer hardware but contracts with a private firm to run the facilities.

There have been occasions where the city manager's function is contracted out. This is a very unusual situation, often a result of political tension between the council and the last manager or as a stopgap until a full-time manager is appointed.

4. *Manual Services*

Contract cities typically contract for the bulk of their manual services. Most cities have contracted or franchised for trash collection since incorporation. Other services commonly contracted out to the private sector include street sweeping, tree trimming, and mowing. One area that was mainly provided by city employees but is increasingly being contracted out is custodial services.

Traditionally, the LA County Public Works Department provided a wide range of both professional and manual public works services, including street repair (not street reconstruction or construction), traffic signal maintenance, sewer maintenance, and the disposal of industrial waste. Table 7.4 summarizes the volume of work commissioned by cities in the 1994/95 fiscal year.

The LA County role in public works has declined in proportionate but not absolute terms over the past three decades. The reasons are threefold. First, private firms have emerged in some areas, challenging the county's role. For example, there are two sizable contractors—Charlie Abbott and Burns Pacific— doing street maintenance work for cities, while two contractors—Superior Signals and Allied Signals—work for cities on traffic signal maintenance. A second reason is that some cities are establishing their own in-house operations. This is especially true of the larger contract cities. Finally, some cities are contracting with other cities rather than with the county. For example, the city of Brea (in Orange County) provides street maintenance services to neighboring cities, such

TABLE 7.4. Manual Services Contracting with LA County

Service	Number of Cities	Range of Expenditure ($)	Average Expenditure ($)
Industrial waste	23	2,000–100,000	18,050
Traffic signal maintenance	25	650–51,750	14,400
Building inspection	22	11,600–713,700	177,000
Street maintenance	25	325–1,421,700	210,000
All services	32	11,500–1,471,300	310,000

Source: LA County Public Works Department. Figures relate to expenditure billed July 1994 through March 1995 (75% of the 1994/95 fiscal year).

as Diamond Bar. Indeed, Brea won the contract following an RFP process for which LA County and Charlie Abbott competed. Similarly, Sante Fe Springs is interested in providing traffic signal maintenance services to nearby cities, while the city of Burbank maintains Glendale's traffic signals. The county's role in tree-trimming and landscaping services is now minimal.

There are a number of general conclusions that can be drawn:

- Contract cities strongly favor contracting for manual services but are less likely to contract for professional services. The two exceptions are legal services and planning/engineering services.

- Service provision by other governments is as important as contracting with the private sector. Contracting for sheriff's services and membership of the Fire and Library Districts are the main approaches.

- LA County's role in law enforcement, fire, and libraries appears stable, but its contracting role for public works and other functions has been steadily and gently declining over time.

- The availability of private firms willing to provide services for government appears to be largely influenced by the willingness of local governments to contract for services. In other words, supply appears to be a function of demand. Moreover, the establishment of intergovernmental contracting has in turn stimulated the development of private contracting for public services.

- The contract city concept has evolved significantly over time. At the time of incorporation, a contract city would contract for virtually all of its services with LA County. Today, a contract city typically contracts with a range of providers, both public and private, and it maintains some in-house capability, especially for professional services. As a result it is possible to detect a degree of convergence between the contract and full-service cities. The former are creating some in-house capability, while the latter are contracting out an increasing volume of services.

Approach to Contracting

The approach to contracting is examined here in relation to the extent to which a strategic approach is in place, the selection techniques, the nature of contracts, and contract management arrangements.

1. *Strategic Approach*

Few of the contract cities appear to adopt a strategic approach to service delivery. Their approach is one of pragmatism and opportunism. Indeed, the Lakewood Plan itself was a piece of opportunism. It was a convenient way of continuing county services at low cost while achieving local control. It was not part of a crusade to create minimal government.

Cities tend to stick with tried and tested service-delivery approaches, and any experimentation tends to be small-scale and at the margins. Few cities have withdrawn from the special fire and libraries districts or terminated contracts with the sheriff. Moreover, few cities have carefully examined the alternative methods. None of the cities visited by the author had, for example, looked carefully at the alternatives to contracting/agreements with the county for law enforcement, fire, and library services.

Although not an explicit or conscious strategy, contract packaging tended to be based on the principle that small is best—where possible, break the work down. This has stimulated small and medium-sized firms to bid for city work. Indeed, it was noticeable that a number of "mom and pop" companies were engaged in contracting for legal services, trash collection, and engineering services. At the same time, it discourages major corporations because the volumes of work are small, the bidding processes elaborate and expensive, and the prospects of retaining the work are uncertain.

2. *Selection Techniques*

Contract cities tend to use competitive sealed bids and RFP procedures. There is a strong preference for the RFP approach over competitive sealed bidding. This is because it gives the local government more discretion and control over whom to select. Moreover, once a contractor has been appointed, the contract is likely to be renewed without formal competition, whether a sealed bidding or an RFP process. This is clearly demonstrated in Tables 7.5A and 7.5B, summarizing Lakewood's and Santa Clarita's contracts. The trash-collection franchise has been in place for well over 30 years with the same firm and has not been subjected to formal competition. The same is true of legal services, street sweeping, and data processing.

Noncompetitive contracting is also the dominant feature of the LA County contracts. Again using Lakewood as an example, the contracts for sheriff's law enforcement services and public works have not been subject to formal competition. This is understandable in the case of law enforcement, as there are few genuine alternative providers, other than those involved in setting up a municipal police force. However, it is harder to understand for public works where there are alternative providers. Some contract cities are beginning to subject the county to competition. For example, the city of Diamond Bar issued an RFP for street maintenance services, and LA County competed against Charlie Abbott and Associates and the city of Brea. Brea won the contract. Such an approach is, however, the exception rather than the norm.

3. *Nature of Contracts*

Some of the contracts are franchises, especially in the trash-collection area. Unlike a normal contract, these franchises make it the franchisee's responsibility

TABLE 7.5A. Lakewood's Service-Delivery Choices

The Service	Delivery Mode
Law enforcement	Contracts with LA County; has never seriously considered setting up its own police department, on grounds of the high cost; did consider supplementing the contract with in-house community relations initiatives in the 1970s, but this came to nothing.
Fire	Member of the LA County Consolidated Fire Protection District; has never considered opting out of the district, on grounds of high setting-up and running costs.
Libraries	Member of the LA County Library District—has not considered leaving but may do so in the future as a result of the current fiscal crisis in LA County and its impact on the district.
Legal services	Has a personal services contract with John Todd, the father of the Lakewood Plan.
Data processing	Owns the computers but contracts with DRC to maintain the facilities. This is an annual contract that was awarded following an RFP process—the contract has not been subject of competition since the original award in the 1980s.
Planning and zoning	In-house.
Budgeting and accounting	In-house.
Personnel administration	In-house.
Management of recreational facilities	In-house.
City engineering and traffic management	Small in-house capability, but mainly contracts out to LA County; this contract has never been subject to formal competition.
Building and safety	Contracts with LA County and has not been subject to any formal competition.
Street sweeping	Contracts with R. F. Dickson, a large street-sweeping firm. This is an annual contract that has been extended without formal competition for well over 20 years.
Grounds maintenance	Some in-house capability; contracts out on a project basis using competitive sealed bidding.
Tree trimming	Some in-house capability (two crews), and lets contracts on a project basis, using competitive sealed bidding.
Street repair	Contracts with LA County.
Traffic signal maintenance	Contracts with LA County.
Trash collection	Franchises with BZ Disposal, a local firm that only works for Lakewood and has been with them since incorporation; the contract has never been out to competitive bid since the first award.
Water supply	In-house water utility for two-thirds of the city, with the remaining third supplied by a private water company.
Wastewater	LA County's responsibility—part of the County Sanitation District.
Custodial Services	Contracted out with a private firm.
Paramedics	Part of the service provided by the Fire District.
Ambulance	A county responsibility (the county contracts with private firms).
Printing	Some in-house capability, with large-scale jobs contracted out.

Source: Lakewood City Administrator's Office, 1995.

TABLE 7. 5B. Santa Clarita's Service-Delivery Choices

The Service	Delivery Mode
Law enforcement	Contracts with LA County. Has never seriously considered setting up its own police department, on grounds of the high cost.
Fire	Member of the LA County Consolidated Fire Protection District. Has never considered opting out of the district, on grounds of high setting-up and running costs.
Libraries	Member of the LA County Library District—has not considered leaving but may do in the future as a result of the current fiscal crisis in LA County and its impact on the district.
Legal services	Contracts with a legal firm, and the contract has not been subject to formal competition. The contract is an open contract that allows the city to give 30 days' notice for termination.
Data processing	In-house.
Planning and zoning	In-house.
Budgeting and accounting	In-house.
Personnel administration	In-house.
Management of recreational facilities	In-house.
City engineering and traffic management	Mainly in-house but uses consultants for more specialized work; used to contract with Willdan Associates.
Building and safety	Mainly in-house, but sometimes contracts out to cope with heavy workloads. Used to contract with Willdan Associates.
Street sweeping	Contracts with a private firm; used to contract with LA County.
Grounds maintenance	Some in-house capability; contracts out on a project basis using competitive sealed bidding.
Tree trimming	Some in-house capability (two crews), and lets contracts on a project basis, using competitive sealed bidding.
Street repair	Contracts with LA County.
Traffic signal maintenance	Contracts with LA County.
Trash collection	Franchises for commercial collections with three firms and also has franchises with three firms for residential collections; the franchises have never been out to competitive bid.
Water supply	In-house water utility for two thirds of the city, with the remaining third supplied by a private water company.
Wastewater	LA County's responsibility—part of the County Sanitation District.
Custodial Services	Contracted out with a private firm.
Paramedics	Part of the service provided by the Fire District.
Ambulance	A county responsibility (the county contracts with private firms).
Printing	Some in-house capability, with large-scale jobs contracted out.

Source: Santa Clarita City Manager's Office, 1995.

to collect a fee from the individual service users. The fee is fixed by the city, and it means that the service is paid for from a separate user fee rather than the general fund.

Most contracts with private firms are annual, or else they are open—that is, they do not define a period. In addition, contracts can usually be terminated at short notice, usually between one and three months, without cause. Most intergovernmental contracts are for a five-year period, but again either the city or LA County has the ability to terminate the contract at short notice.

Contracts that go through a competitive sealed bidding process tend to be specified in much more detail than those that go through an RFP process. Indeed, many of the professional service contracts say very little about what is to be done! Light specification combined with the renewal and easy termination options make for a very flexible form of contracting, which contrasts strongly with the traditional approach to public procurement.

The author came across a few examples of "joint contracting" where cities join together to contract for a service. This is the case for some cities for law enforcement. Lakewood and its neighboring cities have a regionalized multicity contract with the sheriff. This enables the cities to share law enforcement resources, cut costs, and increase flexibility and capability of responding to emergencies. At the same time, cities have the ability to supplement their multicity contract with additional services to meet their needs. The special districts for fire and libraries are, in effect, regional contracts.

4. Contract Management Arrangements

There is no standard approach to contract management. Arrangements and approaches vary markedly. There are, nevertheless, three basic approaches:

- *Hands on:* this usually applies to contracts with private firms. In the case of professional contracts such as city engineering and traffic management services, an appointed city contract officer usually has to approve the recommendations of the contractor rather than delegate it to the contractor. However, there appeared to be little formal monitoring of performance and few, if any, published targets. The monitoring that took place tended to be based on word of mouth and anecdotal. Council members were rarely involved in monitoring issues unless such issues became public problems with media coverage. Monitoring of manual services was more formalized, with appointed monitoring personnel undertaking spot checks and following up complaints. Again, however, there was little formal reporting of performance, and council members had minimal involvement.

- *Hands off:* this usually applies to the intergovernmental contracts, especially law enforcement. Here, typically, monitoring will be the responsibility of a senior official in the city manager's office, but that official will have plenty of other duties. In practice there is little monitoring, except for data supplied by the county on levels of criminal activity and expenditure. There is no monitoring of the fire and library districts. Indeed, these tend to be regarded as outside the responsibility of the contract city.

- *Citizen involvement:* this is relatively small but is on the increase. Lakewood, for example, has a citizen telephone hotline which it uses to track the performance of a number of contractors, such as trash collection, street sweeping, and street repair. Complaints are handled and monitored centrally within the city administrator's office. Another area of increasing citizen involvement is law enforcement. This includes the use of the block captain system to encourage the community to be involved in crime prevention. It also includes regular meetings between police officers and council members and the local community.

Contract monitoring for manual public works services tends to be the responsibility of a separate city engineer or public works director. Where the professional engineering functions are contracted out, the monitoring responsibility for both professional and manual services is usually in the city manager's office.

Impact on Value for Money

Despite the long, bitter battles between the contract cities and the full-service cities over the former's right to exist and particularly over the basis of the intergovernmental contracting, there is no definitive evidence on the relative efficiency merits of the two approaches. Nevertheless, there is some evidence that tends to point to the superiority of the contract city model. This is now covered in relation to law enforcement, fire, libraries, professional services, and manual services.

1. *Law Enforcement*

A number of feasibility studies have been undertaken in recent years which suggest that contracting with LA County is more efficient than establishing a municipal department. Table 7.6 summarizes the results of three studies undertaken in 1991. The sheriff's department, in response to official requests from the cities, undertook the work, for which the latter paid a nominal fee. All of the reports are public documents. None of the proposals was followed up, largely for political reasons. However, the cities did use the studies to change the management of their own police forces.

Table 7.6 shows that intergovernmental contracting is between 23% and 44% more efficient than operating a police department, and this appears to apply to both small and large cities. Why is this? Is it due to intergovernmental contracting or to something unique to LA County and/or the three cities?

The reasons for the lower costs are:

- *The sharing of law enforcement resources.* This allows LA County to provide a police service on a regional basis, spreading expensive uniformed officers over a

TABLE 7.6.   Feasibility Studies to Contract with the County Sheriff

City	Population	Area (square miles)	Police Budget ($)	Cost of Recommended Level of Service ($)[a]	Costs of Duplication ($)
Bell Gardens	42,355	2.39	5.7 m	4.2 m (26% saving)	3.9 m (31% saving)
Long Beach	429,433	53.84	91.26 m	61.9 m (32% saving)	51.1 m (44% saving)
Hermosa Beach	18,200	1.36	4.42 m	3.2 m (27.5% saving)	3.4 m (23% saving)

Source: LA County Sheriff's Department.

[a]The recommended level of service includes some improvements in service levels (e.g., a dedicated narcotics/gang team in the case of Bell Gardens and enhanced traffic enforcement in the case of Long Beach).

wider area. At the same time, the department can respond better to major emergencies. Policing problems rarely follow local government boundaries.

- *Reduced and shared support services.*   This covers clerical and administrative staff as well as sergeants, lieutenants, and station commanders.

There is usually little difference between the salaries of sheriff's officers and city police.

There are counter-examples of contract cities considering and in a few cases establishing their own municipal police departments. The financial implications are harder to establish, but the costs appear to be higher—both one-off set-up costs and the running costs. For example, the city of Hawaiian Gardens recently terminated its contract with LA County in order to set up its own department, spending an extra $750,000 per annum—a substantial increase for a small city.

2.   Fire Services

As with the sheriff, the Fire District is asked from time to time to undertake feasibility studies to take over a city's fire service. Two recent studies have been undertaken and are summarized below:

- *Pomona.*   The Fire District undertook a feasibility study for the city, and this was implemented. Pomona officially joined the district on 30 June, 1995. As a result of the change, the city saved $1.3 million annually, which equates to a saving of at least 10% of the municipal budget. In addition, there was a small one-off receipt due to the transfer of equipment and facilities. The annual cost of the new service was just under $12 million.

- *Hawthorne.* At the time of writing, the city had major financial problems that could have forced it into bankruptcy. As a result, the city was exploring a range of options to cut expenditure, one of which was dismantling the city fire department and joining the Fire District. The Fire District completed the feasibility study in April 1995. It proposed an annual cost of $4.54 million, representing an annual saving of $1.85 million—that is, a reduction of around 29%. In addition, the city would receive a one-off receipt of $375,000. In practice, the savings were even greater because the city was self-insured and these costs were not included in the savings figure but were part of membership of the Fire District. At the time of writing, Hawthorne had not decided whether to join the Fire District.

Joining the Fire District appears to offer lower costs, no reduction of service levels, and in some cases a broader range of services. How can this be? The main factors are economies of scale and geography. The Fire District can usually reduce the number of engines and stations for a city without increasing the fire risk or speed of response. This is especially the case where a city is contiguous with or surrounded by other cities in the Fire District. Cities with their own fire departments have to be self-sufficient in engines and stations. The district is also able to reduce support costs, with fewer fire chiefs, senior officers, and clerical/ administrative support, again achieved by spreading these resources over a larger complement of firefighters.

3. *Libraries*

Table 7.7 provides information on costs and services in a large number of local governments in LA County. One conclusion that is clear is that LA County provides a low-cost library service compared to most other local governments. Out of the local governments listed in Table 7.7, LA County has the third lowest spending per head of population. It is not possible to conclude that the county is more efficient on the basis of the figures, however. It is also clear that the county has less stock per head of population, but its large size may reduce this problem.

4. *Professional Services*

There is little hard evidence available on the cost comparisons between in-house and contracted professional services. The cities visited, however, tended to view contracting as the lower-cost option, even where they had decided to provide the service in-house. Decisions to provide the service in-house were usually made for control rather than cost reasons. It is the case for building and safety work that contracting with private firms such as Willdan Associates is a lower-cost option compared to contracting with LA County. This is because such firms usually agree to provide the same service at a discount on the county's fee.

TABLE 7.7. Service and Cost Information on Libraries in LA County

Local Govt	Pop'n	Area (sq. miles)	Spend per Capita	Library Holdings per Capita	Hours Open per Capita	Pop Served/ fte Staff	Circul'n per Hour
LA City	3.62 m	463.7	$13.09	$1.68	0.04	4,063	61
LA County	3.32 m	3,062.1	$13.57	$1.65	0.03	3,981	122
Glendale	190,200	30.59	$24.81	$2.83	0.05	2,206	141
Long Beach	436,800	50.22	$25.98	$2.55	0.05	2,131	125
Inglewood	113,600	8.85	$22.67	$3.66	0.05	2,323	84
Pomona	138,600	22.86	$14.65	$1.75	0.02	3,401	169
Santa Monica	89,800	8.1	$45.1	$4.09	0.13	1,007	100
Whittier	80,600	12.51	$26.22	$3.0	0.06	1,990	123
Beverly Hills	32,600	5.69	$110.08	$6.46	0.1	444	228
Burbank	98,700	17.1	$33.73	$3.23	0.08	1,701	85
Downey	94,800	12.75	$12.52	$1.33	0.03	3,846	161
Cerritos	54,200	8.9	$38.74	$2.51	0.06	1,408	225
Redondo Beach	62,700	6.55	$26.18	$2.17	0.08	3,171	91
Covina	44,450	6.8	$14.56	$2.33	0.04	3,757	110
Monrovia	37,550	13.75	$15.81	$2.75	0.07	1,095	67
El Segundo	15,650	5.47	$82.33	$6.12	0.59	441	22
Sante Fe Springs	15,550	8.67	$53.8	$4.69	0.16	1,220	45
Signal Hill	8,800	2.2	$16.79	$2.2	0.25	2,551	12

Source: California Library Statistics, 1995 (data on the 1993/94 fiscal year).

5. *Manual Services*

One major study comparing in-house provision with contracting for a range of manual services was undertaken in LA County in the early 1980s (Stevens, 1984). The study found considerable savings related to contracting, without any reduction in service levels. The full results are reported in Chapter 5. There is little other evidence to substantiate the Stevens findings. Most contract cities take it for granted that contracting for manual services is the best financial option. However, there have to be some question marks over whether cities are maximizing efficiency on manual service contracts, because:

—Relatively little attention is given to contract packaging, and few cities have packaged contracts in such a way to encourage larger firms to bid. Officials in Santa Clarita, for example, acknowledged that a rationalization of the commercial and residential trash-collection franchises would probably produce a substantial saving.

—The tradition of noncompetitive contracting can lead to some of the same problems of complacency and reduced cost-consciousness that arise with a long-standing in-house provider.

The Decision-Making Environment

There are major differences between the decision-making environment of the contract cities and the big cities visited by the author on the East Coast and in the Mid West. Most significantly, there was a much lower level of politicization in the contract cities. Decisions about how to deliver services were, by and large, left to the city manager, an appointed official. Moreover, these managers were much more likely to attach high priority to issues such as efficiency rather than party political issues such as who are the winners and losers in any change. A second difference was far fewer self-imposed regulations over the contracting process. Contract cities did not have preference programs, could renew and extend contracts with ease, and did not have the rigid procurement frameworks that were a feature of cities such as New York and Chicago. Finally, decision making was more devolved in the contract cities. Appointed, professional officials made most of the managerial and policy decisions. Even in the case of LA County's intergovernmental contracting, the county supervisors delegated the negotiating and approval process for the contracting to appointed officials.

What accounts for these differences? Clearly the size of the large eastern and mid-western cities means that policies and management issues are inherently more political because they impact on the distribution of resources to various groups within the cities. There is little doubt, however, that the form of government also plays a significant role. All of the contract cities had adopted the council–manager plan of government. Unlike the mayor form of government, this established one power base responsible for policy: the council. The mayor model has at least two power bases (the mayor and the council) and very often more where there are other elected officials. This concentration of power reduces political tension and creates an environment that is more likely to favor less regulation and delegation of decision making. So many of the regulations imposed in mayor cities were attempts by the legislative branch (the council) to control the executive (the mayor).

The second defining feature of the council–manager plan is the appointment of a professional manager with wide-ranging powers to run the government. There is little doubt that such a manager is usually the key individual in a contract city. His or her political masters are part-time amateurs and rely on the manager for information and support. They also have few formal powers—they decide policy on the advice of the manager, and they appoint the manager. The manager has all other powers—the city manager, for example, appoints all other staff, and the senior staff usually do not have contracts and so can be fired easily. City managers are typically career professionals. They will usually have a degree and often an MA in public administration, and most are members of the International City/County Management Association. Their mind-set is more managerial than that of elected politicians, and as a result decisions in contract cities tend to be more influenced by managerial considerations.

A third factor is that the contract cities are nonpartisan, so party politics is less apparent. Moreover, city workforces are usually not unionized.

It would be wrong to conclude that politics is not present in contract cities. Decisions in some areas are highly political, and this reduces the manager's room for maneuver. Here are two examples:

- *Trash-collection franchises.* Trash collectors have a high profile in the local community and often have established a close relationship with one or more council members, including contributing to their political campaigns. Changing the arrangement by introducing regular formal competition for the franchise or rationalizing the number of franchises can be difficult and risky for a manager even if significant savings are possible. These factors were present in both Lakewood and Santa Clarita.

- *Fire and police.* Both areas tend to be highly political. In the case of the Fire District, the firefighters' union is high-profile and active—any attempt to leave the Fire District would be strongly opposed by the union, which itself can be an important factor in supporting elected politicians. The sheriff, as an elected politician, has a tradition of establishing and maintaining a close relationship with elected politicians.

EVALUATION OF THE CONTRACT CITY MODEL

This section examines the contract city model in relation to three questions:

- What is the real purpose of the contract city model?
- Is the contract city model more efficient?
- Are there any lessons for local government service contracting?
- Does the decision-making environment help or hinder smart contracting?

We now turn to the discussion of these issues.

The Contract City Philosophy

Decisions on contracting in California tend to be made on pragmatic rather than ideological grounds—"we'll try it if it saves money." There is remarkably little ideology around the contract city model. Indeed, "home rule" rather than ideas about small government seems to be the driving force behind the model:

Inherent in the contract cities program is that local autonomy and control of municipal affairs remain with the locally elected city council. The result is home rule plus
economy—a city operation without large capital investments and minimal overhead
but retaining grass-roots government. It is decentralized policy with centralized
administration. [County of Los Angeles, Chief Administrative Office, 1977]

Contract cities are proud of their "home rule"—they decide which services
they will provide, how they are to be provided, the form of government that they
will have (e.g., the number of politicians, whether they have a powerful elected
mayor, etc.), and they control zoning. The contracting philosophy is therefore a
means to an end.

Efficiency or Ideology?

There is little doubt that contracting and joining regionalized special districts
is a more efficient way of delivering services compared to in-house provision.
In part, this is due to economies of scale and because governments are more
likely to manage an outside organization vigorously. Another key factor, however, is the increased choice over the delivery method. Contract cities that
contract out or join a special district always have the option of setting up a
municipal operation or contracting with another agency. This choice tends to
prevent the contractor or special district from becoming complacent. This choice
does not apply to the same degree in the opposite direction where a city has an
in-house provider, as it is much more difficult politically to contract out than to
contract in.

Lessons for Service Contracting

There are a number of positive lessons about contracting, most notably:

- *Flexibility.* Lakewood-style contracts tend to be very flexible. For example, it is
  usually possible to extend a contract without going through formal competition
  for many years. It is also possible to terminate a contract with a month's notice at
  will. Moreover, cities usually do not rely on a rigid specification, making it
  possible to adjust the requirement during the contract to respond to changing
  circumstances.

- *Trust.* Smart contracting requires a high level of trust between the government
  and contracting. This is often forgotten in the traditional public sector approach to
  procurement. The highly flexible approach adopted by the contract cities stresses
  trust and gives the appointed officials considerable latitude to make the relationship work.

- *Contracting for core services.* Contract cities are not concerned about contracting for what many would regard as core or sacrosanct public services. Examples

of such services that are contracted out regularly include legal services, financial services, the entire city engineer's function, as well as policing.

- *Intergovernmental contracting.* Many of the contracts are with other governments. The contract city model shows that intergovernmental contracting can work, resulting in a more responsive and lower-cost service.

There are some risks with the contract city approach to contracting. Most significant is the noncompetitive approach to contracting. This can reproduce all of the problems of a complacent in-house provider if the relationship with the contractor is not well managed. Second, the informal approach to contract management can degenerate into no effective contract management. Finally, the "light-touch" approach to specifications can lead to problems in managing a contract as there are no targets or standards to hold the contractor to account against.

The Decision-Making Environment

The council–manager form of government is a significant feature of the contract city approach to contracting. It stresses a professional, managerial approach and devolution of decision making. It also reduces the potential for political tension and conflict because it centralizes policy-making whereas most forms of government in the U.S. have a pluralist approach. Finally, the council–manager model encourages a strategic approach on the part of council members—their job is to set policy and review performance and leave the operational details to the manager.

Many would no doubt express concern over the technocratic approach of the council–manager form of government, arguing that it is not possible to separate policy and administration in a simplistic way. Moreover, it minimizes the role of locally elected politicians in the running of the government. There is some truth in such arguments. It is not possible to separate policy and administration in a simple way, and the council–manager plan does minimize the role of the elected politicians, who do not in practice appear to play a strategic role. Indeed, the author formed the view that the managers developed the policy, with politicians getting involved in minutiae in much the same way as they do in other forms of government. However, the council–manager form of government does result in a more businesslike approach to government. In the case of the contract cities, this promotes smart contracting and better, lower-cost services.

One problem with the contract city model relates to local accountability in the special district concept. Special districts do result in more efficient service provision, but there are real problems over accountability. There is no clear purchaser/provider relationship. In LA County, the five county supervisors serve as the directors of the fire and library districts. These supervisors are elected to represent the 9.23 million people of LA County, yet they also oversee the operation of fire and libraries for the 3 million who live in the two districts. Is this a fair system? Secondly, the relationship is theoretically between the fire and library governing boards and the electors, with the cities having no role. It is hard to believe that this makes sense. Most residents feel distant from the special districts and do not understand what they do and how they can influence things. Residents clearly have a much stronger affinity to their local city, but the latter has little role in the workings of the special district.

CONCLUSIONS

The Ridley image of the private contract city is largely a myth. Certainly contract cities exist, but they do employ some staff and provide services directly and much of the contracting is with other public agencies. Contract cities are not an all-private-sector affair. Moreover, their councillors do meet more regularly than once a year. Indeed, it is nearer to once a week or every other week! The clear distinctions between the contract and full-service cities have also become blurred.

Nevertheless, there is little doubt that the contract cities have been a financial success. They are low-tax, value-for-money cities. Per capita spending for basic city services by contract cities is less than half the level of their full-service counterparts. At the same time, crime rates are low and quality of life is at least as good as the service cities. These are some of the reasons why Californians like living in contract cities. It also explains why an increasing number of full-service cities are taking contracting seriously now.

There are also many lessons to learn from how contract cities buy and manage services. Not all of these lessons are positive. The flexibility of the approach is the great strength, as are the nonbureaucratic approach to contracting, the ease of terminating an unsatisfactory contract, and the need to build trust with the contractor, especially for professional services such as legal advice. The success of contract cities also challenges the conventional wisdom that some services, such as police and fire, can never be contracted out. There is little doubt that contracting for police and fire leads to a responsive, low-cost service. However, high flexibility does have a downside. Contracting with a single supplier without formal competition can become cozy, leading to higher-than-necessary costs being incurred. The pragmatic and opportunist approach to service delivery can also result in missed opportunities.

8

The Indianapolis Experience—
Using Competitive Contracting
to Improve Services and Efficiency

"A Mayor Shows Gore's Team the Way." —*Washington Post*, 25 August 1993

"Innovator in the Heartland." —*City Journal*, Spring 1994

"The New Mayors." —Leader for the *Wall Street Journal*, 30 November 1993

"In Privatizing City Services, It's Now Indy-a-First-Place." —*New York Times*, 2 March 1995

"Indianapolis and the Republican Future." —*Governing Magazine*, February 1994

This is a small sample of many articles published on Indianapolis in recent years in well-respected U.S. newspapers and journals. Indianapolis is widely viewed as the jewel in the crown of urban Republicanism. It is regarded as the role model for Republican city government, with many lessons for running state and federal agencies. The use of competitive contracting is viewed as the main source of its success.

Stephen Goldsmith was elected mayor of Indianapolis in 1992, and within a short period of time he had introduced the most comprehensive contracting program of any major U.S. city. He also transformed the city's fiscal position and improved public safety services in the inner-city areas dominated by ethnic minorities.

One pundit has called him "Robomayor," and the *Washingtonian* suggested in a humorous article that the Republicans would do well to consider him for the presidential nomination in 1996! More seriously, all of the major Republican mayors, such as Riordan from LA, Guilliano from New York, and Schundler from Jersey City, have been to Indianapolis to learn first hand from Goldsmith's success.

Does the Indianapolis experience show that competitive contracting can transform city government? What are the lessons for smart contracting? This is the theme for this chapter.

THE BACKGROUND

In 1970 the city of Indianapolis expanded its boundaries to include all of Marion County. The consolidation is called "Unigov," a unified city–county government. Unigov serves more than 1 million residents. It has three branches—the mayor, a city–county council, and the judiciary.

In addition to his own office, the mayor has five departments—public works, public safety, parks and recreation, metropolitan development, and capital asset management. There are also six independent municipal corporations that include the airport, library, public transport, and health and hospital functions. There are 11 school districts within Unigov's boundaries and special service districts for fire and police. Voters elect the mayor, the city–county members, and a range of county officials such as the auditor, assessor, treasurer, sheriff, and prosecutor.

Indianapolis is a Republican city. Its brand of Republicanism has traditionally been nonideological and paternalistic. Goldsmith was elected on a very different manifesto. He adopted an ideological approach not dissimilar to that of Prime Minister Margaret Thatcher in the U.K. City government was too big and expensive. Many of its tasks should be handed back to the private sector, and its services should be contracted out. It was a privatization agenda. However, after a short period in office the Goldsmith agenda shifted subtly away from pure privatization to competition. Here is Goldsmith in his own words:

Burger King and Domino's, for example, don't work so hard to satisfy their customers merely because they are private. They give great service because they are in competition, and will go out of business if customers don't like what they serve up. If we were simply to privatize without first creating a competitive environment, the benefits would be minimal. [Goldsmith, 3 December 1992, *Wall Street Journal*]

From the Taxpayers' point of view, the ideal situation occurs when the most efficient private sector service provider goes head-to-head with a public sector provider operating at its most efficient level. [Goldsmith, 3 December 1992, *Wall Street Journal*]

We have been very careful over and over again to say that we do not have a privatization effort; instead we have the most comprehensive competition and competitiveness effort of any major city or maybe any governmental entity in the United States. The distinction is critical for a number of reasons: for labor reasons in my own area, and because private monopolies are only marginally more efficient than public monopolies. There is no great value in and of itself for privatization, as contrasted to the competitiveness process. [Goldsmith, Carnegie Council, no date]

The remainder of this chapter examines the Indianapolis story—what happened, the impacts, and the underlying issues. The chapter ends with a discussion of the lessons for other governments.

WHAT HAPPENED?

Table 8.1 presents some of the main highlights in Goldsmith's first term of office. It shows that competitive bidding played a key role in the Goldsmith revolution, but it was only one element in the changes. Goldsmith made sweep-

TABLE 8.1.   Highlights of the Goldsmith Term of Office

1992

- City has a $20 million deficit
- Goldsmith takes office
- "SELTIC" established
- ABC exercise begins
- Competitive bidding for sewer billing

1993

- Competitive bidding for trash collection
- Competitive bidding for running the wastewater treatment facility
- Budget process overhauled to base it on business principles

1994

- Private contractor takes over the running of the wastewater treatment facility on a 10-year contract
- New "Popular Budget" launched
- Property tax maintained at 1992 levels

1995

- Competitive bidding for the management of the city's IT facilities
- Competitive bidding to run Indianapolis International Airport
- Balanced budget achieved
- Budget includes a 15% increase in spending on public safety compared to 1992

ing changes amongst the senior management team in the city. He hired a number of young people from the private sector to replace top city officials. Many of these were lawyers, managers, and accountants, with no prior experience of government.

One month after Goldsmith entered office, he set up the Service, Efficiency, and Lower Taxes for Indianapolis Commission (SELTIC). The objectives were to make the government more efficient, reduce costs, cut waste, eliminate unnecessary services, and pass appropriate services to the private sector. SELTIC was composed of nine businessmen. A study team drawn from the private sector and city departments supported each board member. Each study team focused on one area—for example, transportation, parks and recreation, or public works. All of the study teams were unpaid volunteers, and they totaled 100.

SELTIC inventoried city assets and services and undertook a "core service" analysis: Is the service needed? Should the city continue to provide the service? Are there opportunities to improve efficiency by privatizing or market testing? As a result of SELTIC's work, a wide range of recommendations were made to the mayor. Many of these involved subjecting in-house services to competitive bidding.

Another early innovation of the mayor was to introduce a system of activity-based costing (ABC). In the spring of 1992 he commissioned consultants KPMG to develop an ABC model for the city. The objective was to identify how much each city service and activity costs. Traditional cost accounting makes it difficult to understand the cost of activities because, for example, overheads are not properly assigned to services. Therefore the full costs of services are not identified. ABC tries to measure service costs and allocate overheads in relation to their use by the service. It also includes relevant fixed costs, such as building space and idle equipment. Goldsmith wanted to use ABC to help compare costs of in-house provision with those using private firms. He also wanted to identify opportunities for internal efficiencies by increasing cost transparency and enabling internal comparisons.

One of the early contracting exercises involved sewer billing. In 1992, the city spent almost $3 million to collect annual sewer bills of $40 million. The Indianapolis Water Company (IWC), a private utility, processed the bills, but city employees sent out the invoices to city residents. SELTIC recommended that water billing should be subject to competitive bidding. IWC initially offered to provide an integrated billing service for the city at 95% of costs, but the mayor rejected the approach and decided to follow SELTICs recommendation. IWC won the bid. This produced substantial savings and increased revenues but also meant that residents would in future receive a consolidated bill for city and IWC services.

The city–county consolidation resulted in 25 trash-collection districts, serviced by four firms and the city Department of Public Works. Each trash collector had a local monopoly. There was no competition for the franchises. In 1993, the mayor rationalized the number of districts down to 11 and subjected them to competition.

The city guaranteed that the public works department would retain one district to provide a capability to respond to emergencies. Services in all other 10 districts were up for competition. To prevent a monopoly emerging and to discourage "low balling, no single provider could win more than three contracts."

The bidding process caused the Department of Public Works to examine its approach. In consultation with the staff, the department changed its service-delivery methods, moving from four- to seven-hour days and increasing productivity. The department won three districts and increased its market share within the city. It had submitted the lowest bids. Contracts were signed for periods of between three and five years to stagger future competitions.

The trash-collection competition was a very significant event. It demonstrated that government employees could compete and win against the private sector. The city taxpayers were also winners because costs fell substantially.

The opening of the city's two advanced wastewater treatment operations to competition was one of the biggest and most difficult attempted by any U.S. city. The plants treat sewage before releasing it into the water supply. Over 300 people worked in the plants, and a significant rise in fees was anticipated. The city explored the option of selling the facility to a private operator but backed down as a result of complications because it was funded to a large degree with federal dollars, so the city invited bids from the private sector.

Bids were received from four top utility companies as well as the city employees. The White River Environmental Partnership won the bid. This comprised the IWC, Lyonnaise des Eaux-Dumez, and JMM Operational Services (Lyonnaise's U.S. operating company). The contract was for five years.

In 1994, the city introduced "popular budgets." These combined activity-based costing principles with performance measures, enabling managers, politicians, and citizens to compare the cost of services with performance. This helped to consolidate the emerging performance culture within City Hall.

At the time of writing, the city had embarked on two ambitious competition exercises involving the running of the airport and the computing facilities.

The Goldsmith regime did not focus only on contracting for city services. They used some of the savings to fund improvements in other areas, especially public safety and infrastructure developments.

THE IMPACTS

There can be little doubt that contracting has produced dramatic savings in Indianapolis. However, there are two qualifications. First, most of the Indianapolis contracts are in the early part of their term, and therefore few difficulties have been encountered. Second, the vast majority of savings are estimates, not actuals. Table 8.2 illustrates the position. Table 8.3 shows in more detail what happened in some of the larger competition exercises.

Contracting had other impacts in relation to the city's fiscal position, employees, management structure, processes and systems, and culture. These impacts are now examined.

1. *Fiscal Position*

This covers the budgeted expenditure, the level of expenditure, the state of the reserves, and the levels of taxation. Figures 8.1 and 8.2 show the trends on the budget and expenditure. It is clear that the Goldsmith administration has steadied the city's fiscal position. Budgeted expenditure has fallen slightly. The 1995 operating expenditures were $10 million less than the level in 1992 when Goldsmith took office. Financial control has also improved, with a balanced budget achieved in 1995.

However, these figures are hardly dramatic. There have been substantial savings from the competition programme, but these have not been directly translated into reduced expenditure. A significant proportion of the savings has been diverted to other spending programs within the departments achieving the savings and to the public safety program. Indeed, public safety is taking between 25% and 33% of the savings achieved through the competition program. The level of expenditure is shown in Figure 8.3. There have also been increases in

TABLE 8.2.   Financial Impacts of Contracting, Competition, and Reengineering in Indianapolis

Year	Saving ($)
1992	6.6 million
1993	12.7 million
1994	27.9 million
1995	28.8 million
1996	28.8 million
1997	23.5 million
1998	22.9 million
7-year gross	151.2 million
7-year net present value	131.9 million

Notes: (1) Figures supplied by the Mayor's Office in February 1995. (2) The figures are a combination of actuals and estimates. (3) The figures cover the majority of initiatives, but there are some exceptions where, for example, a competition exercise is underway. There are some significant exclusions such as the bidding exercises for the airport and computing facilities. (4) Most, but not all, of the initiatives relate to contracting.

TABLE 8.3.   Impacts for Competitive Bidding

Activity	Saving	Method	Winners and Losers
Sewer billing	Received savings and increased revenues of $2.35million per year	Public/private competitive bidding	Indianapolis Water Company won the contract
Trash collection	$15 million over three years against a precontract budget of $30 million	Public/private competitive bidding for 10 contracts, with restrictions on how many contracts each bidder could win	The Department of Public Works won the maximum three bids and increased its share of the work
Street repair	25%	Public/private competitive bidding	Department of Public Works
Operation of the two advanced wastewater-treatment plants	$69.8 million over five years, representing a saving of 44%	Public/private competitive bidding	The White River Environmental Partnership
Microfilming	$425, 000 per year, a saving of 63%	Opened to competition and subsequently privatized	Private vendor
Copying and printing	Direct savings of $600,000 per year, a saving of 43%; in addition, indirect savings of $1,300,000 per year were achieved	Public/private competitive bidding	Private vendor
Messenger services	$100,000	Public/private competitive bidding	Pillow Express, a minority-owned business
Golf courses	$300,000 annually, plus one-off sales of $330,000	Outsourcing	Private vendors

Note: Figures based on the 1995 document, "The Indianapolis Experience," produced by the Mayor's Office.

other programs, such as the "Strong Neighborhoods" program. This involves a series of infrastructure improvements in downtown Indianapolis.

Property tax is the main source of tax income in Indianapolis. The Goldsmith administration has held tax constant during its first three years of office.

2.   *Employees*

The number of city employees has fallen significantly, as shown in Figure 8.4. Non–public safety employees have fallen by around 25%, whereas the number of public safety employees has been maintained. The reality is less impressive

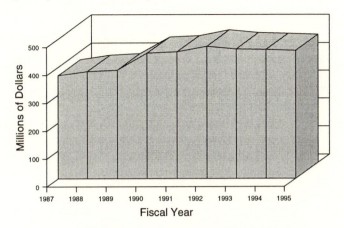

Figure 8.1.   City Budget, 1987–1995

than the headline figures on closer examination, however. The contracting initiatives affect the non–public safety employees, so this is precisely where you would expect the reductions. Moreover, the new contractors do of course employ staff, although they generally make do with fewer staff than the city government. Nevertheless, the reductions in people working on city government work is much smaller than the headline figures suggest. The White River Environmental partnership alone employed around 200 people to run the two treatment plants.

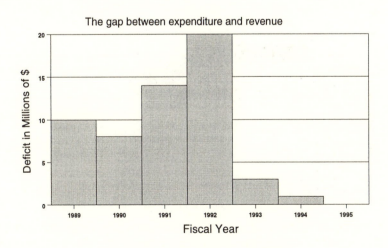

Figure 8.2.   The Deficit, 1989–1995

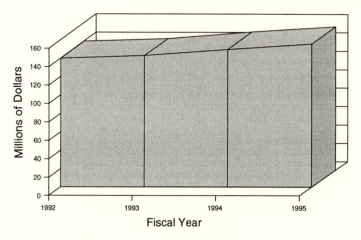

Figure 8.3.   Spending on Public Safety

The second feature of the Indianapolis approach is the heavy emphasis on redeployment. Very few staff were laid off as a result of contracting functions out. Those staff who did not transfer to the contractor were found other positions within City Hall.

3.   *Management*

The contracting program has had a big impact on who the managers are but little effect on the structure. Goldsmith replaced the city officials with a group of young, energetic people from the private sector, many of whom had no

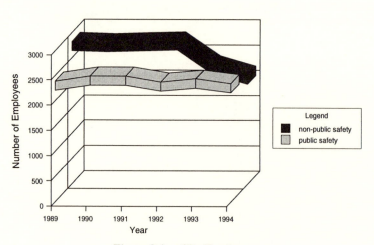

Figure 8.4.   City Employees

prior experience of government. He kept the basic management structure intact, however.

4. *Processes and Systems*

Big changes occurred here. A new form of cost accounting was introduced—activity-based costing. Infrastructure balance sheets were also developed to identify the total investment in infrastructure, the present-day value, and the future requirement to maintain or improve infrastructure. There was also a heavy emphasis on performance measurement—in part, these were needed to produce specifications for contracts. Customer surveys were also undertaken regularly to evaluate service effectiveness. A review process was also developed to question the purpose, efficiency, and effectiveness of all city functions.

5. *Culture*

To an outsider, there does appear to have been a significant shift in culture in Indianapolis. Clearly, Goldsmith and his senior executives and managers are enthusiastic about the program of changes. They are not the people to go to find real evidence of culture change. The expected opponents provide a much more accurate picture of what is happening on the ground. The unions have opposed many of Goldsmith's reforms and have fought and lost some of them in the courts. However, it is also true that the unions have supported staff in the process of public/private competition. A number of council members have been won over by the process. Here, for example, is a quote from Stephen Fantauzzo, the Indianapolis Executive Director of AFSCME, in the *Indianapolis Star*:

For the first six months [Goldsmith was in office], we fought him. Then [former] Department of transportation Director Mitch Roob came to us and said, "If we change privatization to let your workers bid for city work—is it something we can talk about?"

Fantauzzo's reply to Roob's question was:

If we get a level playing field, and you are serious about open competition, and if you give our people training, we will compete. ["Privatization Efforts Are Winning over City Workers," 26 March 1995]

Discussion of Underlying Issues

This section evaluates the Indianapolis experience. Is the hype justified, and what are the lessons for other jurisdictions? The section is divided into four issues—costs and benefits, tools and processes, strategies, and the decision-making environment.

1. *Costs and Benefits*

There can be little doubt from the evidence presented that there are significant benefits resulting from the contracting program. It has saved money. It has helped to contain expenditure and restore the city's fiscal position. It has helped to contain taxes. It has provided resources for improvements in public safety and downtown renewal.

However, it would be easy to get carried away with this good news. First, the Indianapolis program is still at a very early stage. Consequently, most of the savings quoted are estimates, not actuals. It is perfectly possible that not all of the savings will materialize—this has happened with outsourcing elsewhere. Second, contracting certainly appears to have worked well to date, with no major scandals or performance problems. However, it is difficult to assess whether this will remain the case, because of the early stage in the city's program. In most cases, the city and contractors are still in the "honeymoon period." What will happen, for example, with the second round of contracting? Third, the impact of the program on the city's level of expenditure and the number of people employed by or for government is much less than the hype suggests. The growth in city spending has stopped with a small reduction, and this has been accompanied by a modest reduction in the number of city employees. But there have not been massive reductions in spending or a dramatic downsizing in the number of people working for government, either directly or indirectly.

2. *Tools and Processes*

One of the most impressive aspects of the Indianapolis approach has been the emphasis on putting sound management processes in place before embarking on a major contracting program. Many other cities have begun their contracting without really knowing how much in-house services cost and what standards of service are being achieved. This was certainly true of the large mayor-run cities visited by the author, such as New York, Baltimore, and Chicago.

Perhaps the most significant process is activity-based costing. Traditional government accounting provides misleading information on costs because services consume overheads differently. These overheads are inside and outside the departments in which the services are provided. Financial support, for example, might be located in a separate department and property costs might be handled centrally, whereas purchasing might be devolved to the department but not correctly assigned to the relevant services. Moreover, these overheads have grown significantly over the last 30 years with the developments in technology, the provision of a wider range of government services, and the growth in complexity of services.

ABC involves assigning resource costs to activities based on whether the services generate the cost. Traditional cost accounting allocates overheads on an arbitrary basis. ABC assigns costs to services on a more rational basis. However, it does not usually involve full-cost absorption, where every overhead is assigned to services to establish the full cost of each service. Often this requires a great deal of effort, cost, and complexity. Most ABC approaches involve an element of absorption but fall short of full absorption to keep the system simple and relatively painless.

Indianapolis has used a simple ABC model, which does provide a better picture of the costs of services. Nevertheless, the city still undertakes a detailed costing of services when deciding whether to award a bid to an in-house bidder or an outside firm.

3. Strategies

There are important lessons here for other jurisdictions. Indianapolis has adopted a much more strategic approach to contracting than have other local governments, and this is to its advantage. There are a number of significant features of the Indianapolis strategy:

- *Putting the foundations in place first.* Systems such as activity-based costing and performance measurement were developed in advance of contracting. Most local governments develop aspects of these as they are embarking on contracting. Developing the systems in advance enables the local government to make objective decisions about making or buying. It also helps pinpoint any action that can be taken ahead of contracting.

- *Undertaking a comprehensive review of services.* The typical U.S. local government contracts on a piecemeal basis and usually selects a service because there is an internal crisis. Indianapolis undertook a careful of review of all of its services over a period of time using SELTIC. The review involved recording what was done, what assets the city held, and what were the alternative options. It then looked at the alternatives and examined a range of options. Contracting was only one of the options examined, although it was the most common recommendation. Should the city outsource? Should in-house teams be allowed to compete against outside firms? Should the function be reengineered internally? This comprehensive approach resulted in some innovative proposals such as public/private competition and long-term contracts for the management of utilities. Again, the review encouraged a more rational approach to contracting.

- *Public/private competition.* Indianapolis was not the first U.S. local government to encourage in-house teams to compete against outside firms. It was not Goldsmith's initial preference to promote public/private competition. However, once Goldsmith accepted the approach as valuable, he did promote it in a more wide-ranging and comprehensive way than any other U.S. local government. Phoenix, for example, the real pioneer of public/private competition, has largely used it only in the public works area.

- *Developing a clear vision.* Contracting was part of a much wider vision for local government in Indianapolis. Some services had been defined as core services that needed to remain in-house, such as fire and police. All others were subject to review and testing. Moreover, there was a clear agenda on the direction of the program—savings to address the fiscal problems, improve public safety, and revitalize the downtown. This provided a clear agenda for managers to work toward.

4. *The Decision-Making Environment*

Indianapolis enjoyed a number of advantages over other mayor cities which made a radical contracting program more possible. First of all, the city is less politicized than other mid-western and northeastern cities. It is an old-fashioned Republican city. It also has friendlier, less radical unions than cities such as New York, Chicago, and Philadelphia. Goldsmith did encounter resistance to his initiatives but not the prolonged strikes of Mayor Rendell in Philadelphia. Nor did the Indianapolis unions have the muscle of their New York counterparts to block contracting moves by the mayor through the city council legislation. Indianapolis also has a strong mayor charter, which meant that Goldsmith had more power *vis-à-vis* the city council to push his proposals through. Weak mayors such as Daley in Chicago and Riordan in Los Angeles would inevitably find it harder.

What was unique about Goldsmith was that he took management very seriously. He is a part-time lecturer in public administration at the Universities of Indiana and Harvard and has written extensively on government and public administration. Unlike many other mayors, he appeared to know what was required in management terms to make contracting work—putting in place more accurate information, recruiting private-sector managers rather than lifelong public officials who had supported his campaign, and delegating responsibility to his executives to get on with the job. As a result, he created a strong managerial culture among senior executives. Goldsmith was an unusual animal—a manager-mayor.

DISCUSSION AND CONCLUSIONS

Indianapolis deserves its reputation for innovation with service delivery. There is little doubt that it has one of the most radical programs of contracting of any government in the U.S. It has also achieved substantial savings in the process. The quality of management has improved dramatically, with much better information on costs and performance levels than is typical in local government.

However, the story needs to be treated with some caution. First, the savings are mainly estimates, not actuals. Second, much of the savings have been diverted to other expenditure programs, with the impact on city expenditure overall fairly modest. Consequently, contracting has not led to smaller government. Indeed, it is possible to argue that Indianapolis has shown how to have more government for less investment!

The area where Indianapolis has been most innovative is the way it has contracted for services. Three innovations, in particular, deserve mention:

- The public/private competition, which improved value for money without destroying morale amongst city workers

- The strategic review of city services to examine the best way to deliver a service. This involved looking at a wide range of options, not just contracting

- The implementation of activity-based costing, which meant that more intelligent decisions could be made about service delivery.

9

Careless Contracting in New York City— The Problems of Designing a Contracting System to Avoid Corruption

"The City's contracting operations are awash in a sea of paper, plagued by inordinate delays, and clouded by unclear and inconsistent rules and procedures which slow City business to a crawl and discourage vendors from stepping forward to bid. As a result, the City often pays far more than it should for goods and services, wasting millions of taxpayer dollars. At the same time, the widespread reluctance of vendors to do business with the City offers opportunities for bid-rigging and corrupt side-deals." —New York State Commission on Government Integrity (1989)

"A series of New York City government scandals in the mid-1980's exposed wide-scale corruption in City contracting. Leases, concessions, and contracts worth millions of dollars were awarded on the basis of bribes. Funds needed for essential goods and services ended up in the wrong hands and public mistrust of government grew deeper." —City of New York (1992b)

Few people agree on anything in New York City government, except for one thing: New York is a model of how *not* to manage a city. Nowhere can this be demonstrated better than in the city's approach to contracting for goods and services. Insiders and outsiders, describing archaic practices, incompetence, and delay in the city's contracting processes, have done countless studies over the last decade. The city's history also includes a small number of celebrated contracting scandals. These have made and destroyed promising careers and help explain the control-orientated administrative culture of the organization and the framework for contracting that exists today.

This chapter examines the contracting regime in New York, its problems, and the attempts to reform it. The truth behind New York is rather less exciting than the fast image. Nevertheless, it illustrates the difficulty of contracting for goods and services without having a smart purchaser in place. The chapter also shows the problems of pursuing reform in a highly politicized environment. It is divided into six sections:

- Background information on the city, its government, and its finances.

- A description of the contracting regime.

- An assessment of the problems experienced with contracting.

- An outline of the attempts to reform contracting.

- An analysis of the underlying issues affecting contracting that make reform difficult.

- Some conclusions.

THE ORGANIZATIONAL AND FINANCIAL CONTEXT

New York City is a unique local government in a number of respects. The first of these is its size. The city is the largest local government in the U.S., with a residential population of 7.5 million. In expenditure terms, with an annual budget of nearly $32 billion, it is the fourth biggest government in the U.S., surpassed only by the federal government, New York State, and the State of California. It is also unusual for the wide range of functions for which it is responsible. It provides all the usual local government services such as fire, police, libraries, waste management, recreation, town planning, and transportation. In addition, it provides a wide range of social services, schooling, a major public university, prisons, the largest municipal health system in the U.S., and the city's water-supply and sewerage systems.

The city is also closely linked through mayoral appointments to a number of public corporations such as the Metropolitan Transit Authority, the Health and Hospitals Corporation, the Housing Authority, and the School Construction Authority. The major portions of the budgets for these organizations are not included in the city's $32 billion budget. The city employs around 225,000 staff.

New York has a mayoral form of government. There are a number of elected officials in addition to the mayor—five borough presidents, a comptroller, a city council president, and 51 council members. Until 1990, the city's most senior elected officials (the mayor, borough presidents, comptroller, and the city council president) comprised a body called the Board of Estimate, which combined legislative and executive powers, including the responsibility for awarding contracts. In November 1993, after decades of Democratic control, a new Republican mayor was elected—Rudolph Giuliani. A key element of the mayor's agenda was to clean up contracting in the city and to examine the scope for privatizing and exposing city services to competition. Giuliani's background is as a prosecutor who made his name in handling corruption scandals, including the Mafia scandals that dogged the Koch administration in its twilight years.

In 1988, the U.S. Supreme Court ruled that the Board of Estimate's voting structure was unconstitutional because it violated the principle of one person one vote. The city's approach to contracting had also been subject to a number of high-powered studies that exposed corruption, incompetence, and a huge waste of resources. These included:

—The State–City Commission on Integrity in Government, 1986 (Sovern Commission).

—The Institute of Public Administration, *Contracting in New York City Government*, 1987.

—The Mayor's Private Sector Survey, *The New York City Service Crisis: A Management Response*, 1989.

—New York State Commission on Government Integrity, *A Ship Without A Captain: The Contracting Process in New York City*, 1989 (Feerick Commission).

In response to the Supreme Court, a Charter Revision Commission was established to review certain areas of city government. Part of the commission's mission included revising the arrangements for contracting. A revised charter was adopted in 1989. The Board of Estimate was abolished, and the mayor's role as head of the executive was strengthened. A new independent Procurement Policy Board (PPB) was created to establish policies, rules, and procedures for all contracting by the city for goods, services, and construction. The PPB comprised five members: three appointed by the mayor and two by the comptroller. The PPB's role was only advisory, advising the mayor and comptroller on practice, and the council on law. There was a clear expectation that the PPB would clean up contracting and develop a more professional approach. An executive director—Connie Cushman, a former staff member of the Feerick Commission—was appointed.

New York City's budget for fiscal year 1995 provided for expenditure of $31.6 billion. The major items of expenditure included the department of social services ($7.3 billion), police department ($2.1 billion), board of education ($7.7 billion), and servicing debt ($2.3 billion). There were four main sources of revenue—a property tax ($7.3 billion), other local taxes ($10.2 billion), state grants ($6.3 billion), and federal grants ($3.5 billion).

The city's finances are legendary for their precarious nature. The city narrowly escaped a series of bankruptcies in the 1970s. Under state law, the city must balance its budget on an annual basis. Moreover, the city's budget is structurally out of balance—that is, the growth in expenditure is outpacing the growth in revenues—and the gap is set to grow in future years. This means that there is an annual crisis each year when the next year's budget is being finalized and there are regular crises during the financial year to keep expenditures within budget. In fiscal year 1995, the Financial Control Board of the State of New York estimated that there was a risk of a $1 billion deficit and projected this as increasing to $2 billion in 1996 and $3 billion in 1997.

Some of the main areas of risk cited by the State Financial Control Board include:

—a shrinking tax base

—growth in expenditure above the rate of inflation, especially for personal services

—a major growth in debt

—underfunding of maintenance requirements, which will add to debt problems in future years

—the inability of the Board of Education to stay within its budget

—a lack of management and control over budgets for contracted services and goods.

The financial difficulties faced by the city explain why attempts are underway to improve value for money from contracted services and why the issues of privatization and competition are being seriously entertained.

THE CONTRACTING REGIME IN NEW YORK CITY

The city already contracts for a wide range of goods and services. For the fiscal year 1995, the city allocated $2.9 billion for almost 9,000 service contracts, nearly 10% of the city's expense budget. These are shown in Table 9.1.

A substantial amount of the city's capital program is also contracted out to the private sector. This varies significantly from year to year, but in fiscal year 1994 it amounted to $6.8 billion. Finally, the city purchases a wide range of goods: in fiscal year 1994, purchases of goods in excess of $10,000 amounted to $745 million.

Tables 9.2 and 9.3 show the pattern of service contracting. Table 9.2 shows that the vast amount of service contracting is done in social services, whereas Table 9.3 shows that the lion's share of expenditure in social services agencies is on contracting. Most of the social services contracting is with nonprofits rather than for-profits. New York contracts out very little of its basic municipal services, as Table 9.4 shows. Moreover, most of the contracting in these areas is for support rather than core services, although precise data are not available on this. Using the 1992 ICMA survey of service-delivery methods as a baseline, New

TABLE 9.1. Service Contracts in 1995

Area	Estimated No. of Contracts	Dollars (millions)	% Total Dollars
1. Social service–related and health services, such as child welfare, day care, homeless programs, employment services, and mental hygiene	2,903	1,737	58.9
2. Youth- and student-related services, such as pupil transportation and payments to contract schools	1,282	413	14.0
3. Maintenance and operation of infrastructure, such as lighting, streets, and water supply	1,062	358	12.2
4. Other services, such as custodial, security, secretarial, advertising, and economic development	1,016	190	6.4
5. Professional services/consultants, such as accounting, engineering, and systems development	808	150	5.1
6. Maintenance of equipment (e.g., data processing, office equipment, and telecommunications)	936	56	1.9
7. Cultural-related services	713	19	0.6
8. All other	183	27	0.9
Total	8,903	2,950	100.00

Source: New York City Contract Budget for Fiscal Year 1995.

TABLE 9.2. Service Contract Budget Categories

Category	% of Contract Budget
Social services	70.0
Infrastructure maintenance and operation	10.1
Building maintenance and operation	5.4
Equipment maintenance and operation	2.1
Security services	1.8
Support services	1.4

Source: 1993 City of New York Contract Budget.

TABLE 9.3.   Agencies That Contract Out More Than 50% of Their Budgets

Agency	% of Budget
Department for the Aging	78.9
Department of Mental Health	73.7
Department of Youth Services	52.2
Department of Employment	51.4
Human Resources Administration	51.3

Source: 1993 City of New York Contract Budget.

York is unusual in the extent to which it contracts out social services; it also does less contracting than other jurisdictions for traditional municipal services. The Department of Environmental Protection does contract out a great deal of its activities (33.9%), including core services relating to water supply and wastewater systems. For example, most local governments' contract for around 35% of human services compared to almost 75% in New York City. Similarly, around 30% of local governments contract for infrastructure and maintenance operations compared to 10% in New York (see Miranda & Andersen, 1994).

Contracting in New York has traditionally been noncompetitive. In areas such as sanitation and parking enforcement there would be a competitive bidding process but few bids, despite the fact that there is no shortage of suppliers. There have been strong allegations of Mafia control and a number of corruption cases (see Newfield & Barrett, 1988). In the human services, until very recently, contracts with nonprofits would be regularly renewed without going through a competitive process.

Under the city charter there are four key players in the contracting process: (1) the City Council, the legislative body, which agrees the mayor's budget; (2) the Procurement Policy Board (PPB), which advises on the operational frame-

TABLE 9.4.   Contracting for Traditional Municipal Services

Category	% of Budget Contracted Out
Police	0.5
Fire	0.7
Corrections	1.6
Elementary and Secondary Education	4.5
Sanitation	4.8
Parks and Recreation	5.1

Source: 1993 City of New York Contract Budget.

work and establishes the rules for contracting; (3) most importantly, the mayor, who is responsible for identifying which areas are subject to contracting, contractor selection, and contract management; (4) the comptroller, who registers contracts to enable payments to be made. The comptroller is also responsible for auditing the contract system.

While the mayor is ultimately responsible for contracting decisions and management, in practice the bulk of contracting is decentralized in New York. Contracting decisions, monitoring, and management take place at agency level (there are around 40 agencies). Contracting decisions for goods and major construction projects are centralized. Around 1,500 employees are involved in contracting for more than 50% of their time and a further 1,500 involved for less than 50% of their time.

There is a high level of oversight in the contracting process. Nine agencies have oversight responsibilities, as set out in Table 9.5. While the PPB advises on the framework for contracting, it does not get involved in individual cases.

Arrangements within agencies vary. However, decision making and contract management tend to be handled at program level, with a coordination and oversight role being exercised by senior contracting officers working closely with the relevant commissioner. It is common for agencies to mirror external oversight requirements with their own internal processes.

The contracting process comprises five basic elements. These are:

—developing the service specification

—identifying who is interested in doing the work (this is done through advertising and a bidders list)

—selection of the approved contractor

—where applicable, negotiation with the preferred contractor to finalize all aspects of the contract

—obtaining the required approvals from the various oversight agencies within the city.

There are five main contracting methods used in New York City: competitive sealed bids, requests for proposals, sole-source negotiations, renewals, and arrangements for small purchases. Competitive bidding is the most common method used and applies to around one-third of all contracts/purchases. This is the preferred method for the city. Requests for proposals (RFPs) are the second most common method, covering around 20% of all contracts. RFPs are the preferred approach for technical, consultant, and personal service contracts. Around 4% of the financial value of contracts is awarded on a sole source basis—that is, without going through a competitive process. Sole sourcing has to be fully justified when, for example, there is a patent or copyright issue or there is only one supplier. Renewals were used for almost one-third of all contracts in 1994.

TABLE 9.5.   The Oversight Agencies

Agency	Oversight Function(s)
Office of Management and Budget	Prepares and monitors the city's contract budget; monitors expenditures throughout the fiscal year. Reviews financial plan and budgets for contracts and major contract changes; prepares financial reviews for large contracts which are subject to scrutiny by the Financial Control Board.
Mayor's Office of Operations	Ensures that the mayor's policies and priorities are followed by agencies contracting decisions; reviews projects and sometimes gets involved in/assumes leadership for project management of major contracting exercises.
Department of Business Services	Ensures that contractors provide equal opportunities to all employees and applicants.
Mayor's Office of Construction	Reviews and supports project management for construction and construction-related professional services not subject to competitive bidding (i.e., those projects subject to RFPs and RFQs); also reviews certain change orders and contract overruns.
Mayor's Office of Contracts	Develops and polices the contracting processes; reviews awards and extensions for contracts over $10,000 not subject to public bidding ($15,000 for construction contracts) and contract amendments; oversees public hearings for contracts exceeding $100,000; maintains information on the responsibility of contractors; polices agency compliance with the PBB rules.
Law Department	Reviews contract documentation to ensure legality and enforceability as well as compliance with various city ordinances.
Department of Investigation	Undertakes checks on contractors.
Department of Finance	Checks contractors for tax compliance.
Office of the Comptroller	Reviews all contracts prior to registration; audits a sample of contracts

Most of the renewals were in the human service area. The city is changing its approach here in two respects. First, it is keen to encourage more competition in human service contracts. Second, it is developing a more structured approach to contract renewal, using multiterm contracts. These allow the city to exercise renewal options within multiterm contracts, subject to satisfactory performance by a contractor.

There are a number of other common requirements for all four types of procurement. These are set out below:

- *Vendor responsiveness:*   the agency contracting officer must ensure that the recommended contractor has met the city's administrative requirements.

- *Vendor responsibility:*   a check carried out by the agency. A secondary check is made by the Department of Investigation and the Department of Finance on whether the firm can do the job and has the integrity to justify the award of public money.

- *Certification:*   in many cases for noncompetitive bidding contracts greater than $10,000, the mayor's Office of Contracts checks to ensure that the agency has followed all the necessary rules.

- *Registration:*   further checks on business integrity, the solicitation process, contract award, and the availability of funds by the comptroller before allowing funds to be paid to the contractor.

Competitive contracts with a value over $10,000 ($15,000 for construction contracts) have to be advertised in *The City Record*, the official city publication that announces invitations for bids and proposals. Agencies also use bidders lists to identify potential contractors. The use of prequalified bidders lists—to limit the number of bids/proposals to be evaluated—is small but growing.

The contract decision-making rules in the city vary depending on the procurement method used. Nevertheless, six principles tend to be emphasized:

- *Value for money:*   competitive sealed bids must be awarded to the "lowest responsive and responsible bidder," and RFPs also regularly attach high priority to low-cost bids.

- *Competence:*   the contractor must demonstrate that it can meet the obligations of the contract.

- *Integrity:*   contractors must be trustworthy and honest.

- *Fairness:*   there is a clear preference to open contracts up to competition wherever possible.

- *Equity:*   contractors should be equal-opportunity employers and should be able to demonstrate this with high levels of minority representation.

- *City Policies:*   contractors should meet city and state laws, which are set out below.

There are a number of constraints on the city's procurement process. These fall into three categories. First, there is the "Wicks Law"; this is a state law that applies to public works projects with a value in excess of $50,000. The law requires multiple contracts for construction projects. In practice, this means separate contracts for electrical, plumbing, heating, and ventilation work. Second, there are various PPB and Charter rules that require public hearings to be held. For example, a hearing must be held for any contract (except for those subject to competitive sealed bidding) worth over $100,000. In addition, the council has the right to hold a hearing under a local law where the mayor is proposing to privatize an in-house service. Finally, as part of the city's collective bargaining agreement the unions have the right to put in a counterproposal after a private contractor has been selected but before the contract has been awarded. The city used to have a system of price preferences favoring certain minority-owned businesses (MBEs); these were New York City-based contractors and firms who used recycled materials. This was abolished in 1994.

THE PROBLEMS OF CONTRACTING

Five problems with New York's approach to contracting—time-consuming processes, poor contract management, a low level of competition, fraud and corruption, and financial waste—are examined below.

Time-Consuming Approach

Contracting in New York City is slow and inefficient. Indeed, contract award can take up to double or treble the amount of time needed in other jurisdictions. Recent city workshops held to examine complex contracting in the Departments of Environmental Protection and Health identified the following timescales for the contract award process:

—Department of Environmental Protection: 446.5 days (21 months)

—Department of Health: 239 days (11 months).

There are a number of reasons for the time-consuming approach adopted, namely:

- *The amount of oversight.* There are nine oversight agencies, as well as the City Council and the Procurement Policy Board. The average amount of time needed for processing contracts by oversight agencies is 93–107.5 business days. The breakdown of the volume of oversight is shown in Table 9.6.

- *Parallel internal oversight.* Agencies generally establish internal oversight controls to parallel external oversight. For example, in the Department of Environmental Protection, over half of the 21 months' processing time for contract award was taken up by internal requirements for defining, approving, and evaluating proposals.

- *Sequential and duplicative nature of review.* Much of the oversight activity could be undertaken in parallel rather than sequentially. Some of the oversight is undertaken sequentially, which adds unnecessarily to timescales. At the same time, some of the review activity is duplicative. For example, the comptroller reviews vendor responsibility toward the end of the process before deciding whether to "register" a contractor. However, the contracting agency will already have undertaken a review to determine "vendor responsibility" much earlier in the

TABLE 9.6. Processing Time by Oversight Agencies

Agency	Number of Days
OMB	10
MOC (Contract Review)	8–16.5
MOC (Public Hearing)	30
VENDEX	3
Division of Labor Services	13
Department of Investigations	17
Corporation counsel	3
Comptroller	5–11

Source: Deloitte Touche, 1994.

process. The fact that information is fragmented on a range of information systems does not help.

- *Volume of paperwork.* The PPB rules themselves comprise some 288 pages. Consultants Deloitte and Touche recently reviewed the city's contract award process and estimated that it involved over 20 million pages of paper annually at a cost of over $5 million! Once again the causes are duplication, fragmented systems, sequential processes, and the sheer volume of oversight controls.

- *Unproductive public hearings.* These are required for any contract award over $100,000 that has not gone through a competitive sealed-bid process. They delay contract award by at least 30 days. However, testimony is gathered in only 3% of hearings.

Quality of Contract Management

New York City devotes a considerable amount of time to contract award. By contrast, contract management appears to be largely neglected. This problem was acknowledged in my interviews with staff in front-line and oversight departments in 1994/95 as well as pointed out in other reviews such as the 1994 Deloitte and Touche study and the 1993 Fall report to the PPB. The quotation below from the PPB report demonstrates the scale and seriousness of this shortcoming:

There is a virtual absence of contract management throughout the City. Once a contract is in place, compliance with contract terms and conditions is taken for granted. Assuring performance and successful contract completion is the exception not the norm. Even in human services contracts, the lion's share of monitoring concentrates on compliance with form and process requirements, often in trivial detail, and neglects true assessment of the outcome, or the impact, of the contractor's performance. [City of New York, 1993b]

A number of issues can be pinpointed here:

- *Few incentives for good performance.* According to the State of New York Financial Control Board, there is little interest in contract performance. City processes focus on contract award. There are few oversight requirements in relation to contract performance. Those that do exist relate to the barest details of financial performance—when contract payments are set to exceed the maximum limit agreed by the Office of Management and Budget (OMB). The biggest pressure for performance often comes from outside city government. The need to avoid a media scandal probably does more than any internal requirement to keep managers alert. Unfortunately, this does little to encourage good performance.

- *Poor specifications.* Many city specifications rely on input and process measures rather than on outputs or outcomes. This was confirmed by a sample analysis undertaken of recent contracts in the departments of youth services, parks, and aging.

- *Inadequate financial data.* The State of New York Financial Control Board keeps the financial position of the city under close review. This includes an annual report on the city's financial plan. The most recent review on the 1995/98 Financial Plan expressed serious reservations about the quality of information and control over the city's contract budget. In particular, the board found that the most basic financial disciplines were not in place. They claimed that there were no proper budgets for contracts. Second, virtually no variance analysis was undertaken to establish how performance compares to the budget. Moreover, the city's financial systems were unable to track expenditure on the many contracts that straddle more than one financial year (the number of such contracts is increasing because the PPB has been encouraging greater use of multiyear contracts). The city is addressing all of these issues—the 1996 contract budget, for example, modifies contract budgets every month, tracks expenditures against them, and monitors multiyear contracts.

TABLE 9.7. Level of Competition for Contracts

Requests for Proposals	*Number of Bids*	*Competitive Sealed Bid*
Single bidder	6.7%	12.8%
2 bids	5.1%	3.7%
3–5 bids	19.4%	14.8%
6–9 bids	20.7%	13.4%
10 or more bids	48.2%	55.3%

Source: City Comptroller's statistical supplement to the 1993 report on contracting.

The Level and Quality of Competition

On the basis of figures supplied by the comptroller, competition for city work appears healthy and improving. The comptroller's Comprehensive Annual Contracts report for 1993, for example, reveals the levels of competition shown in Table 9.7.

The comptroller believes that a minimum of three bids is needed to ensure a reasonable level of competition. In this light, the figures look respectable as over 88% of competitive sealed bids and 83% of RFPs received at least three bids. However, a closer analysis of the situation shows it to be more problematic than the raw data suggest. First, the assumption that three bids are needed to ensure competition can be questioned. In professional circles, three to five strong bids would be seen as sufficient, but this is rather different to three bids. It is common to receive some weak bids, especially where specifications are poor and the contracting processes not well understood. More significantly, it was clear from discussions with city officials and representatives of the business community that firms do not view the city as a good business partner. This is despite the best efforts of the Department of Business Services to communicate with the private sector through advice and publications on how to do business with the city. Indeed, many view the city as a customer of last resort (i.e., they would only do business with the city if there were no alternative). This means that many of the better firms will not bid for city work. The reasons cited by the business community (see New York Chamber of Commerce . . . , 1993) for this situation are as follows:

- *The complexity and time-consuming nature* of the city's contract award process.

- *The city as a late payer.* Indeed, such is the level of delay in payments that many contractors have to take this into account when submitting their contract prices. Moreover, it is well known that late payments have caused severe and sometimes terminal cash-flow problems for small firms. The city has agreed to pay interest for late payments in excess of 30 days.

- *The city is unfair and partial in its contracting.* The city's appeal and alternative dispute-resolution processes are not seen as independent, because city officials are represented on the panels. More seriously, contractor selection is widely viewed as a matter of whom you know rather than what your proposal involves and your track record. It does not matter whether this perception is true, because it still discourages firms from bidding.

Fraud and Corruption

New York City's history includes a number of high-profile cases of fraud and corruption, from the Boss Tweed scandal involving the construction of City Hall in the mid-1800s right through to the scandals that dogged the Koch administra-

TABLE 9.8.   Sample of Upheld Registration Objections

The Contractor	*Allegations/Outcomes*
DeMatteis Corporation	Submitted false and misleading information about a prior city investigation; the principal owner was also alleged to have ties to organized crime and was the subject of litigation in relation to bid rigging in the concrete industry.
Standard Industrial Services	Made false statements about tax payments and committed various environmental violations.
Discount/Diversified	Formed new companies to conceal poor past performance.
Independent Taxi Owners Group	Principal was indicted for fraud.
Marathon Orbit	Submitted fraudulent bonds on city contracts.
Dentom Transportation	Made false statements and was indicted for bribery.

Source: City Comptroller, 1992.

tion in the mid-1980s. Many of these cases concerned contracting fraud. A number of key elected and appointed officials in the Koch administration were imprisoned following the revelations of a bribery ring in relation to parking violations contracts. More recently in 1993, there was another parking violations bureau scandal, this time involving the budget director in the Dinkins administration, the Lockheed Company, and a contract worth around $500 million.

One way of understanding the complexity and levels of oversight in New York City's contracting systems is as a series of responses to corruption and media scandals. What is surprising, however, is the low level of detected fraud. For example, the comptroller has an audit responsibility to detect and prevent fraud and corruption. The comptroller's 1993 review identified some 30 objections to contract registration on grounds that corruption was suspected. This is a mere 30 cases valued at less than $29 million compared to a total population of some 9,000 contracts. More than half of the cases were overruled by the mayor after the investigations were completed. These levels of objections and those overruled and upheld were similar in the preceding years. In addition, there were 105 nonresponsibility determinations (NDRs) in 1993. Only half of the NDRs related to a lack of business integrity on the part of the contractor.

Table 9.8 shows a sample of upheld registration cases for the fiscal year 1992. Not only is there a low level of detected fraud, but that which is detected does not fit the conventional view of corruption. It tends to relate to a failure to provide accurate information rather than outright corruption in relation to city contracts. Clearly, the city's elaborate contracting requirements and its high moral position on what constitutes business integrity are contributing factors to the level of detected fraud.

Value for Money and Contracting

It is difficult to know how much waste there is in New York's contracting, because basic financial management disciplines are not in place. The city relies on line-item budgeting rather than activity budgeting, which records the planned and actual costs of activities. Moreover, little information exists on performance. It is therefore difficult for the city to make, in an informed way, the "make or buy" decision. Moreover, the budgeting and monitoring of spending on contracting is inadequate. Despite these problems, it is clear that there is significant waste, although it cannot be quantified precisely. A modest 10–15% improvement in value for money in contracting would contribute greatly to solving the city's structural-deficit problems by reducing revenue and capital expenditures.

The reasons for suspecting considerable waste are simple; the city's approach to contracting is based on the need to avoid scandals rather than to ensure good service and value for money. The cost of oversight agencies alone exceeds $200 million per year, and these agencies add little to contracting in the city. They do, of course, have other functions. The real waste occurs in the contract prices that are higher than they should be because of the low level of competition, the discouragement to good firms, and the costs of delay.

REFORM MEASURES

City officials are well aware of the contracting problems in New York and have been engaged in a series of reforms since the establishment of the PPB. These fall into four main categories.

Reforming the Procurement Framework

The first task that the newly established PPB completed was a revised, single set of rules for contracting, although a variety of approaches is permitted to accommodate different circumstances. This included a separate approach for human services contracting which requires that certain types of contract be subject to a competitive process by 1997. The norm for human service contracts had been to renew them without competition. The rules also included guidelines for prompt payment and a new dispute-resolution mechanism.

Professionalizing the Purchasing Function

In 1992, Mayor Dinkins launched a Procurement Improvement Initiative (PII) to consolidate and professionalize the procurement function in the largest mayoral agencies. Resources were made available to create an Agency Chief Contracting Officer (ACCO) post in each agency and establish a Procurement Training Institute (PTI). Twenty-seven agency chief and deputy-chief contracting officer posts have now been established and filled. The PTI has provided 5 days of introductory training for nearly 1,700 contracting staff, and of these some 300 have achieved buyer-level certification through the National Institute of Governmental Purchasing. In addition, the PTI offers many beginner- and intermediate-level courses on a wide range of procurement topics. Around 50 to 70 city contracting staff also participate in professional purchasing associations.

Reengineering the Process

Reengineering of the process has involved four elements: computerization, devolution, streamlining processes, and financial savings.

- *Computerization.* A number of computer improvements are underway. The most ambitious was the Integrated Contract and Procurement Management System (ICPMS), which aimed to automate all procurement functions on one system. This project was shelved because of the cost and uncertainty of success. It has been replaced with a program of smaller IT improvements which are being implemented. For example, electronic mail is being introduced in some agencies, as well as project management systems.

- *Devolution.* Two pilots are underway which involve some delegation of responsibility to agencies and a reduction of the roles of oversight agencies. For example, some sign-offs by the city's Chief Purchasing officer (in the mayor's Office of Contracts) and OMB have been passed on to the departments of health and environmental protection. However, to date, devolution has been very limited in scope, but more is planned such as increasing the threshold for requiring central oversight of contracts and moving from pre- to post-contract award audits.

- *Streamlining.* Procurement processes in the department of health and environmental protection have already begun to reduce the processing time for contracts—by 34 days in health and 27 days in environmental protection.

- *Financial savings.* A progam of savings for contracting is also underway. As of July 1994, departments were reporting savings of some $49 million, which represents a little over 0.5% of the expenditure on contracting.

Encouraging Public/Private Competition

The mayor has identified a number of city services for possible privatization, and a process for encouraging public/private competition for city services has been unveiled. The mayor is considering privatizing and contracting for a range of services currently provided in-house, such as park maintenance, fleet maintenance, sign repair, data entry, building cleaning, homeless shelters, and hospitals. Many of the obvious candidates—the airports, wastewater treatment and trash collection, for example—have, however, been ruled out for political reasons. There is also talk of encouraging competition between city employees and the private sector, as is the case in cities such as Indianapolis and Phoenix. However, little has happened so far. The only recent example of contracting-out city services previously provided in-house is in the Parks Department, where a small number of parks districts have been subject to a competitive bidding process. So far, contracts for two districts in Queens and two in the Bronx have been awarded, and there are plans to go through a similar exercise for four other districts.

THE UNDERLYING ISSUES—THE OBSTACLES TO SMART CONTRACTING

Significant improvements have flowed from the reforms: procurement professionals are in post in all of the large agencies, processing time for contracts has fallen, and money is being saved. However, the reforms fall far short of addressing the underlying issues. As a result a number of problems remain:

—The contracting rules remain extraordinarily complex.

—Processing time for contract award is still very long.

—Full computerization is a long way off and may not be attainable in the medium term.

—Decision making remains very centralized, with high levels of oversight.

—Basic contracting and financial management disciplines are not in place.

It is necessary to examine why reforms have failed to make a major impact on the contracting problems of the city. There are eight underlying reasons that illustrate the nature of obstacles to smart contracting: the political process, the organizational culture, organizational capacity, the strength of the unions, the lack of responsibility, the impurity of the contracting regime, the absence of accurate, relevant, and timely information, and, finally, the size of the city organization.

The Political Process Inhibits Smart Contracting

Political management is institutionalized in New York City. This is by far the biggest obstacle to smart contracting. What should be managerial issues become political decisions, such as whether a contractor can meet the contract and the selection of contractors. For example, the purpose of the responsibility determination is to ensure that contractors have the business integrity to justify the award of tax dollars. Most jurisdictions focus on whether the contractor can meet the specification, but in New York City the emphasis is on the general integrity and morality of the contractor. Even this relatively straightforward issue has become politicized and has the effect of reducing competition. The city comptroller, an elected official, can object to contract awards, for example. The mayor has the right to respond and can overrule the comptroller. In practice, however, there is a negotiation process between the mayor's office and the comptroller.

... the responsibility decision in New York has become politicized as never before and nowhere else. I believe it is not too strong to say that the responsibility decision today has become a political football kicked around among the Mayor, the Comptroller, and the City Council. [City of New York, 1993c]

Another example of this can be found in the human service area. The tradition here has been to award *de facto* long-term contracts to nonprofits without going through a regular competitive process. In recent years, the city has been exposing human services to regular competition. In home care for the elderly, for example, 5 of the 75 recently awarded contracts went to for-profits following a competitive process. However, the nonprofits that lost the competitions sued the city and won an injunction to prevent the contract awards.

These examples clearly demonstrate the limits on competition because of the political process. City politics is intertwined with the leadership of nonprofits. So it was not surprising when the Youth Services Department proposed changing suppliers following a competitive process in which there was a huge row involving the mayor, the council, and the borough presidents. There were genuine problems with the whole exercise, but it revealed the politics of selection of nonprofits for contracts. In such circumstances there is a risk that contracting to nonprofits in human services could become a new form of patronage politics.

The real issue, however, is the form of government in New York. First, the mayor system involves an elected politician as the head of the executive branch rather than a professional manager with experience of running a large business. With the history of New York City, this encourages an overt system of political management where professional, technical, and managerial considerations receive little priority. Second, power is dispersed in the mayor-council model and even more so in New York with the other elected positions of comptroller and borough presidents. With such a system, it is inevitable that the various elected officials carve out roles of influence for themselves, which affects contracting. Again, this does little to encourage a professional approach to contracting. Third, with political considerations and a lack of a managerial culture at the top of the organization, it is hardly surprising that this percolates down the city organization.

There is a further constitutional problem. The charter reforms have failed—and in some ways have made it more difficult—to sort out the contracting in the city. Most fundamentally, the PPB's role is flawed. Its role is too limited in scope: it is purely advisory; its rules only apply to mayoral agencies, not arm's-length city bodies such as the schools board; and it lacks an overall audit responsibility. Even if the PPB remit were broadened, it would not be able to fulfill it because of the small number of staff—it only has five professional staff. The PPB has also found it difficult in practice to be genuinely independent because the mayoral agencies and the comptroller often work to limit the board's influence. More fundamentally, the mayor and comptroller make the appointments to the PPB. The recently departed executive director to the PPB claimed that some administration members would come to meetings adopting a "party line." The intention of the PPB had been to provide an independent, expert view on contracting. In this respect it has only been partially successful due to understaffing, but also because most of the appointees have little expertise in contracting. Indeed, it is hard to understand why a PPB-type structure was adopted, given the emphasis on expertise. An alternative, simpler, and less political approach would have been to appoint an expert in contracting heading an arms-length agency with wide-ranging powers.

The Organizational Culture

There are a number of features of the organizational culture which impact on the practice of contracting and discourage a professional approach:

- *Risk aversion.* This is more important than performing well. There are much greater penalties for making mistakes—being criticized within the agency or by an oversight agency, an elected official, or the press or being fired if the post-holder is in an executive position. By contrast, there are few incentives to perform well. Officials are not judged or paid on results, and the mayoral system often results in managerial promotions and appointments being made on political grounds rather than on merit. This approach is common in the public sector, but risk aversion has reached new heights in NYC.

- *Lack of trust.* The city's contracting processes (and other managerial processes) emphasize control and try to eliminate judgment and discretion. In part, this reflects an assumption that officials lower down the organization cannot be trusted to perform without a great deal of guidance. As a result, there is a control system, lots of supervision, and elaborate and comprehensive rules. Unfortunately, as one senior official in the mayor's office said, "The check, review and pass on mentality only provides the illusion of control."

- *Obsession with process.* Compliance with rules is the order of the day in the city. A good example of this was the introduction of the PPB rules, followed by a detailed memorandum issued by the mayor's office to help agencies interpret them. Moreover, agencies spend an inordinate amount of time rigorously following every detailed step rather than using common sense.

- *Managerial subservience.* The tradition of political management, political appointments, and the ease with which "disloyal" senior managers are replaced discourages managers from speaking out and defending a managerial agenda. The easiest and best way to survive is to comply, even if it does not make sense!

Organizational Capacity Shortcomings

New York City's precarious financial position means that tough budget cuts have become a feature of life. Not surprisingly, the emphasis is on reducing spending on nondirect services. A number of interviewees with experience in service departments suggested that this practice has damaged the thinking capability of departments. As one interviewee commented: "A number of agencies are close to being brain dead." This practice makes it difficult for departments to think strategically and manage change.

Strong Unions

The major union in the city is the Association of Federal, State, County and Municipal Employees (AFSCME), with the other significant unions being those of the firefighters, police, and teachers. The city is highly unionized, with virtually all nonsenior management posts filled by union members. The unions are a powerful feature in New York City. They can help determine which candidates for elected positions succeed and which ones fail. This is because of the number of votes they can influence (i.e., union members and their relations and friends) and their role in campaigning during elections. The current mayor is one of the few to get elected against union support. The unions have enjoyed considerable success in opposing attempts to privatize or contract out city services. They helped, for example, to get the council to pass "Local Law 35", which allows the council to hold a hearing where the mayor proposes contracting out a service currently performed in-house. They also negotiated the right to submit a bid after private sector bids have been received for a service currently performed in-house, which gives city employees a built-in advantage where privatization is proposed. Their power also impacts on the role of managers, who find their autonomy constrained by the actions of councils or mayors who are responding to union concerns.

Responsibility without Power

The form of government in New York City combined with high levels of oversight dilutes managerial responsibility. This is exacerbated by the frequent use of centralist crisis-management measures, such as freezing contract awards and payments late during the financial year. This discourages managers from feeling responsible for their portfolios. This makes for bad management because decisions are often taken by elected and appointed officials who are far away from the action on the ground and know little of the issues. The managers on the front line also lack an incentive to actively manage their areas.

Overloading the Contracting Regime

As noted earlier the contracting regime has a wide range of objectives, from achieving value for money right through to minimizing corruption and promoting local firms, minority businesses, and equal opportunities. Most of these objectives are highly desirable, but their cumulative impact on contracting is serious. It also makes it difficult to achieve any of the objectives, because there is a lack of focus on what is most important. How, for example, are trade-offs to be made when no one single contractor meets all of the requirements? This dilemma is clearly articulated in the following excerpt from a PPB report:

Now put yourself in the position of the Mayor or his delegate in the following case, where three companies each qualifies for preference on a different ground, or a combination of grounds. In competitive sealed bid procurement for a $25 million purchase, the low bidder is from out of town, but is a certified minority and offers products with high-recycled content. The next low bidder also offers recycled products, and is a local company, but is not a certified M/WBE. The next low bidder—still within 5% of the low bid—is a certified minority, but is not a local company, does not offer recycled products and cannot sign the McBride principle rider. By coincidence, two of the three have recently placed well-known lobbyists on retainer, and the president of the third has been a long time campaign contributor to the Mayor.

On what basis does the Mayor or his delegate decide—using unreviewable discretion—what best serves the City's best interest? How much more does he agree to pay for the procurement, and to whom? How does the man or woman in the street view this decision, whatever the outcome?

And what cost is there, in terms of delayed response to the initial purchase request, for the system that places responsibility for this decision at the very pinnacle of the pyramid of the purchasing bureaucracy, and at the very end of the chain of activities that go into selecting a contractor? [City of New York, 1993c]

A second related problem is the focus of oversight. Typically the key oversight agencies, such as the mayor's Offices of Contracts and OMB and the comptroller, have multiple objectives and wide-ranging responsibilities. Single-purpose agencies are nearly always more successful, because they have clarity of purpose and limited functions (Wilson, 1989). Unfortunately, most of the oversight agencies in New York have wide-ranging functions and multiple objectives. This makes it difficult to make progress in any one area because they are invariably pursuing so many other objectives.

Information Problems

In essence, the city lacks relevant and timely information to manage the contracting process. There is not a proper contract budget in place, and it is not possible to track expenditure accurately. Performance information is patchy in many cases and nonexistent in some areas. Information is also fragmented on a bewildering number of manual and computerized systems, with little ability to transfer data from one system to another. Indeed, there are five separate systems but no central repository of information. Moreover, there is little ability to link information stored on the systems.

Is New York City Too Big?

It is difficult to avoid the question of whether the city's size makes it unmanageable. To put it in perspective, the New York economy is larger than that of Russia and its government is bigger than the national governments of many Western countries. Many of the world's largest multinationals have been going through a genuine devolution revolution since the 1980s. This involves radical devolution of power. By contrast, New York remains highly centralized, and reforms emphasize administrative decentralization rather than real devolution. For example:

—The PPB rules provide a common framework for all city agencies.

—The reengineering exercise and the ICPMS propose an integrated contracting system for the city.

—The plans for public/private competition involve a centralized approach with decisions being made in the mayor's office.

All of the reforms assume that the city is and should remain one organization with a common framework for contracting. This approach has to be questioned. Will reform of such a large bureaucracy ever be able to succeed without breaking it up?

CONCLUSIONS

New York City is a unique local government. The problems it is experiencing with contracting illustrate very well why the black box of contracting arrangements, processes, and systems matters. Poor contracting costs the city dearly, with financial waste and poor services.

The principal obstacle to smart contracting in the city relates to the strong tradition of political management. This relates to the mayor-council form of government, with the tradition of a political executive and dispersed power between elected officials. Another significant obstacle is the sheer size of the organization. Is it possible to develop smart contracting practices in such a large organization with centralist systems and processes?

10

Competition Affects Everybody—
Contracting for Support Services
in Milwaukee

Milwaukee is a Great Lakes manufacturing city with a population of around 630,000. Over 60% of the city's population is white, and the bulk of the minority population is African–American. In recent decades, Milwaukee's economy has diversified, with service jobs replacing lost manufacturing jobs.

The city has a mayor-council form of government. The city attorney, comptroller, and treasurer are also elected. At the time of writing, the mayor, John Norquist, was in his second term, which ended in 1996.

Milwaukee employs around 8,500 staff. It provides a comprehensive range of local government services. These include police, fire, public works, water, libraries, public and environmental health, a municipal court, and a range of development services. A number of arms'-length agencies are responsible for services such as low-income housing and the convention center and arena. The city does not own or run an airport, nor is it responsible for the electricity utility. A separate school board runs the schools in the city, and there is a sewerage district for the metropolitan area.

The city has a solid reputation for service delivery, clean government, and fiscal prudence. Although a conservative city, the Norquist administration has instituted a number of reforms. These range from major changes in service delivery such as the introduction of community-based policing as well as a number of managerial initiatives. The latter include an integrated strategic planning and budget system, managerial devolution, and, the subject of this chapter, the Internal Service Improvement Project (ISIP).

FINANCIAL POSITION

In 1995, the city's gross annual expenditure was projected to exceed $1,000 million. This included a capital program of $93 million. Nearly 75% of expenditure was on personnel, and the big-spending services were police, fire, water, and public works. Expenditure levels were held constant by the Norquist administration, with a 1% reduction in real terms between 1988 and 1994.

The main source of income is intergovernmental revenues, which makes up 37% of the city's income. Milwaukee, along with other governments in Wisconsin, receives a share from a pool of state-collected taxes (mainly income, sales, and motor fuel taxes). The main local tax is a property tax, which accounts for around 23% of the city's income. A wide range of service charges, fees, and other local taxes make up the balance. Since 1988, the property tax levy has fallen by nearly 20% in real terms, and the rate has been reduced by 17%.

Milwaukee has an above-average level of debt. Nevertheless, it has a sizable contingency fund and healthy reserves. Unlike many other large cities, it has avoided using reserves to cover revenue expenditure. It is also funding an increasing amount of its capital program with cash rather than loans. These factors help explain why the city enjoys an AA+ bond rating.

THE INTERNAL SERVICE IMPROVEMENT PROJECT

In 1991, the city undertook a survey of the "customer" departments for internal support services. The survey revealed widespread dissatisfaction with the cost, speed, and quality of internal support services. As a result, a program was developed to reduce the costs and improve the quality of internal support services. This became known as the ISIP. The approach was borrowed from the STEP program developed by the Department of Administration in the state of Minnesota (Barzelay, 1992).

The ISIP approach comprised four elements:

1. Classifying support services by their nature and function into one of three categories. "Policy/regulatory" services were those that established policies and standards and/or enforced them. Other services were classified as "monopolies", as they could only be provided through a single source. Finally, there were "competitive" services where city departments could buy from the in-house supplier or outside contractors.

2. Separating regulatory from support functions, wherever possible, to ensure that support functions had a customer focus.

3. Exposing "competitive" services to competition by transferring their budgets to the customer departments and allowing the latter to seek bids from outside contractors.

4. Encouraging the "competitive" services, known as Internal Service Agencies (ISAs), to operate more like private businesses.

Table 10.1 provides a list of the 35 support services and how the city classified them. Sixteen of these services were classified as competitive and, as such, were earmarked to take part in the ISIP. However, the city decided to experiment first with a small number of ISAs and customer departments. The experiment began in 1992, and the participating ISAs are shown in Table 10.2. In 1992, five competitive bidding exercises were undertaken, and these are summarized in Table 10.3.

All five bidding exercises were won by outside contractors. ISAs lost three of the competitions solely on price. One was lost on a combination of price and quality, and in the remaining competition the ISA bid failed to conform to the specification. The baseline for four of the five services listed in Table 10.3 (excluding the building inspection) was the relevant ISA bid, and these amounted to $88,600. Consequently, savings from the competition exercises represented nearly 43%. The value of the winning bid for building inspection was nearly $118,000.

Despite the financial advantages of bidding exercises, most departments chose not to undertake them for most services. No competitions were required for training or for major building renovation. However, the city feels that the benefits of ISIP extend well beyond the competitions. City officials cited a number of other benefits, including the following:

- The threat of competition enabled a number of customer departments to negotiate better prices with ISAs. For example, the Budget and Management Division achieved a 38% reduction on a $10,000 contract for computer maintenance.

- Some ISAs have been contracting out services required by internal customers where they do not have the capacity or cost advantage in-house. For example, Municipal Equipment contracts out transmission and engine rebuilding and brake repairs, which the private sector can perform at lower cost. Training have also done this. Instead of losing in direct competition, ISAs are subcontracting to the private sector where they have a clear cost or capacity advantage.

- There is improved customer satisfaction with ISAs. A follow-up to the 1991 survey showed a significant turnaround, with most customers satisfied with performance. Satisfaction levels varied from 65% for information systems (IS) projects to 100% for training. These improvements related to a lowering of costs, speedier performance, and better customer service. A good example of this can be found in Central Reproduction and City Records Center (CRCRC). CRCRC implemented a "printer liaison" program and a network of customer contacts to enhance communication, speed turnaround, and improve responsiveness to customer needs.

- The more entrepreneurial ISAs are beginning to press for greater flexibility to enable them to operate more like businesses. For example, they are seeking more

TABLE 10.1. Classification of Support Services

Services	Function	Annual Expenditure
1. Policy/regulatory	Budget analysis	$781,000
	Management analysis	$339,000
	Purchasing	$1,548,000
	Legal services	$3,099,000
	Collection and claims service	$437,000
	City clerk reference service	$5,527,000
	Accounting and payroll services	$2,780,000
	Auditing services	$687,000
	Real estate services	$366,000
	Labor negotiation	$794,000
	Recruitment and staffing	$1,042,000
	Fringe-benefit administration	$1,501,000
	Position classification	$512,000
	Recruitment and staffing for the fire and police commission	$488,000
	Radio maintenance for police	$639,000
	Total	$20,600,000
2. Monopoly	City hall delivery service	$74,000
	Mainframe computer service	$4,231,000
	Translation/interpreter service	$46,000
	Telephone services	$1,083,000
	Communications cabling	$250,000
	Total	$5,684,000
3. Competitive	Title searches	$103,000
	Printing and reproduction	$694,000
	Microfilm and records storage	$379,000
	U.S. mail preparation and delivery	$95,000
	IS project development and design	$2,230,000
	Microcomputer hardware and software maintenance	$514,000
	Training and development services	$333,000
	Employee physicals	$79,000
	Employee assistance program	$62,000
	Building design and inspection	$166,000
	Building maintenance	$3,500,000
	Custodial services	$2,200,000
	Electrical service	$1,200,000
	Vehicle maintenance and repair	$2,754,000
	Vehicle and operator rental	$22,665,000
	Total	$37,740,000

Source: Draft City of Milwaukee report on the implementation of the ISIP Program, 12 August 1993.

TABLE 10.2.   The ISIP Program

Internal Service Agency	Start Date	Number of Departments as Customers
Purchasing[a]	1 January 1992	7
Computer Maintenance	1 May 1992	All
IS Projects	1 January 1992	6
Minor Building Repair and Maintenance	1 June 1992	2
Major Building Renovation	1 January 1992	1
Training and Development Services	1 January 1992	All

[a]Proposed changes in purchasing arrangements were withdrawn in October 1992.

flexibility to hire and fire staff, changes to employment terms and conditions, and greater freedom from city procurement regulations.

Costs were incurred in setting up the ISIP scheme. City officials spent time developing and monitoring the initiative, and new accounting systems had to be developed to track service costs rather than simply record input costs. Additional staff efforts and the accounting changes were absorbed within existing budgets.

The ISIP scheme has expanded since 1992 in two respects. First, a group of services—central reproduction and records—have been added to the program. Second, there has been an increase in the number of competitive bidding exercises. Bridges and Buildings, for example, have been required to compete for maintenance of a few buildings each year. Individual departments have also looked to alternative providers for training, computer services, and vehicle rental, but not on a large scale. Indeed, most ISA services continue to be provided without going through a competition.

TABLE 10.3.   Impact of ISIP in 1992

Customer Dept	ISIP Service	Savings
Police	Computer maintenance	$22,755
Libraries	Building repair and maintenance	$9,441
Administration	Computer maintenance	$3,788
Fire	Building repair and maintenance	$1,770
Building inspection	IS project development[a]	–
Total	All	$37,754

[a]The in-house bid did not comply with the specification, and as a result it is not possible to establish a saving level as this was a small one-off project which was part of a larger budget for IS.

Analysis of ISIP

Table 10.4 summarizes my assessment of Milwaukee against the smart contractor model. Overall, ISIP has been a worthwhile experiment that has produced benefits. However, at present ISIP can only be viewed as a modest change rather than a management revolution. The financial impact on the city has been small scale and generally more modest than the savings usually achieved through contracting services out. Moreover, even though competitive bidding exercises have produced significant benefits for the city, few have been attempted, despite the fact that there is a ready market for a whole range of services inside ISIP and beyond. The approach could produce significant cost reductions if it is applied more widely to support and direct services where there is an established market. Good examples here would be trash collection and legal advice, both of which are contracted out by many jurisdictions.

Further comments on four selected issues—the financial effects, customer roles and relationships, the impact on ISAs, and the extent to which a strategic approach has been adopted—are set out below.

1. *Financial Effects of ISIP*

While high levels of savings are being achieved when bidding exercises are undertaken, the overall impact of ISIP to date has been modest. First, very few areas have been exposed to competition, and those that have been are relatively small-scale activities. This explains why the absolute levels of savings achieved have been small—$37,754 in 1992 (less than 0.01% of the expenditure on support services). However, it is clear that the ISIP has exerted a downward pressure on internal service costs. This is shown in Tables 10.5 and 10.6 for the Information Systems Division and for Municipal Equipment.

Tables 10.5 and 10.6 show that service costs have fallen over time. This is all the more impressive as wages have risen during the period as a result of union agreements. One of the reasons for the improvement in efficiency has been the use of subcontracting by ISAs. This is shown in Table 10.7 below for Municipal Equipment.

As a result of ISIP, the Municipal Equipment Department undertook market research and decided to discontinue providing services where it was clearly not competitive.

In addition to cost savings, overall levels of expenditure for support services have fallen since the introduction of ISIP, but the changes are not dramatic. The changes in expenditure are shown in Table 10.8. This shows that expenditure increased for Training and for Municipal Equipment and decreased for Information Systems and CRCR. There was little difference in the changes when compared to expenditure patterns of the city generally. It would be a mistake to equate resource levels with costs and efficiency. Nevertheless, while ISIP may have improved timeliness and customer satisfaction and resulted in more effi-

TABLE 10.4.   How Does Milwaukee Fare against the Smart Contractor Model?

Principle	Evaluation
1. Challenges the status quo	Yes—challenged the way support services were provided but ignored direct services.
2. Examines the competition	Little attempt was made to assess the alternative providers of support services when the initiative was conceived; however, individual departments and ISAs have begun to benchmark ISAs against market rates.
3. Thinks creatively	Limited attention given to the alternatives to ISIP; little consideration at city or departmental levels given to how work should be packaged; however, ISAs have given much more thought to how their services are provided as the initiative has evolved.
4. Prepares carefully	Training was provided and a sensible implementation time-scale used; the quality of financial data was also much better than is the case in most cities.
5. Has a customer focus	A key strength—ISAs did develop a much stronger customer orientation and customer departments had power and choice; however, many customers did not use their freedom reflecting improved satisfaction.
6. Copes with the political process	Well handled but the cost has been a small-scale initiative with only modest returns so far.
7. Behaves corporately	Managed corporately—however, because decisions on competitive services have been devolved, there is a risk that decisions in the future might ignore corporate considerations.
8. Competent in contracting techniques	Appeared to be the case.
9. Clarity over roles	The roles were clear—the mayor sponsored the scheme, the administration director coordinated it at city level, and departments were responsible for their purchasing decisions.
10. Clean and independent	No evidence of corruption. However, some conflicts of interest exist such as the location of the Municipal Equipment ISA in Public Works.

cient use of resources, it is clear that its impact on expenditure levels has been at best marginal to date. Moreover, it is not clear what happens to ISIP savings. It is apparent that many of the benefits are hidden. For example, city departments clearly benefit from the decision of Municipal Equipment to stop offering certain types of equipment for rental, but these savings are not separately identified and will probably be diverted to other areas of expenditure within the departments' budgets.

TABLE 10.5.   Information Systems Division—Price Changes 1992–1996

Service Category	1992 Prices	1993 Prices	1994 Prices	1995 Prices	Proposed 1996 Prices
A. *Data center services*					
Print lines (per 100 lines)	$0.277	$0.216	$0.216	$0.216	$0.216
Print pages (per 1000 pages)	$21.45	$16.41	none	none	none
Reader I/Os (per 100 I/Os)	$4.22	$3.56	$0.072	$0.072	$0.063
Disk I/Os (per 100 I/Os)	$0.117	$0.072	$0.072	$0.072	$0.063
B. *Data communications services*					
Mainframe terminals	$2,500	$1,230	$1,200	$1,200	$1,200
Mainframe printers	$2,500	$1,360	$1,200	$1,200	$1,200
Screen printers	none	$260	$260	$260	$260
PCs/mainframe emulation (per unit)	$2,500	$1,100	$1,100	$1,100	$1,100

Source: City of Milwaukee, 1996.

2.   *The Customers*

ISIP has empowered customer departments. Previously ISAs would determine the service requirements and levy charges, and customer departments had little or no say in the matter. Under ISIP, customer departments control the budget decide service requirements and who the supplier will be. It is clear from

TABLE 10.6.   Operator Hourly Rates in Municipal Equipment

Rate Description	1993	1994	1995
Mechanic	$44.43	$48.60	$48.79
Tractor operator	$45.93	$42.32	$38.07
SE operator	$35.32	$34.19	$31.36
Truck driver	$34.44	$33.35	$30.49
Driver/worker	$34.36	$33.27	$30.53
Administrative fee	$10.67	$10.27	$9.93

Source: City of Milwaukee, 1996.

TABLE 10.7.   Daily Equipment Rental Rates for Municipal Equipment

Equipment Description	Market Rate	ME Rate 1995	ME Rate 1996 (proposed)
Auto	$32.00	$12.16	$10.49
Aerial lift	$275.00	$336.78	none
Backhoe	none	$175.95	$183.24
Front loader	$300.00	$607.23	none
Pickup truck	none	$36.68	$23.57
Prentice loader	$330.00	$118.47	$128.55
Van—cargo	$35.00	$8.13	$56.30
Van—passenger	$55.00	$38.90	sold

Source: City of Milwaukee, 1996.

the satisfaction surveys undertaken that customers on the whole like the system and acknowledge improved performance by ISAs.

What is surprising, however, is that so few competitive bidding exercises have been undertaken. This is all the more surprising given the dissatisfaction with ISA services prior to ISIP and the high level of savings achieved through occasional bidding exercises. Why, then, has there been so little enthusiasm for competitive bidding? One view is that a range of improvements were secured in negotiations with ISAs, eliminating the need for bidding exercises. An alternative view is that customer departments are unsure of their purchasing skills and are wary of creating uncertainty with bidding exercises. While there are examples of negotiations producing benefits for customers, the stable financial picture suggests little significant change in costs. There has been an increase in bidding exercises since 1992, but the norm remains to keep the service in-house.

TABLE 10.8.   Changes in Expenditure Levels

Area	1992 (actuals)	1993 (actuals)	1994 (actuals)	2-Year Change
Information Systems	$7,067,184	$6,437,573	$6,293,132	−10.9%
CRCRC	$1,116,557	$1,024,298	$1,063,088	−4.8%
Municipal Equipment	$23,801,612	$25,455,790	$28,514,915	+19.8%
Training	$309,431	$329,707	$358,936	+16.0%

Source: City of Milwaukee, 1996.

3. The Impact on Internal Service Agencies

ISIP has had a major impact on ISAs. Staff in ISAs received training in customer care and business planning prior to the introduction of ISIP. More fundamentally, there has been a major change in the "soft" area of culture change. ISAs no longer see themselves in a protected position. At grass-roots level, a stronger focus on customers has developed. There has also been a change at management level. A stronger management culture is developing: ISAs are beginning to think more like businesses—looking for opportunities to expand their business base outside the city and seeking greater flexibility over various city regulations. There has been a small amount of organizational change, with greater devolution of responsibility and a slimming of the number of middle-management posts, but as Table 10.9 shows this has had relatively little impact on staffing. The only ISA to experience a significant decrease was Information Systems.

As is often the case in the U.K., the in-house contractors appear to have adjusted to the change more quickly than their counterparts on the purchasing side. However, there are a number of constraints that limit their ability to operate as genuine businesses. ISAs have to comply with city financial, personnel, and purchasing regulations. Most seriously, their freedom to hire and fire is restricted, and they must abide by city/union agreements on pay. This means that it is difficult to shed poor performers, and at the same time it is not possible to reward high achievers. Purchasing arrangements are centralized, and even small purchases are subject to citywide rules that can make it time-consuming. For example, there are competitive bidding procedures for commodity purchases over $500 and services over $2,000. Finally, ISAs cannot expand their markets, as the city decided against allowing ISAs to bid for contracts in neighboring local governments.

4. Is a Strategic Approach in Place?

The evidence on whether Milwaukee adopted a strategic approach to ISIP is mixed. On the positive side, the implementation was well engineered politically.

TABLE 10.9.   Direct Labor Hours for ISAs (as specified in the City Budget)

ISA	*1992*	*1993*	*1994*	*1995*
CRCRC	27,300	26,250	27,122	27,000
Information Systems	186,400	141,209	142,530	139,430
Municipal Equipment	643,570	582,785	588,500	596,280
Training	7,200	7,200	8,100	8,280

Source: City of Milwaukee, 1996.

Ann Kinney championed the ISIP scheme, first as budget director and later as administration director. She enjoyed the support of the mayor and gained the support of key customer departments such as police, fire, and libraries. The focus was kept on support services, and politically contentious areas such as legal services (the responsibility of the city attorney) or employee relations (an area in which the unions and the council maintain a close interest) were carefully avoided. This tended to minimize opposition to the approach. A gradual approach was also taken, with some initial training and a steady expansion in the scheme. This reduced the risk of mistakes and media scandals. This was a successful political strategy because the project got off the ground and gained support. The cautious approach may also be justified in the long term if the city is able to expand the scheme to include a much wider range of support and direct services. This seems unlikely in the short term with a mayoral reelection approaching at the time of writing.

Decisions about allowing competition for services should be based on factors such as the need to exercise detailed control over the function, whether a market exists for the service, and to what extent the in-house service is competitive. There are nevertheless business reasons for questioning aspects of the contract strategy:

- *Rationale of the distinctions.* The distinctions between regulatory/policy, monopoly, and competitive services are not relevant to the issue of whether the service is provided in-house or subject to competition. The distinction helps only to decide who should be the purchaser for each function. In any event, the classification was not applied consistently. For example, it is difficult to understand how the bulk of legal advice could be anything other than a support function, yet it was classified as a policy/regulatory function. The same point could be made about the payroll function. Indeed, in U.K. local government, both functions are now subject to compulsory bidding on the grounds that they are support rather than core services.

- *Process orientated.* The ISIP system appears to be concerned mainly with process. There are no published targets for reducing costs, or improving services, and the author's interviews failed to establish whether a private agenda existed.

- *Market factors.* Little attention was paid to the marketplaces for local government function before deciding which activities to include in ISIP and how to expose them to competition. The approach adopted to packaging activities for competition was to break up areas of work into very small projects. This may well be the best way to maximize competition by allowing small firms to compete. However, no consideration appears to have been given to alternative approaches, such as inviting bids for much larger packages of work over a longer time-scale (either within departments or across the city as a whole).

- *Conflict of interest.* Regulatory functions were separated from pure support functions in the case of ISAs. However, the biggest ISA—Municipal Equipment—remained in the Public Works Department, by far the largest customer for vehicles and equipment. There is clearly a conflict of interest in Public Works. The author's impression is that the purchaser side arrangements were overlooked. The need to separate purchaser and provider interests will become a much bigger issue when the scheme expands to all "competitive" services. New purchasing staff did not receive any training in how to undertake bidding exercises and contract management. Again, this will need to be addressed as the scheme expands.

CONCLUSIONS

The Milwaukee story shows that it is possible to subject white-collar as well as blue-collar support functions to competition. It also shows the strength of adopting a "bottom-up" approach to competition—devolving decision-making power to front-line departments. Although this was not a conscious decision, this has the long-term effect of downgrading political considerations and up-grading managerial factors in decisions about how to provide services. The other big strength about Milwaukee was the careful approach to implementation. A cost-accounting system was established in advance, a step missed by the vast majority of local governments. A sensible implementation time-scale was also adopted, giving both purchaser and provider sides time to learn the rules of the new game.

The one area where the Milwaukee ISIP needs further development relates to special factors affecting public/private competition. These are:

- *Organizational clarity.* It is vital in public/private competition to separate internal purchaser and provider interests to ensure both fair competition and that the purchaser side is genuinely independent, thinking primarily of customer and service issues rather than production issues.

- *Training.* The purchaser side needs training just as much as the provider side. Indeed, there are good grounds for arguing that the purchaser side's needs are greater. Unlike the providers, purchasers are being asked to think in a completely different way.

- *Outputs and outcomes.* Public/private competition can easily degenerate into a bureaucratic process, where form becomes more important than substance. This is why the purchaser side needs to be able to demonstrate with results the benefits of the preferred approach.

11

Alarm Bells Ringing—Can Putting Out Fires for Profit Work?

In the year after the city of Scottsdale, Arizona, combined its fire and emergency ambulance services, it increased paramedic units by 56%, put a paramedic in every fire station, and added 12 firefighters to the city's department. All of this was achieved at no additional cost to the city's taxpayers. Is this a good example of a local government improving services? Well yes, if you also consider that the city of Scottsdale has a private fire and emergency service. Scottsdale has developed an innovative public/private partnership with the Rural/Metro Corporation to provide a comprehensive emergency service to residents, businesses, and visitors, with impressive results. If you have a medical emergency in Scottsdale, a paramedic is on the scene, on average, in 3 minutes, 2 seconds—more than twice as fast as U.S. national standards. The level of fire safety is also superior to most as a result of one of the most far-reaching fire prevention programs in the U.S.

Rural/Metro now serves around 8 million people in 10 states. Its growth in recent years has been nothing short of phenomenal: for the six months ended 31 December 1994 the company reported a net income of $3 million on a $76 million total revenue, compared to income of $1.7 million and a total revenue of $47 million for the same period one year earlier. This represented a 62% jump in revenues. In 1995, its turnover was expected to double. So how has this been achieved? This chapter examines the Scottsdale story. What are the origins of Rural/Metro? Does it work? What are the lessons?

TABLE 11.1. Service Delivery for Emergency Services

Area	*Mainly Direct Provision*	*Another Public Agency*	*Private Providers*	*Volunteers*	*Total Responses*
Fire service	79.8%	12.9%	3.5%	14.0%	1,299
Emergency medical service	61.8%	20%	21.9%	12.0%	1,200

Source: 1992 ICMA survey of local governments summarized in Miranda & Andersen, 1994.
Note: The figures in the columns are not mutually exclusive, and as a result the percentages exceed 100%.

EMERGENCY SERVICES IN THE U.S.

There is no requirement in the U.S. to have a fire service. Nevertheless, virtually every local authority provides fire protection. The vast majority of local authorities set up municipal fire departments to provide the service (see Table 11.1). A sizable minority provide the service through an "intergovernmental agreement." This could mean one city buying the service from a neighboring local authority, or a group of authorities establishing a special fire district to provide the service to all the member authorities. A small number of U.S. cities contract with for-profit firms, such as the Rural/Metro, for fire protection. A very small proportion of the U.S. population does not have a municipal fire service. In such areas, individuals choose whether or not to subscribe to a private fire-protection scheme. The latter arrangement is normally in a rural area.

Emergency services in the U.S. are predominantly in the private sector, as is, of course, the U.S. health system. Individuals pay an emergency-service carrier after using the service. States regulate the standards and charges. As an individual needing attention and depending on your health insurance, you are free to choose which emergency service to use. Emergency services are part of the health industry rather than local government. Local governments get involved by franchising one or more emergency-service providers to its emergency telephone number, 911 (the equivalent of 999 in the U.K.). In many cases, the local authority itself will provide the emergency service, with its own paramedics and in some cases with a combined fire/paramedic service. The trend in recent years has been to award the franchises to private firms.

FROM VOLUNTEERS TO MULTIMILLION-DOLLAR CORPORATION

When Lou Witzeman founded the Rural/Metro Corporation in 1948, he had no idea that it would grow to become one of the largest emergency-service firms in the U.S. The area where Witzeman lived was an "unincorporated" part of

Maricopa County, just outside the city of Phoenix. An unincorporated area is not part of a city and receives only minimal local government services from the county council. Witzeman and his fellow residents did not even have a public fire service. In 1948, Witzeman had a fire at his home and the Phoenix Fire Department refused to help as he lived outside the city boundaries. Witzeman was angry and decided to do something about it. He asked neighbors to contribute to buying a community fire engine. With one engine and four fire-fighters covered by subscriptions, the Rural/Metro was born. Witzeman's ethic was simple: keep finding new and better ways to provide a quality service at a reduced cost. The idea was so popular that by 1980 Rural/Metro was providing fire protection to 20% of Arizonans.

The city of Scottsdale began contracting with Rural/Metro in 1952. The contract has been renewed ever since. Ownership of Rural/Metro changed in 1978 when Witzeman retired: he sold it to the people he thought would do the best job running it—the employees. Today, every employee—from a fire fighter to a clerk—has stock in Rural/Metro. The company grows apace—it operates 800 appliances, covering 80 communities throughout Arizona, Arkansas, Florida, Georgia, Nebraska, New York, Ohio, Oregon, South Carolina, Tennessee, and Texas. This year, Rural/Metro broke into Europe with a contract in Holland.

DOES IT WORK?

Effectiveness of the Fire Operation

There is little doubt that Rural/Metro's results are impressive. The 1989 University Science Center study compared the company's performance in Scottsdale with 9 municipal fire departments in cities of comparable size and land area. These included nearby Phoenix and Tucson. Phoenix has an international reputation as a well-managed city. For example, in recent years it has been rated the best-managed big city in the U.S. by *Financial World Magazine* and in 1993 it won the Bertelsmann Prize for being one of the two best-managed cities in the world!

Rural/Metro fared well on all the comparisons:

- Scottsdale had the lowest number of structure fires of all 10 cities, at 1.1 per 1,000 population compared to 1.8 for Phoenix and 2.0 for Tucson. Controlling structure fires is an important measure of fire-service effectiveness because these fires tend to be the most dangerous and costly fires.

- Scottsdale also had the lowest level of financial loss due to fires. Financial loss is a measure of fire safety and fire-service effectiveness. Per capita dollar loss for Scottsdale was $13 compared to an average of $22 for the 10 cities. The equivalent figures for Phoenix and Tucson were $29 and $13, respectively. The loss figures related to a three-year period to control for any extraordinary losses.

- The number of fire deaths in Scottsdale was 15% below the average for the 10 cities. Again the figures for each city were collected over a three-year period. Plano (Texas) and Glendale (Arizona) had the lowest fire-death rates at zero. The fire death rate for Scottsdale at 2.3 compared to the average of 2.9. The fire-death rates for Phoenix and Tucson were 10.3 and 4.0, respectively.

No one of these statistics provides a perfect measure of fire-service performance and safety. Fire dollar loss, for example, can be affected by the estimating methods used and the variations in property values. Fire deaths are also a function of citizen safety as well as the performance of the fire service. Nevertheless, the combination of the three indicators and the high performance of Rural/Metro on each front against a carefully selected sample of similar cities provides powerful evidence of good performance.

Cost to the City of Scottsdale

All the available evidence suggests that Scottsdale receives a high level of service at a low cost. This includes comparative data and an analysis of the costs of creating and operating a municipal department for Scottsdale.

Table 11.2 shows the cost per capita for Scottsdale, Phoenix, as well as the national average for fiscal years 1993/94 and 1994/95. Scottsdale performs better than Phoenix and the national averages. There are, of course, difficulties with comparisons using raw data on costs. Such comparisons take no account of variations in service levels, fire-prevention policies, accounting conventions, geography, as well as the nature, type, and density of development. Nevertheless, the raw data still strongly suggests the low costs of the Scottsdale operation. This is because of the size of the gap between Scottsdale and the national average and the comparison with Phoenix when combined with the service performance information covered earlier.

The 1989 University Science Center study provided further evidence of Rural/Metro's good performance on costs. The study examined and costed a proposal to establish a municipal fire operation in Scottsdale (Table 11.3). A citizen group

TABLE 11.2. Cost Per Capita for Fire Protection

City	1993/94	1994/95
Scottsdale	$48.78	$50.78
Phoenix	$99.89	$102.10
National average	$78.98	$81.35

Source: City of Scottsdale and Rural/Metro Corporation. The 1993/94 data are actuals, whereas the 1994/95 figures are based on budget estimates.

TABLE 11.3.   **Costing the Municipal Alternative for Scottsdale**

Budget Items	Costs in $
Net operating budget	6,503,264
Capital budget	1,119,121
City expenses	300,976
City overheads	1,495,751
Total	9,019,111

Source: University Science Center, 1989.

Note: The City of Scottsdale's net operating budget for its private Fire Department in 1989 was $5,148,275.

prepared the proposal with advice from a fire chief from a municipal department in another city. The study concluded that the municipal alternative would be much more expensive and would not improve services. Indeed, the study estimated that the annual costs would be around 53% more expensive! There would also be set-up capital costs of over $1 million.

There are sound reasons for questioning aspects of the comparison. For example:

- The municipal alternative includes city overheads of 23% to help run the fire service. This is supposed to cover costs such as payroll, personnel, and purchasing, and the figure of 23% is already used by the city to allocate overhead costs to service budgets in the budget process. This is an exceptionally high figure that probably overstates the real cost of overheads substantially. Unfortunately, it is not possible to test this with available data, because Scottsdale does not have an activity-based accounting system.

- The municipal alternative involves increased manning of appliances and shorter hours for fire-fighters. These were features of the citizen-group proposal, but it is possible to argue that this distorts the comparison—the comparison covers both the public/private difference as well as variations in labor practices.

These qualifications would reduce the level of savings, but the contracted-out option would still remain substantially cheaper.

Does Scottsdale Really Get More for Less?

What accounts for the difference? Is it a genuine? Is it due to private service delivery? There is a lot more to the Rural/Metro difference than using green rather than red fire trucks. Indeed, the underlying factors are the emphasis on

prevention, cost efficiencies, the management culture, the hidden costs of regulation, and the risks associated with a contract. These are expanded on below.

The Emphasis on Prevention

Since 1974, the city of Scottsdale, on the advice of Rural/Metro, has had
various requirements on smoke alarms and sprinklers. In 1985, the city adopted
the most comprehensive fire-sprinkler ordinance (local law) in the U.S. This
requires all new developments, 50% of renovated structures, and change of
occupancies, regardless of size and use, to be sprinklered. It is now estimated
that around half of all the city's properties are sprinklered. A thorough prevention program that includes fire-safety inspections during the plan check stage
and follow-up surveys one-year later supplements these requirements. The city
also has one of the most extensive public fire-safety programs in the U.S. The
prevention philosophy has also spread to the emergency-response service. This
includes, for example, a blood-pressure-monitoring program in place in all fire
stations for members of the public, a major public program of cardiopulmonary
resuscitation training, and a home-pool safety initiative. The emphasis on prevention is the major reason for the high level of fire safety. It also enables Rural/
Metro to achieve significant economies, which reflect in the city's low costs.

Cost Efficiencies

Fire prevention and the use of non-unionized labor are the foundations of the
Rural/Metro efficiencies. All of the efficiencies involve simple rather than sophisticated measures. The major efficiencies concern staffing, which accounts
for around 80% of the cost of a fire service. Rural/Metro uses fewer fire-fighters
per engine (2 as opposed to 3 or 4 in other cities) and they work longer hours (68
hours per week compared to 56 hours in nearby municipal fire departments).
Pay is roughly comparable with municipal operations. Rural/Metro uses a
unique combination of full-time, part-time, and voluntary staffing. In addition to
the full-time career fire-fighters, the Rural/Metro uses fire reserves that are
available on major incidents and for covering for full-time fire-fighters. It also
has a unique fire support program. Some 40 city employees are available to
work on major incidents. All fire reserves and fire support staff go through a
thorough training program and are on call at certain times of the day/week.
Cross-utilization of employees is achieved by, for example, training fire-fighters
to undertake safety inspections and as paramedics. This enables Rural/Metro to
make good use of the fire-fighters during most of their working week when there
are no fire incidents. The sprinkler program also enables Rural/Metro to achieve
efficiencies in other areas, such as greater spacing between fire hydrants and
using fire hoses with a smaller diameter. Rural/Metro is also able to take advantage of economies of scale and use the latest technology, where the development
costs can be spread over a large number of contracts. Finally, being outside the

public sector enables Rural/Metro to avoid costly and lengthy procurement procedures.

Management Culture

Rural/Metro boasts an organizational culture as impressive as the multinationals cited by the likes of Tom Peters as being at the leading edge of management practice. Innovative management practice is encouraged through a genuine "bottom-up" approach whereby staff at the sharp end help shape and improve the running of the business. "Focus groups" and "task teams" provide regular feedback and ideas to the management on how to improve the way things get done. This management culture is perhaps at odds with the traditional "command and control" style of most quasi-military operations. Involvement of staff at all levels in the organization is carefully nurtured through intensive training for all. Training is both job-related and "relationship"-oriented, with as much emphasis on training in management and interpersonal skills as the technical areas. Fire officers who struggle with a more "democratic" style of management are even offered outsourced counseling. This open style has, according to Ann Stein, the human resources director at Rural/Metro, blown away the idea that the "great decisions" are made by the few behind closed doors. Rural/Metro has demonstrated its commitment to training with money and action: 4% of the employee budget goes on training and development. This includes supporting staff on Certificate, Bachelors, and even MBA programs. Innovative personnel practices also support the culture, such as "360-degree feedback" and rewarding staff for not taking sick leave (e.g., if you do not use your 10 days' sick leave you get a 5-day leave credit!). What does this all add up to? "A fun place to work," in the words of Rural/Metro President and Chief Executive Robert Manschot.

The Hidden Costs of Regulation

It is clear that the prevention and efficient working practices save the city of Scottsdale substantial amounts of money and make the city a safer place to live in, work in, and visit. However, it needs to be recognized that some of the costs of the Rural/Metro approach are hidden and excluded from the traditional cost–benefit equation. This is because the costs of the prevention program are borne by individuals and organizations. These costs are unknown, although there are many studies that suggest that sprinkler and smoke-detector programs pay for themselves over a period of years.

The Risks of Outsourcing

The economists warn of the danger of contracting for a service where the "transaction costs" are high (e.g., Williamson, 1975). This covers contracts that rely on, for example, equipment and facilities owned by the contractor or contract employees with a great deal of knowledge specific to the contract operation. Where these conditions exist, economists argue that in-house provision is preferred to minimize the risks of an outside monopoly and to avoid the high costs of change and monitoring. Does the Rural/Metro contract run such risks? Yes, as there is no real competition for the fire-prevention element of the Scottsdale contract. The only genuine alternatives to Rural/Metro are the establishment of a municipal department or an intergovernmental agreement with a nearby city such as Phoenix. Both alternatives would be difficult to organize, and the municipal fire department would require high one-off set-up costs. This is especially so as Rural/Metro owns around one-third of the vehicles and major pieces of equipment. The reasons why these risks have not materialized to date are a combination of pressure, goodwill, and good luck. Rural/Metro has always been the subject of attack from citizen groups and fire-fighter unions, and this helps reduce the danger of complacency and monopoly creeping in. Concerned citizens and unions for example, initiated the 1989 study. Fortunately for Scottsdale, Rural/Metro is a responsible company keen to look after its long-term interests by providing a good, low-cost service. Indeed, until 1989, the city did not have anybody responsible for monitoring the company's performance and the contract itself was little more than a "gentleman's agreement." Since 1989 the city has appointed a contract manager, introduced a five-year performance contract, and instituted a policy of increasing its share of vehicles and equipment over time. These measures should go a long way toward reducing the risks of outsourcing.

THE LESSONS

The fire service is widely viewed as a core local government service. Does the Rural/Metro story prove that private fire protection can work? Are there any other lessons?

For-Profit Fire Prevention

There is little prospect of a return to the days of fire insurance using private fire companies. Fire safety is a community issue that cannot be adequately catered for on an individual basis. Some people would not participate in insurance schemes and would endanger the rest of the insured community because a raging fire is no respecter of who pays their premiums! However, it would be possible to contract out a public fire service to a private company. The question is, would such an arrangement be desirable?

The Scottsdale story shows that fire fighting and prevention can be contracted out. There would, of course, be great opposition to proposals to contract out the fire service, using arguments such as the dangers of putting a price on people's lives and the undesirability of fire fighting for profit. Most of these arguments are emotional and do not, however, stand up to serious scrutiny. Governments put a price on people's lives all the time when they decide how much to spend on the fire service, the sort of service they want, and the nature of fire-related regulations through, for example, the system of building control.

A more powerful argument against contracting is that there is little to be gained and big risks for fire services. First, there is a weak market. Second, there would be high transaction costs associated with contracting out fire fighting that would result in high monitoring costs and the danger of creating powerful private monopolies. Moreover, the entry costs to firms would be high.

The technical tasks of drawing up a specification and monitoring performance for the fire service would certainly be no more difficult than those for many other services subject to contracting (e.g., social services and legal advice). High transaction costs could be minimized by local governments retaining ownership of facilities, vehicles, and major items of equipment and by applying progressive personnel policies to protect staff displaced by contracting.

Perhaps a more fundamental issue is whether the Rural/Metro approach to management could be copied by municipal fire departments. Clearly, the manning levels for fire engines could only be adopted if a similar amount of sprinkler and smoke-detector coverage could be achieved. Similarly, the requirements on, for example, hydrants and fire hoses could only be adopted when combined with an aggressive prevention policy. The emphasis on devolved management and teamwork could be adopted, and some of the more progressive local governments are beginning to do this.

The Preventative Fire Service

There is a strong tradition of public education and fire-prevention measures through, for example, building regulations. However, the investment in fire prevention in the vast majority of local governments does not compare with that practiced in Scottsdale. Could it work elsewhere? One of the obvious problems is that many cities, unlike Scottsdale, are largely developed. Introducing tough regulations on sprinklers and smoke alarms would therefore have little impact for a very long time indeed. Any attempt to require such devices for existing properties would be resisted on grounds of cost for the individuals affected and the inspection costs to local authorities. However, there could be corresponding savings, such as reduced building standards. What are powerful ideas, however, are the cross-training and cross-utilization of fire fighters and fire prevention officers, as well as the programs aimed at helping individuals and organizations install and maintain smoke alarms and sprinklers.

An Integrated Emergency Service?

There are obvious attractions and some hidden dangers in integrating fire prevention with the ambulance service. Many would view an integrated fire and ambulance service as "common sense." Both are emergency services often responding to the same incidents. There could well be efficiencies to be gained. There are some obvious organizational difficulties, especially where different organizations handle fire and emergency services. A second danger relates to the service costs. An increasing number of U.S. local governments are combining their fire and paramedic services. However, the merger appears to be based on fire taking over paramedic services, in many cases with fire-fighters replacing paramedics. This can prove a costly approach because fire-fighters are more highly paid. Moreover, the majority of emergency calls (around three-quarters) are medical calls rather than fire incidents.

CONCLUSIONS

The Scottsdale story demonstrates some of the risks of contracting for a service with a single supplier in a weak market. However, it also shows how such a contract can be structured and managed to minimize the risks and produce real benefits to taxpayers, residents, businesses, and visitors.

While the case study explodes the myth that emergency services can and should only be provided by the public sector, it is difficult to imagine a rush by local governments to contract out fire and emergency services. However, as local government becomes more constrained financially, the possibility of intergovernmental agreements and perhaps even a contract with a private firm will move up the agenda. In the meantime, serious consideration should be given to the Rural/Metro prevention philosophy and the innovative management practices. This is because many of the strengths of the Rural/Metro success stem from its innovative policy and management practices rather than from the fact that it is a private firm.

12

The English Contracting Revolution

Privatization and contracting in U.S. cities have captured many of the headlines in recent years. Few people realize that one of the most comprehensive systems of local government contracting now exists in England. The English system started in 1980 when a national law was passed requiring all local governments to subject capital projects to a system of competitive bidding. This system is called Compulsory Competitive Tendering (CCT). In the early years, there was nothing especially revolutionary about this. There had always existed a well-established marketplace for construction works, and the contracting techniques for construction were well understood.

The idea of the national government mandating competitive bidding for local governments was unusual. It became revolutionary when it was extended to a much wider range of local government services in 1988. Then, five manual services, including trash collection and grounds maintenance, were included in the CCT regime. Significantly, the law was an "enabling" Act that allowed the government to add more services easily without having to go through the whole legislative process again. More services have been added since 1988, such as the management of recreation facilities. More recently, a whole range of professional services has been included, such as financial services, legal advice, and computing. The full range of services included in the CCT regime is shown in Table 12.1.

There are a number of differences between U.S. and English local government contracting. These include:

TABLE 12.1.   The Services Included in the CCT Regime

Local Government, Planning and Land Act 1980
- New building (including renewal)
- Building repair and maintenance
- Highways construction and maintenance

Local Government Act 1988
- Refuse collection
- Building cleaning
- Other cleaning (e.g., street sweeping)
- School and welfare catering
- Other catering (e.g., city halls)
- Vehicle maintenance
- Grounds maintenance
- Management of sport and recreation services—added in 1989
- On-street parking—added in 1994
- Security—added in 1994
- Vehicle-fleet management—added in 1994
- Legal—added in 1994
- Construction and property services—added in 1994
- Housing management—added in 1994
- Information technology and services—added in 1995
- Finance—added in 1995
- Personnel—added in 1995

- *Public/private competition.*   English local governments nearly always "contract in" by encouraging their employees to compete with the private sector. U.S. local governments mostly contract out, although there are some high-profile exceptions such as Phoenix and Indianapolis.

- *Complete and partial contracting.*   English local governments tend to favor "complete contracting" more than their U.S. counterparts. This means, for example, that many contracts are for 100% of a function. Many U.S. local governments retain a proportion of the work in-house or contract with more than one firm.

- *Big is beautiful.* Many U.S. governments contract with small firms, many of them local, family-owned businesses. In England, contractors tend to be much larger enterprises. Clearly, this is a reflection of the preference for complete contracting.

- *Support Services.* U.S. local governments have focused on contracting for manual services, such as trash collection. English local governments, by contrast, have been more prepared to contract out professional support services, such as computing and financial services.

- *Intergovernmental contracting.* There is considerably more intergovernmental contracting in the U.S. than in England. Indeed, intergovernmental contracting is constrained by law. Local governments can only supply services to other governments if they have "surplus capacity" and supply the service "at cost." Of course "surplus capacity" and "at cost" are subject to interpretation, but the net effect is to restrict such contracting.

- *Intragovernmental contracting.* English local governments do much more "internal contracting" than their U.S. counterparts. This is where internal support services are provided on a quasi-contract basis within the organization. This is much more than an accounting technique. It involves transferring the budget from the support function to front-line departments and giving the latter the freedom to buy the service from outside.

THE CCT REGIME

There are a number of rules for the CCT process, including:

- *Advertising.* All contracts with a total value in excess of around $300,000 have to be advertised in the *European Journal* to encourage European-wide competition.

- *Timing.* There are minimum and maximum periods for each stage of the bidding process.

- *Overhead costs.* There are national guidelines for comparing the costs of public sector bids against the private sector, to ensure that all relevant indirect costs are included in the in-house bid.

- *Packaging and contract conditions.* There are regulations to prevent "anticompetitive behavior" by cities and counties—that is, packaging contracts and including contract conditions to discourage or distort genuine competition.

- *Appeals and complaints.* The national government has introduced a procedure for investigating allegations of anticompetitive behavior. Ultimately, it can force the local government to rebid the work and cease the in-house operation if the allegations are confirmed.

The purpose of these rules is to create a "level playing field" between the public and private sector contractors. The Conservative Government was concerned that many Labour Party–dominated cities would attempt to ensure that the in-house employees win at all costs.

As the system has matured, a market for local government services has emerged. Some well-established firms, such as Cadbury Schweppes and EDS, moved into local government services. New firms have also emerged, and some of these resulted from management buy-outs (MBO). For example, MRS, a

TABLE 12.2. The Impact of CCT

Area	Average no of Bids	In-House Contractor % Share of Market	Annual % Savings
Refuse collection	3.3	64.4%	11.3%
Street cleaning	3.5	63.7%	(2.6%)
Building cleaning	4.6	40.8%	12.7%
School and welfare catering	1.9	75.1%	(2.8%)
Other catering	2.3	67.8%	4.9%
Vehicle maintenance	2.6	74.9%	1.3%
Grounds maintenance	4.1	57.8%	10.9%
Management of sports/ recreation services	1.7	84.8%	(5.0%)
All services	3.0	58.8%	6.5%

Notes: (1) The average number of bids and the in-house percent share of the market are based on a survey carried out by the Local Government Management Board. (2) The savings are based on a sample survey of 40 local governments carried out by Walsh & Davis (1993) for the Department of the Environment. (3) Figures in parentheses in Column 4 refer to increases in spending. There are reasons for some of the increases which go beyond CCT: for example, the increase in spending on street sweeping was due to higher standards mandated by a new law rather than CCT.

major trash-collection and street-sweeping company, was established as an MBO of Westminster City's waste-management bid team. However, the private sector has not got its own way all the time. As Table 12.2 shows, local government employees have, in fact, won around 60% of the contracts for manual services. Some local governments have saved 20–30% through contracting. However, the average level of savings for all services by all local governments, according to the latest national government research, is only around 7%, but this has been increasing as competition develops (Walsh & Davis, 1993). Most significantly, savings are being achieved irrespective of whether the bids are won by the public or private sectors. These levels of savings may appear low compared to those being achieved by some U.S. local governments. However, the English savings are nationwide, and as a result the total level of saving is substantial.

VOLUNTARY COMPETITIVE TENDERING (VCT)

A number of local governments decided to contract out white- and blue-collar services in advance of the national legislation. One of the main reasons for doing this was to avoid the bureaucracy of compulsory systems. One example of a

TABLE 12.3.   City of Westminster's Contracting Program (December 1992)

Function	Total Budget before Contracting (in £s [~$1.6])	Annual % Saving
Finance		
Printing	400,000	8.8
Staff catering	410,600	5.6
Building cleaning	546,820	14.8
Payroll	292,600	7.7
Sundry debtors	90,435	16.2
Vehicle maintenance	605,200	40.8
Mech. and elec. maintenance	1,122,000	15.5
Material supply	659,403	39.4
Facilities management of buildings	1,667,000	8.6
Investment portfolio	410,500	32.6
Facilities management of IT	7,771,500	20.3
subtotal	13,976,058	20.3
Social services		
Establishment cleaning	253,905	+ 22.5
Transport	259,464	45
Day nurseries cleaning	265,300	40
subtotal	778,669	22
Housing		
Estates ground maintenance	327,400	4.2
Estates cleaning	2,173,000	+40.5
Home-ownership service	626,000	52
Responsive repairs	4,000,000	8.8
Estate cleaning (different estates to the item covered earlier)	1,368,702	16.5
subtotal	8,495,102	1.8

local government, that went down the VCT route is the City of Westminster in the heart of London. Table 12.3 provides details of its extensive contracting program.

Since 1992, Westminster has continued to expand its program and make substantial savings. Two areas of service have subsequently been subject to VCT: white-collar services such as legal and financial services, and a range of social service functions. Other notable features of the Westminster approach include:

TABLE 12.3.   *(continued)*

Function	Total Budget before Contracting (in £s [~$1.6])	Annual % Saving
Education and Leisure		
School cleaning	752,450	18
Sports grounds	675,300	23
School catering	2,550,120	20
Leisure centers	2,906,600	15
Special-needs transport	259,464	+77.3
subtotal	7,143,934	14.5
Planning and Transportation		
On-street parking	6,138,400	20
Grounds maintenance and patrolling services	1,544,560	4
Multidisciplinary project team	1,929,800	10
subtotal	9,612,760	15
Environmental Services		
Refuse collection and street cleansing	14,572,300	18
Public conveniences	1,465,500	33
Waste transfer and salvage baling	834,268	41
subtotal	16,872,068	20
Managing Director		
Communications Group	490,600	5
Legal Services		
Civil litigation	342,100	12
Total	57,221,181	15.6

Source: Westminster City Council, December 1992.

—Only five of the 32 contracts were awarded under the CCT regime; the remainder were done on a voluntary basis.

—Only five contracts were won by in-house teams.

—Two of the contracts were won by MBOs, the most significant being the refuse-collection and street-cleansing contract.

RELATED DEVELOPMENTS

There are a number of changes closely related to CCT that have had a major impact on English local governments. These are:

- *Education reform.* Under the 1988 Education Reform Act, all but a few schools are now managed locally (LM schools). In practice this means that they have delegated powers over staffing and financial management, with a very limited role for the parent local government. The local government also has to distribute resources to schools on the basis of a formula, with the number of pupils attending the school being the main criterion for attracting resources. Local governments can retain a small percentage (no greater than 7% of the total schools budget) for support services and other initiatives. A second development has been the introduction of grant maintained (GM) schools. Unlike LM schools, these receive their funding direct from the national government and get the full 100% of the budget as no money is held back. Schools can become GM following a ballot among parents. One of the effects of LM and GM has been to encourage the development of a market for educational support services such as school meals, cleaning, personnel, and information systems support. Local governments have set up in-house arms'-length support services to supply services to LM schools on a payment basis, with the budget for support services devolved to schools as part of the formula. Some local governments have also begun to supply services to GM schools.

- *Transfers of council housing to housing associations.* Throughout the 1980s, the national government encouraged the development of housing associations as providers of low-rent social housing. This was a role traditionally provided by local governments and many local governments, had very large housing stocks. The London Borough of Southwark, for example, had over 50,000 rented properties, while the city of Leeds had well over 70,000 properties. Housing associations are nonprofit organizations that received their funding from a national agency called the Housing Corporation. The Conservative Government gradually diverted funding away from local governments to housing associations. At the same time, a number of local governments sold their housing stock to established or newly created housing associations. This involved transferring stock and tenants to a housing association in exchange for a capital receipt.

- *Community care.* The national government agreed to transfer funding from the national Department of Social Security to local government to recognize the change in responsibility for mentally ill people in the community. In future, local governments, not the health service, would be responsible for mentally ill people living in the community. As part of the transfer, the government required local governments to spend up to 85% of new moneys in the independent sector—that is, the for-profit and nonprofit sectors. This has led to a substantial increase in contracting in social services.

- *Market testing in central government.* National government departments and agencies have had to go through a regime similar to CCT in the 1990s. The framework has been more flexible, but the net effect has been similar—more support services being contracted to the private sector and extensive public/private competition. For example, in Her Majesty's Custom and Excise Department approximately 5,000 of the 25,000 staff in the department have been involved in market testing (CIPFA and Chief Executives' Forum, 1996). In this case, savings have averaged between 20–25% annually and the majority of bids

(90%) have been won in-house. In another example, the Benefits Agency, a huge organization with an operating spendiing of around $4 billion, market tested around $150 million of accommodation and office services. Overall, around 60% of contracts were won in-house and annual savings averaged 32% (CIPFA and Chief Executives' Forum, 1996).

- *The Private Finance Initiative(PFI).* This initiative was launched in November 1992 to encourage greater use of private sector capital and management for public services. A common application of PFI involves the private sector finding the capital to provide a public service facility such as a road, school, leisure center, or hospital and then running the facility for an agreed period. In return it receives an operating fee from the relevant public sector agency. This is sometimes called Design, Build, Finance and Operate (DBFO). In effect, it converts public sector capital requirements into revenue and extends private sector management of public services.

All of these developments have encouraged the development of a market for a wide range of public services. In addition, a number of the providers span all sectors—local governments, national government departments, and national government agencies.

EVALUATION OF THE ENGLISH EXPERIENCE

The English experience can be evaluated against the features of smart contracting:

—achieving positive consequences

—healthy competition

—challenging the status quo and thinking creatively

—comprehensive, corporate, and systematic approach

—careful preparation

—cutting red tape

—clean and independent contract management

—competent in service contracting

—customer-friendly approach.

1. *Achieving Positive Consequences*

This can refer either to savings or to increases in service standards and/or quality. Comprehensive evidence has shown that savings have been made, but they have been modest (Crossland et al., 1993; Szymanski & Jones, 1993; Walsh, 1991; Walsh & Davis, 1993). Moreover, there have been significant variations for the same service from local governments even in areas where the same contractors operate. One of the prime reasons for the variation is the degree to which a local government favors or opposes contracting. This strongly influences whether outside contractors will mount a bid, and this in turn affects the in-house bid (i.e., they will be under greater pressure to reduce costs if outside bids are being strongly encouraged by the local government).

2. *Healthy Competition*

This varies enormously by service area, geography, and local government. In general, competition tends to be highest in the south of England, where local governments are keen to encourage outside bids and for certain services where there are a number of contractors such as refuse collection, cleaning, and grounds maintenance. A number of local governments are not receiving any bids in new areas of CCT such as housing management, finance, and personnel services. One reason is that these are new areas where the market is weak and the contractors focus on those contracts where they are most likely to succeed.

Over time, however, markets have developed. Ten years ago, for example, there were no major contractors for the finance function, but now there are. CAPITA is one such example. The company was an offshoot of the public finance accountants. Today it is quoted on the London Stock Exchange, has a market value of around £250 million, and has contracts with numerous local governments, central government agencies and departments, as well as utility companies.

Figure 12.1 shows the average level of interest shown by contractors at each stage of the bidding process.

3. *Challenging the Status Quo and Thinking Creatively*

The author's impression based on practitioner and consultancy experience in the U.K. is that most local governments have been unimaginative in their approach to contracting. Most prefer to organize contracts, for example, on the basis of their historical organizational structures and highly prescribed specifications stressing inputs and work methods. However, there is a growing number of exceptions, such as facilities management contracts, wide-ranging professional services contracts, output specifications, and extensive use of customers in specifying and monitoring contracts. Table 12.4 shows some of the innovations.

4. *Comprehensive, Corporate, and Systematic Approach*

Overall, English local governments have adopted a corporate approach to competition. In part this has been forced on them by legislation. It was clear from the outset that a wide range of services would eventually fall within the scope of CCT, and therefore many authorities began preparations at a corporate

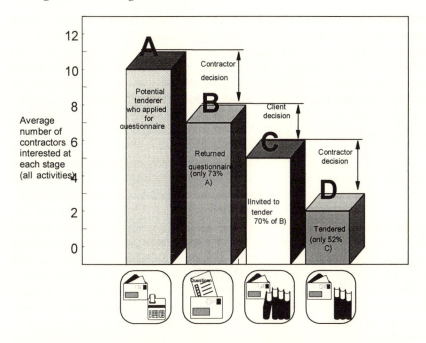

FIGURE 12.1.   Level of Contractor Interest in Bidding for Contracts (Audit Commission, 1993)

level. This meant, for example, restructuring the organization, both officers and politicians. Many local governments combined some or all of the in-house provider groupings that would be subject to CCT into Direct Labor or Service Organizations (DLOs and DSOs). Research for the Department of the Environment showed that a multipurpose DSO was the common approach for blue-collar functions (Walsh & Davis, 1993). A major reason was to achieve economies of scale. Less common was an integrated client or purchaser side for CCT functions, although it was found for functions such as cleaning and catering (Walsh & Davis, 1993). There were also some changes to the committee systems. Typically, local governments would establish a DSO committee composed of council members to oversee the work of the DSOs.

5. Careful Preparation

The experience here was more mixed. One of the problems that many local governments found was making the transition to competition too quickly. It was not uncommon for local governments to be restructuring the organization and running the bidding process concurrently. This created obvious problems. There was a great deal of uncertainty among staff on the provider and purchasing sides. More importantly, however, the client/purchasing side was often not prop-

TABLE 12.4.   Examples of Innovative Contracts

Contract	Approach
City of Nottingham—Street-Cleansing Contract	Moved away from methods-based contract to an output specification based on standards of cleanliness
City of Coventry—Street Contracts (covered refuse collection, street cleansing, grounds maintenance, lighting, and roads)	Made strenuous efforts to involve service users in the contracting process by: • publicizing the services and standards • developing a "one-stop shop" to provide information and record and deal with complaints about the services • varying the monitoring according to the standard of performance • rewarding contractors who perform well above standards by reducing the monitoring and sharing the savings with them • penalizing contractors financially who fall below the standards consistently.
London Borough of Brent — Revenue and Benefits Service	Used a partnership approach to the contract; this involved asking each bidder to specify its partnership proposals such as joint investments in the service, the use of "open-book" accounting to deal with variations in an open way, and sharing savings from value-for-money improvements. The multinational corporation EDS won the contract with a plan to improve the service with new technology, joint working with the council, and a range of secondments.

Source: CIPFA, 1996.

erly in place and the expertise typically resided in the provider grouping. As a result, local governments were determining their contract strategies and managing the process with a weak client. This meant that preparations were often dominated by the provider side. It is also one of the reasons why so many contracts were won by DSOs initially and why savings were modest. Since the early CCT experience, the client side has strengthened considerably (Audit Commission, 1993).

The legislation prescribed a common approach to the bidding process, as follows:

—*Publication of notice*:   A notice is placed in the press, including the *European Journal*.

—*Expression of interest*:   Bidders register an interest in the contract without making any commitment.

—*Questionnaire and outline details*:   Bidders complete details of their track record and financial standing.

—*Formal notification of interest*:   Each bidder decides formally whether or not to submit a bid.

—*Invitation to tender*:   Bidders receive a formal invitation to bid, which includes the service specification and contract conditions.

—*Tender submission*:   A sealed bid is submitted.

—*Evaluation and award*:   The local government compares the bids against its criteria and selects one bid.

—*Start*:   The successful bidder begins work.

Maximum and minimum periods of each stage of the process were also prescribed to prevent an approach favoring DSOs. One of the advantages of a clear and explicit approach was that it was fair and known to all parties— contract management, the DSO, and outside bidders.

Another problem was the lack of good management information both on expenditure and service (Walsh & Davis, 1993). In preparing the specification, the contract management function often had to rely on poor financial informa- tion which could not, for example, break down expenditure by activities. In many cases, detailed information on current service levels was not available. As a result, DSO staffs were often better informed than the contract management function. This inevitably benefited them in the first round of bidding.

6.   *Cutting Red Tape*

The CCT system is clearly bureaucratic. If a local government has an in-house bid, it has to follow a battery of rules and regulations. This is why some of the local governments keen on contracting have adopted a VCT as opposed to CCT route or simply outsource a function without having an in-house bid. The CCT regime is designed to provide a level playing field for contractors bidding for work against DSOs in local governments who want their DSOs to win the contract.

The legislation and regulations attempt to prevent such anticompetitive behavior, but this has the effect of making the system more cumbersome. Table 12.5 lists some of the ways that local governments do frustrate the aims of CCT.

7.   *Clean and Independent Contract Management*

The CCT legislation has encouraged an organizational split between the pur- chasing and providing functions within the local government (see Figure 12.2). A survey by the Audit Commission in 1992 (Audit Commission, 1993) found the following arrangements:

TABLE 12.5.   Anticompetitive Behavior

Examples of Anticompetitive Behavior

---

1. Select a service for CCT where there are few potential providers
2. Package work to make it unattractive to the private sector (e.g., grouping dissimilar services together)
3. Produce a very detailed specification that gives the contractor very little room for maneuver
4. Make it clear that the local government would adopt a hostile attitude to the contractor

---

   Source: CIPFA, 1996.

- Leisure management and refuse collection tend to have a single department as the purchasing function

- Building cleaning, vehicle maintenance, and grounds maintenance tend to be carried out by a central department or a lead department on behalf of the rest of the organization. This is called the client–agent role.

Whatever the arrangement, the DSO has to operate at arm's length from the purchasing function. Moreover, the legislation requires that the DSO be treated just as any other bidder.

The number of cases of contracting fraud in English local government is very low. The results of a recent study by the Audit Commission are shown in Table 12.6. Clearly, it is difficult to identify corruption. Nevertheless, the number of known cases is low, and there has been no increase in cases despite a significant increase in the amount of contracting during the 1990s.

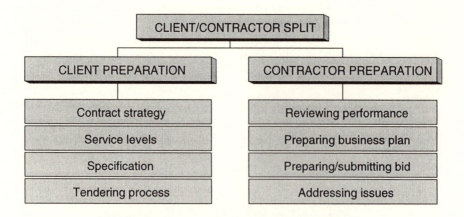

FIGURE 12.2.   The Client/Contractor Split

TABLE 12.6.   Contract Corruption, 1990–1996 (number of cases)

1990/91	*1991/92*	*1992/93*	*1993/94*	*1994/95*	*1995/96*
12	15	20	15	15	11

Source: Audit Commission, 1996.

8.   *Competent in Service Contracting*

Overall, local governments developed sound contract management functions within a short time. However, given the speed of the change there were inevitably teething problems. The Audit Commission (1993) highlighted these as follows:

—poorly defined and overdefined specifications

—unenforceable contract conditions

—inadequate tender-evaluation procedures

—inefficient contract monitoring

—bureaucratic contract administration.

There were significant variations in the quality and cost of the client side. Table 12.7 shows the variations on the cost side.

TABLE 12.7.   The Cost of the Client Side

Activity	Average total cost as % of total annual expenditure	Lower Quartile	Upper Quartile
Catering (education and welfare)	1.4%	0.6%	2.1%
Leisure management	1.5%	0.6%	1.7%
Other catering	1.8%	1.0%	2.7%
Refuse collection	3.8%	2.4%	5.6%
Building cleaning	4.4%	1.8%	5.4%
Other cleaning	5.6%	3.5%	7.3%
Ground maintenance	5.7%	3.4%	7.1%
Vehicle maintenance	12.5%	6.5%	16.7%

Source: Audit Commission, 1993.

9. *Customer-Friendly Approach*

Overall, local governments viewed contracts from a technical perspective. Most did not think about service users a great deal, and even fewer involved the latter in setting specifications and monitoring performance. This has begun to change, however, in at least two ways:

—setting up systems to monitor and act upon customer complaints

—consulting customers on service requirements (this has been a key feature, for example, of management contracts for housing estates).

SOME LESSONS FOR THE U.S.

The Case for Public/Private Competition

Public/private competition has a number of advantages over traditional contracting out:

- *Motivates employees*—public sector employees have the opportunity to win the work.

- *Helps develop markets*—the English example shows how contracting policies can influence and shape the marketplace.

- *Promotes business practices*—the English in-house teams soon started learning from the private sector. This meant that many of the benefits of competition were realized even if the bid was won in-house.

- *Produces good results*—in-house bids are just as efficient as private sector bids.

- *Provides continuity*—clearly this helps ensure a smooth transition if the same management and staff are involved.

The Public/Private Competition Tool Set

Six areas in particular may be of interest:

- *Organizational separation and "Chinese Walls."* The starting point for public/private competition is to separate the contract management function from the in-house contractor. This involves accounting for the contractor as a separate entity. In England, this is called a "trading account." It also involves organizational separation. Finally, it requires that the in-house contractor be treated in the same way as any other bidder. So, for example, the in-house contractor cannot receive any privileged information and must submit the bid at the same time and in the same format as the other bidders.

- *The issue of "twin-hattedness."* This is about the appropriate level for separating contract management from in-house contractors. An increasing number of English cities and counties, especially the larger ones, are separating the contract managers from the in-house contractors at the highest level possible, to minimize the dangers of conflicts of interest. This means avoiding "twin-hattedness," where both functions are under the same Service Director. Sometimes the separation even affects elected officials, with one committee responsible for contract management issues and another looking after the in-house contractor.

- *Devolution.* Many local governments have given their in-house contractors greater freedom to enable them to compete. For example, financial, personnel, and procurement rules are being relaxed so that in-house contractors can behave more like commercial firms. Some in-house contractors have even renegotiated employee terms and conditions to stay competitive. This has meant departing from the national bargaining system.

- *Employee participation.* Bids by local governments are prepared by the managers of the relevant team. Experience shows that managers who involve their staff in the process prepare the best bids.

- *No more business-as-usual.* In-house contractors cannot rely on winning the contract by bidding on the basis of how things have always been done. They have to rethink how they operate, such as work methods and the use of technology. It also means asking tough questions about whether they can win with existing numbers of staff, pay, and conditions.

- *Costing of services.* There is a systematic approach to the costing of in-house bids, with care being taken to minimize the amount of overheads. Indeed, every local government has by law to prepare a statement of support-service costs for external scrutiny.

- *Preventing in-house low-balling.* In-house contractors must meet financial objectives set by the national government, currently a rate of return of 6% on capital employed. This measure helps prevent internal low-balling.

Planned Approach Rather than Piecemeal Development

Another feature of the English approach is the heavy stress on planning. The structure of the organization has been fundamentally changed in many local governments at both council-member and officer level, for example. There have also been significant changes to information systems and terms and conditions.

Employee Protection

The most controversial aspect of CCT has been whether and to what extent employees affected by CCT should receive a measure of protection. In the early years of CCT, where an in-house team lost its bid against an outside contractor most, but not all, of the displaced personnel would be taken on by the new employer, usually with changed (often reduced) pay and conditions. However, there would usually be a shortfall, as the main area for savings has been reduced staffing. Local governments would do their best to redeploy staff, but some layoffs were needed, especially where a large contract, such as trash collection, was involved.

In the last two years, the issue of employment protection has moved to the top of the agenda as a result of European Community (EC) legislation. The EC directive on "Acquired Rights" was passed to protect employees affected by company takeovers. As a result of a number of court decisions, it became apparent that the directive could apply to contracting out by local governments in certain situations. Where it does, employee numbers and terms and conditions have to be protected for a "reasonable" period of time. This has resulted in a drop-off of private sector interest in contracting because it means that contractors' ability to make savings would be more limited. They would have to take on all staff who want to transfer over and would have to protect their pay and benefits for a reasonable period, perhaps a year. They would also be responsible for lay-off costs of former local government staff.

CONCLUSIONS

English local governments have moved from being service-delivery organizations to "enabling councils" that arrange services through external and internal contractors. This transformation has occurred in less than ten years. It is difficult to see U.S. local governments being mandated to subject services provided by government employees to competitive bidding. Nevertheless, an increasing number of U.S. local governments are experimenting with public/private competition. They could learn some lessons from the other side of the Atlantic, especially the need for organizational separation, devolution, and systematic methods for evaluating the costs of government bids.

13

Conclusions

The aim of this book has been to show that management is the critical ingredient in determining where and how successful contracting will be. Chapters 7 and 12 showed that contracting for services that appear unsuitable can work in the right conditions. At the same time, services that are suitable for contracting can be badly managed. Great variations in the effectiveness of contracting were found. Perhaps the two extremes were Indianapolis and New York. These differences in performance are not accounted for by market conditions or the nature of the services but by culture, history, quality of management, and nature of the governmental system.

WHAT IS THE ROLE OF CONTRACTING?

Chapter 3 demonstrated that in-house provision remains the most popular method of delivering local government services. Contracting is the second most popular option. Contracting with other governments and nonprofits is the main approach for social services, while contracting with the private sector is the most common for public works and a few professional services such as legal advice. Intergovernmental agreements are used for services such as fire protection, police, and libraries, but in-house provision remains by far and away the most common approach.

In theory, those services that are easiest to contract out are tangible and easy to monitor and there are a number of potential providers who can do the work. In practice, these considerations do not explain the incidence of contracting very

well. They explain to an extent the incidence of contracting with the private
sector, but not contracting with nonprofits and other governments. Even in the
case of the private sector, however, the theory would encourage the expectation
that contracting would be the most popular service-delivery option where all
three conditions are in place. In fact, this is not the case, as in-house is the most
popular method of delivering public works services, even trash collection. Contracting with nonprofits has been more driven by politics, whereas contracting
with other governments is often an attempt to achieve economies of scale for
services where there are few if any alternative providers.

Another key finding of the book is that a local government somewhere at
some time has contracted out every service. Even core professional services
such as planning, legal advice, and key public services such as fire protection
have been and are being contracted out. Moreover, some of these contracts work
well for the local governments concerned (see Chapters 7 and 12).

The case studies and evidence in this book demonstrate clearly that contracting can be a superior way of delivering public services. The Indianapolis, Cali-
fornian contract cities, and Scottsdale examples all show that contracting
delivers good value for money without damaging service quality. However,
other cases show that there are major risks in contracting and, as a result, the
potential is not always realized. This was clearly an issue in New York and
Baltimore.

Another issue relates to which services are contracted out. U.S. local governments have generally been reluctant to outsource support services. This is less
the case in England, where a number of local governments have contracted out
financial services, personnel support, and legal advice on a competitive basis.
Indeed, contracting for support services is now part of the mandatory system of
competition in England. There should be questions about the wisdom of making
contracting mandatory for such services, but it is beyond doubt that such contracting can work well in many cases. This was also demonstrated by the
Milwaukee case study in Chapter 11. There are a number of advantages to
contracting for support services. First, it can help the local government focus on
the strategic issues rather than get lost in the minutiae of finance and personnel
administration. Second, it provides an opportunity to make sure that support
services become more user-focused. Third, it can produce savings. However,
one of the lessons from the English experience is the risk of creating a contracting bureaucracy with too many small contracts for services where there are few
alternative providers to government employees.

If they are to secure the benefits, local governments therefore need to think
carefully about how they do contracting.

WHAT ARE THE MOST EFFECTIVE STRATEGIES?

A Strategic Approach

Few U.S. local governments think about contracting—and, indeed, alternative methods of service delivery—in a strategic way. This is a key weakness. It means that decisions are often made in a piecemeal way without fully exploring all of the options. As a result, contracting is often unimaginative as it replicates some of the worst features of in-house provision. For example, contracts often mirror the local government's existing organizational structure and old standards and have strict rules over how the service is delivered (see Chapters 5, 9, and 10). Contracting a service out provides an opportunity for a fresh approach and it is important to use the approach, to encourage some innovation in how the service is delivered (Chapter 6). Indianapolis was the local government that stood out as an example of best practice here. The administration had examined a wide range of services provided by the city and looked at a range of alternatives, not just contracting. Local governments across the U.S. would do well to follow the systematic approach adopted by Indianapolis.

Public/Private Competition

Public/private competition is rare in the U.S. yet there is a compelling case for doing it on a much larger scale for a wide range of services. First, it is more motivating for employees than straightforward outsourcing. They have a chance to show the local government what they can do. Second, it can produce good results. This is well demonstrated in Chapters 8 and 12. Third, it can have an impact across the government. This is because the process forces the in-house bidders to change the way they operate, dropping many of the traditional government methods in favor of a more businesslike approach. Such reforms soon catch on elsewhere in the organization. This was clearly the case in England. Public/private competition there was applied to public works functions first. It did not take long for the in-house providers to start questioning the level, quality, and cost of the support services that they were getting. This led to contracting systems with the support services.

However, public/private competition needs to be handled in a sensible way. First of all, a level playing field needs to be in place. This affects the costs that are included in the in-house bid, but also the process: all bidders should be treated equally. Second, a strong contract management function needs to be established. Otherwise there is a risk that the contracting process (the specification and monitoring) will be dominated by the provider, because that is where the expertise rests. Finally, the local government should relax the organizational rules under which the in-house provider operates. Without this relaxation, the room for maneuver will be limited and the ability to innovate and improve efficiency and effectiveness will be equally limited.

It was clear from the international comparison that the infrastructure for managing public/private competition is much more advanced in the U.K.

Intergovernmental Agreements

Chapter 7 showed that contracting with other governments could improve value for money significantly. This is because larger governments can achieve economies of scale. Contracting by a small government with a large government can therefore achieve central administration with local control. However, there were significant accountability problems where special districts were used rather than the contracting model. This is because special districts are remote public bodies governed by supervisors who are elected by literally hundreds of thousands of voters.

Secure Foundations

A vital ingredient for successful contracting—and for effective service delivery generally—is good information on current costs and performance. In the absence of good information, it is nigh impossible to make sensible decisions about make or buy, yet this is precisely what many local governments have done. This can result in the wrong decision either way—contracting out a service resulting in higher costs, or keeping an expensive service in-house because not all of the relevant costs were included in the original assessment. Poor information on service performance will make it difficult to produce an intelligent service specification, and it will also make contract management problematic.

The best ways to avoid these problems are activity-based costing and performance indicators. Activity-based costing provides a true cost of services, including all of the relevant overheads. It may also help a local government avoid changing the service-delivery method as it could pinpoint some obvious ways of increasing efficiency within current arrangements. Performance indicators provide a measure of service standards. Ideally the local government should have a balance of measures that cover inputs, outputs, and outcomes. Such performance indicators are indispensable in managing contracts.

Careful Packaging

A strong lesson for English local governments is the need for a more flexible approach to contract packaging. Too many local governments transfer a public monopoly to a private monopoly. Greater use of partial and multiple contracting as practiced by many U.S. local governments would avoid monopoly situations arising. This approach would also allow many more small and medium-sized firms compete for local government work.

On the U.S. side, local governments should be much more wary of "pepperpot" contracting. This requires a strategic approach to packaging of contracts, but also means that the organizational implications of changing service delivery should be taken into account. When a large number of services are contracted out, the local governments structure will need to be streamlined to reduce overhead costs and to establish a strong, independent contract management function(s).

Strong Contract Management

Contract management in most local governments is weak. The evidence is clear-cut—weak specifications and minimalist monitoring. The cause, however, is an underdeveloped contract management function. It is vital that staff are assigned to the contract management function before any contracting work begins. It is also important that these staff have status within the organization and receive appropriate training. Where a local government is using public/private competition, it will be necessary to split the contract management function from the in-house bidder to avoid any conflict of interest and to ensure that expertise is developed on the purchasing side.

Purchasing professionals have an important contribution to make to the contract management function. Unfortunately, in too many local governments their role is one of administrative oversight rather than adviser. Moreover, their role is often restricted to traditional contracting for goods and services rather than the contracting-out of in-house services.

WHICH CONTRACTING PROCESSES ARE MOST APPROPRIATE?

The book showed that contrary to conventional wisdom a great deal of local government contracting is noncompetitive. There is a case for noncompetitive contracting where, for example, it is important to establish a partnership with the provider. This is true of professional services, for example, where the local government is looking to the contractor to recommend innovations. However, it is less appropriate for straightforward contracts in the public works arena. There is a major risk that noncompetitive contracting here replicates some of the worst excesses of in-house provision.

A second lesson is the need for a streamlined contracting process that devolves responsibility to the managers responsible for the service and keeps oversight to a minimum. This makes contracting with government more attractive to contractors. It also promotes a sense of personal ownership among the local government managers. They do, of course, need to be held responsible for the latter—councils should regularly scrutinize the performance of contractors and the management by staff. Finally, a streamlined approach increases the speed of contract award and reduces the cost of the process.

In the U.K. Commonwealth countries, mandatory systems of contracting have been introduced for a wide range of local government services. Should a similar system be adopted in the U.S.? Such an approach would break with the U.S. tradition of state governments permitting a measure of independence at local level. Indeed, it is probably not a practical proposition, given the U.S. tradition. There would be benefits, however—savings, a more systematic approach to contracting, and the development of a markets for a wide variety of services. It also needs to be recognized that the English model was a response to a very different situation to the one that exists in the U.S. First, the local governments are much larger. They also traditionally provide most services in-house. Finally, because people are less mobile, there is not the amount of competition between local governments for taxpayers ("voting with their feet"). Moreover, the English experience has produced problems. Most significantly, because most councils oppose the system, there is a constant battle between national and local governments. This results in very detailed legislation that greatly restricts flexibility. It also means that much of the energy is channeled into gamesmanship between local and national governments.

WHO SHOULD DO THE CONTRACTING?

Contract management in the broadest sense is highly politicized in many local governments. This needs to change if contracting is to be truly effective. It needs to be professionalized. This will be difficult in mayor councils, especially those with a tradition of partisan politics. It also means that many more day-to-day decisions need to be delegated to professional managers rather than to politicians. This is not a straightforward process, and it is likely that the decision-making process will need to be reengineered.

References and Bibliography

ACIR (1989). *Residential Community Associations: Private Governments in the Intergovernmental System?* Washington, DC: Advisory Commission on Intergovernmental Relations.

AFSCME (1990). *Annotated Bibliography on Privatization* (unpublished briefing paper).

AFSCME (1993a). AFSCME Fights the Privateers. *The Public Employee Magazine*, 58 (4) (May/June), 4–15.

AFSCME (1993b). *So What's Wrong with Contracting Out?* (unpublished briefing paper.

AFSCME (1994). *Government for Sale. An Examination of the Contracting Out of State and Local Government Services* (4th edition). Washington, DC.

Ahlbrandt, R. (1973). Efficiency in the Provision of Fire Services. *Public Choice*, 16.

Alchian, A. A., & Demsetz, H. (1972). Production, Information Costs, and Economic Organization. *American Economic Review*, 62, 777–795.

American Bar Association (1979). *The Model Procurement Code for State and Local Governments.* Washington, DC.

Armington, R. Q., & Ellis, W. D. (Eds.) (1984). *This Way Up: The Local Official's Handbook for Privatization and Contracting Out.* Chicago, IL: Regnery Gateway.

Arrow, K. J. (1985). The Economics of Agency. In: J. W. Pratt & R. J. Zeckhauser (Eds.), *Principals and Agents: The Structure of Business.* Boston, MA: Harvard Business School Press.

Audit Commission (1993). *Realising the Benefits of Competition: The Client Role for Contracted Services.* London: HMSO Publications.

Audit Commission (1996). *Protecting the Public Purse: Ensuring Probity in Local Government.* Abingdon, Oxon: Audit Commission Publications.

Barzelay, M. (1992). *Breaking through Bureaucracy.* Berkeley, CA: University of California.

Beales, J. R., & O'Leary, J. (1993). *Making Schools Work: Contracting Options for Better Management.* Los Angeles, CA: Reason Foundation.

Beales, J. R. (1994). *Doing More with Less: Competitive Contracting for School-Support Services.* Los Angeles, CA: Reason Foundation.

Bennett, J. T., & Johnson, M. H. (1981). *Better Government at Half the Price: Private Production of Public Services.* Ottawa, IL: Caroline House.

Borcherding, T. E., Pommerehne, W. W., & Schneider, F. (1982). *Comparing the Efficiency of Private and Public Production: The Evidence from Five Countries.* Zurich: Institute for Empirical Research in Economics, University of Zurich.

Bradley, R. (1995). Downtown Renewal: The Role of Business Improvement Districts. *Public Management* (February), 9–13.

Byrners, P., Grosskopf, S., & Hayes, K. (1986). Efficiency and Ownership: Further Evidence. *Review of Economics and Statistics, 68.*

California Contact Cities Association (n.d.). *1954–1991 An Historical Review* (unpublished). Los Angeles, CA.

California Contact Cities Association (1989). *Information Bank on Contract Service Providers* (unpublished). Los Angeles, CA.

California Tax Foundation (1981). *Contracting Out Local Governmental Services in California.* Sacramento, CA.

Chi, K. S. (1994). Privatization in State Government: Options for the Future, *State Trends Forecasts.* Lexington, KY: The Council for State Governments.

CIPFA and Chief Executives' Forum (1996). *Achieving Value for Money through Competition. 27 Case Studies of CCT/Market Testing Experience in Great Britain.* Belfast, Northern Ireland: CIPFA.

City of Indianapolis (1995). *The Indianapolis Experience. A Small Government Prescription for Big City Problems* (unpublished).

City of Milwaukee (1993). *Internal Service Improvement Project (ISIP) Implementation* (unpublished).

City of New York (1992a). *Contracting Guide. A "How To" for Small Business Owners.* City of New York Department of Business Services.

City of New York (1992b). *No More Business as Usual: Keeping City Contracts out of the Hands of Dishonest Contractors.* Report of the Comptroller (September).

City of New York (1992c). *Procurement Improvement Initiative Report.* Report of the Mayor's Office of Contracts, the Procurement Policy Board and the Mayor's Office of Operations (March).

City of New York (1993a). *Procurement Improvement Initiative: 1993 Interim Report.* Report of the Mayor's Office of Contracts (April).

City of New York (1993b). *Statistical Summary Supplement to the Comptroller's Comprehensive Annual Contracts Report for the Fiscal Year ended June 1993.* Office of the Comptroller.

City of New York (1993c). *Stormy Seas: "A Ship Without a Captain" Four Years*

Later. Report of the Executive Director to the NYC Procurement Policy Board (22 October).

City of New York (1994a). *Executive Budget Fiscal Year 1995* (November).

City of New York (1994b). *Guidelines For Public/Private Competition.* Mayor's Office (September).

City of New York (1994c). *Procurement Policy Board Rules* (1 September 1991, with updates until October).

City of New York (1994d). *Procurement SWAT Team Summary of Results.* Report of the Mayor's Office of Operations (July).

City of Phoenix (n.d.). *Public/Private Competitive Process Overview.* City Auditor's Department (unpublished).

City of Scottsdale (1991). *Contract with the Rural/Metro Corporation* (unpublished).

Cohen, M. D., March, J. G., & Olsen, J. P. (1972). A Garbage Can Model of Organizational Choice. *Administrative Science Quarterly, 17* (1), 1–25.

Collins, J. & Downes, B. (1977). The Effects of Size on the Provision of Public Services: The Case of Solid Waste Collection in Smaller Cities. *Urban Affairs Quarterly, 12* (3), 333–347.

Community Associations Institute (1993). *Community Associations Factbook* (1993 edition). Alexandria, VA.

County of Los Angeles Chief Administrative Office (1977). *Los Angeles County Contract Services Program* (unpublished).

County of Los Angeles, Fire Department (1994). *Agreement for Services between the Consolidated Fire Protection District of Los Angeles and the City of Pomona, and Annexation of City to District.*

County of Los Angeles, Fire Department (1995). *Proposal for the Consolidated Fire Protection District of Los Angeles to Provide Fire Protection, Hazardous Materials, and Emergency Medical Services for the City of Hawthorne.*

County of Los Angeles, Sheriff's Department (1991a). *City of Bell Gardens Police Service Proposal 1991.*

County of Los Angeles, Sheriff's Department (1991b). *City of Hermosa Beach Police Service Proposal 1991.*

County of Los Angeles, Sheriff's Department (1991c). *City of Long Beach Police Service Proposal 1991.*

CQ Researcher, The (1994). Special Issue on Private Management of Public Schools, *The CQ Researcher, 4* (12), 25 March, 267–273.

Crain, W. M., & Zardkoohi, A. (1978). A Test of Property Rights Theory of the Firm: Water Utilities in the United States. *Journal of Law and Economics, 21.*

Crossland, K., Halsall, P., Davis-Coleman, C., Jones, T., & Atkins, J. (1993). *Client Management and Refuse Collection Contracting.* London: CD.C Publishing.

Cushman, C. (1994a). *New York City Meets the Model Code: Lessons from Experience.* Unpublished.

Cushman, C. (1994b). *Professional Purchasing: A Catalyst for "Reinventing Government."* Unpublished.

Deacon, R. (1979). The Expenditure Effects of Alternative Public Supply Institutions. *Public Choice, 34*, 381–397.

De Hoog, R.H. (1984). *Contracting Out for Human Services. Economic, Political and Organization Perspectives.* Albany, NY: State University of New York Press.

Deloitte and Touche (1994). *Reengineering The Procurement and Contract Management Process: Final Report for the City of New York* (16 June).

Department of the Environment (1994). *CCT and Local Government in England. Annual Report for 1994.* London: Department of the Environment.

Department of Housing and Urban Development (1983). *Public Housing Authority Experience with Private Management: A Comparative Study.* Washington, DC: Office of Policy Development and Research.

De Tocqueville, A. (1981). *Democracy in America.* New York: Random House.

Dilulio, J. J. Jr (Ed.) (1994). *Deregulating the Public Service: Can Government Be Improved?* Washington, DC: Brookings Institution.

Dilulio, J. J. Jr., Garvey, G., & Kettl, D. F. (1993). *Improving Government Performance: An Owner's Manual.* Washington DC: Brookings Institution.

Donahue, J. D. (1989). *The Privatization Decision.* New York: Basic Books.

Donlevy, J. W. (1994). *Intergovernmental Contracting for Public Services.* Reason Foundation "How To Guide." Los Angeles, CA: Reason Foundation.

Dow, G. K. (1987). The Function of Authority in Transaction Cost Economics. *Journal of Economic Behavior and Organization, 8,* 13–38.

Eagleton Institute of Politics (1986). *Alternative Methods for Delivering Public Services in New Jersey.* New Brunswick, NJ: Rutgers University.

Education Alternatives, Inc. (n.d.). *A Public–Private Partnership That Works* (unpublished). Baltimore, MD.

Eggers, W. D. (1993). *Designing a Comprehensive State Level Privatization Program.* Reason Foundation "How To Guide." Los Angeles, CA: Reason Foundation.

Eggers, W. D. (1994). *Competitive Government for a Competitive Los Angeles.* Los Angeles, CA: Reason Foundation.

Eggers, W. D., & Ng, R. (1993). *Social and Health Service Privatization: A Survey of County and State Governments.* Los Angeles, CA: Reason Foundation.

Feigenbaum, S., & Teeples, R. (1982). Public versus Private Water Delivery: A Hedonic Cost Approach. *Review of Economics and Statistics.* Claremont, CA: Claremont Graduate School.

Feigenbaum, S., Teeples, R., & Glyer, D. (1986). Public versus Private Water Delivery: Cost Comparisons. *Public Finance Quarterly, 14.*

Feldman, R. D., & Ingoldsby, T. M. (1993). *Techniques for Mining the Public Balance Sheet.* Reason Foundation "How To Guide." Los Angeles, CA: Reason Foundation.

Ferris, J. M. (1988). The Public Spending and Employment Effects of Local Service Contracting. *National Tax Journal, 41* (2), 207–217.

Ferris, J. M., & Graddy, E. (1986). Contracting Out: For What ? With Whom? *Public Administration Review, 46,* 332–344.

Ferris, J. M., & Graddy, E. (1988). The Production Choices for Local Government Services. *Journal of Urban Affairs, 10,* 273–289.

Ferris, J. M., & Graddy, E. (1991). Production Costs, Transaction Costs, and Local Government Contractor Choice. *Economic Inquiry,* 541–554.

Florestano, P. S., & Gordon, S. B. (1980). Public vs Private: Small Government Contracting with the Private Sector. *Public Administration Review, 40,* 29–34.

Foldvary, F. (1995). *Public Goods and Private Communities: The Market Provision of Social Services.* Brookfield, VT: Edward Elgar.

Frazier, M. (1980). Privatizing the City. *Policy Review, 12* (Spring), 91–108.

Gillespie, E., & Schellhas, B. (Eds) (1994). *Contract with America. The Bold Plan by Newt Gingrich, Rep. Dick Armey and the House Republicans to Change the Nation.* New York: Random House.

Gillette, C. P. (1994). *Public Authorities and Private Firms as Providers of Public Goods.* Los Angeles, CA: Reason Foundation.

Gomez-Ibanez, J. A., & Meyer, J. R. (1993). *Going Private. The International Experience with Transport Privatization.* Washington, DC: Brookings Institution.

Guardiano, J. R., Haarmeyer, D., & Poole, R. W. Jr. (1992). *Fire-Protection Privatization: A Cost Effective Approach to Public Safety.* Los Angeles, CA: Reason Foundation.

Harney, D. F. (n.d.). *Privatization and Service Contracting in Arlington County, Virginia* (unpublished).

Harney, D. F. (1994). *Service Contracting: A Local Government Guide.* Washington DC: ICMA.

Hilke, J. (1993). *Cost Savings from Privatization: A Compilation of Findings.* Reason Foundation "How To Guide." Los Angeles, CA: Reason Foundation.

Hirsch, W. Z. (1965). Cost Functions of an Urban Government Service: Refuse Collection. *Review of Economics and Statistics, 47.*

Institute of Public Administration (1987). *Contracting in New York City Government. Final Report and Recommendations* (November).

International City/County Association (1989). *Service Delivery in the 90s: Alternative Approaches for Local Governments.* Washington, DC.

Jensen, R. W. (1987). *The Phoenix Approach to Privatization. Competition is the name of the Game.* Unpublished paper.

Johnston, M. (1982). *Political Corruption and Public Policy in America.* Monterey, CA: Brooks/Cole Publishing.

Kelman, S. (1990). *Procurement and Public Management. The Fear of Discretion and the Quality of Government Performance.* Washington, DC: AEI Press.

Kemper, P., & Quigley, J. M. (1976). *The Economics of Refuse Collection.* Cambridge, MA: Ballinger Publishing.

Kettl, D. F. (1993). *Sharing Power. Public Governance and Private Markets.* Washington, DC: Brookings Institution.

Kitchen, H.M. (1976). A Statistical Estimation of an Operating Cost Function for Municipal Refuse Collection. *Public Finance Quarterly, 4* (1), 56–76.

Kolderie, T. (1986). Two Different Concepts of Privatization. *Public Administration Review, 43* (4), 285–292.

Lavery, K. (1992). The "Council Manager" and "Strong Mayor" forms of Government in the USA. *Public Money and Management, 12* (2), 9–14.

Lavery, K. (1994). Local Government US Style. In: R. Hambleton & M. Taylor,

People in Cities. Bristol: School for Advanced Urban Studies, University of Bristol.

Lavery, K. (1995). Privatization by the Back Door: The Rise of Private Governments in the USA. *Public Money and Management, 15.*

Local Government Management Board CCT Information Service (1994). *Survey Report No 10.* London: LGMB (December).

Macauley, S. (1963). Non-Contractual Relations in Business: A Preliminary Study. *American Sociological Review, 28.*

Madison, J. (1961). *The Federalist Papers.* New York: New American Library (first published in 1788).

Mahtesian, C. (1994). Taking Chicago Private. *Governing Magazine,* April.

Marlin, J. T. (1984). *Contracting Municipal Services.* New York: Wiley.

Martin, L. (1993). *How to Compare Costs Between In-House and Contracted Services.* Reason Foundation "How To Guide." Los Angeles, CA: Reason Foundation.

Mayor's Private Sector Survey, The (1989). *The New York City Service Crisis: A Management Response.* City of New York (September).

McDavid, J. C. (1985). The Canadian Experience with Privatizing Residential Solid Waste Collection Services. *Public Administration Review, 45.*

McKenzie, E. (1994a). *Directions in Public Policy Regarding Residential Private Governments in the Intergovernmental System.* Unpublished paper presented to the Annual Meeting of the American Political Science Association, 1–4 September.

McKenzie, E. (1994b). *Privatopia: Homeowner Associations and the Rise of Residential Private Government.* New Haven, CT: Yale University Press.

Mehay, S. L., & Gonzalez, R. A. (1985). Economic Incentives under Contract Supply of Local Government Services. *Public Choice, 46.*

Melman, S. (1970). *Pentagon Capitalism.* New York: McGraw-Hill.

Miller, G. J. (1981). *Cities by Contract. The Politics of Municipal Incorporation.* Cambridge, MA: MIT.

Miranda, R., & Andersen, K. (1994). Alternative Service Delivery in Local Government, 1982–92. In: *Municipal Yearbook.* Washington, DC: International City/County Management Association.

Miranda, R., & Lerner, A. (1995). Bureaucracy, Organizational Redundancy, and the Privatization of Public Services. *Public Administration Review, 55* (2).

Moe, T. M. (1984). The New Economics of Organization. *American Journal of Political Science, 28,* 739–777.

Morley, E. (1989). Patterns in the Use of Alternative Service Delivery Approaches. *Municipal Yearbook.* Washington, DC: International City/County Management Association.

Morlok, E. K., & Moseley, F. A. (1986). *Potential Savings from Competitive Contracting of Bus Transit.* Philadelphia, PA: University of Pennsylvania, Department of Civil Engineering.

Morlok, E. K., & Viton, P.A. (1985). The Comparative Costs of Public and Private Providers of Mass Transit. In: C. A. Lave (Ed.), *Urban Transit.* San Francisco, CA: Pacific Institute.

Moulder, E. R. (1994a). *Privatization: Involving Citizens and Local Government*

Employees. Baseline Data Report, 26, 1. Washington, DC: International City/County Management Association.

Moulder, E. R. (1994b). *Public Works: Service Delivery Choices*, Special Data Issue. Washington, DC: International City/County Management Association.

National League of Cities (Ed.) (1993). Privatization: Contracting Local Government Services. *Issues and Options, 1*, 8.

National Performance Review (1993). *Creating a Government That Works Better and Costs Less.* Washington, DC: U.S. Government Printing Office.

Newfield, J., & Barrett W. (1988). *City for Sale. Ed Koch and the Betrayal of New York.* New York: Harper & Row.

Newman, O. (1980). *Community of Interest.* New York: Anchor Press/Doubleday.

New York Chamber of Commerce and Industry and New York City Partnership Privatization Task Force (1993). *Putting The Public First. Making New York Work through Privatization and Competition.*

New York State Commission on Government Integrity (1989). *A Ship Without a Captain: The Contracting Process in New York City.* Feerick Commission (December).

New York State Financial Control Board (1994). *Downsizing and Restructuring the FYs 1995–1998 Financial Plan* (July).

NIGP (1993). *1993 Survey of Procurement Practices.* Reston, VA: National Institute of Governmental Purchasing.

Niskanen, W. A. (1975). Bureaucrats and Politicians. *Journal of Law and Economics, 18,* 617–643.

Niskanen, W. A. (1991). The District of Columbia: America's Worst Government? *Policy Analysis, 165,* 18 November.

Office of Management and Budget (1984). *Enhancing Government Productivity through Competition: Targeting for Annual Savings of One Billion Dollars by 1988.* Washington, DC: Office of Federal Procurement Policy.

Osborne, D., & Gaebler, T. (1992). *Reinventing Government. How the Entrepreneurial Spirit is Transforming the Public Sector.* New York: Penguin Books.

Perry, J. L., & Babitsky, T. T. (1986). Comparative Performance in Urban Bus Transit: Assessing Privatization Strategies. *Public Administration Review, 46.*

Petrovic, W.M., & Jaffee, B.J. (1977). *Aspects of the Generation and Collection of Household Refuse in Urban Areas.* Bloomington, IN: Institute of Real Estate and Applied Urban Economics, Graduate School of Business, Indiana University.

Pirie, M. (1985). *Dismantling the State: The Theory and Practice of Privatization.* Dallas, TX: National Center for Policy Analysis.

Poole, R. W. Jr. (1980). *Cutting Back City Hall.* New York: Universe Books.

Prager, J. (1994). Contracting Out Government Services: Lessons from the Private Sector. *Public Administration Review, 54,* 2.

Putnam, R. D. (1993). The Prosperous Community: Social Capital and Public Life. *The American Prospect,* Spring, 35–42.

Putnam, R. D. (1995). Bowling Alone: America's Declining Social Capital. *Journal of Democracy, 6* (1) (January), 65–78.

Reason Foundation (n.d.). *Directory of Private Service Providers*. Los Angeles, CA.

Reason Foundation (1989). *SAVINGS ASAP: An Analysis of the City and County of Los Angeles*. Los Angeles, CA.

Reason Foundation (1994). *Privatization '94*. Los Angeles, CA.

Rehfuss, J. A. (1989). *Contracting Out in Government*. San Francisco, CA: Jossey Bass.

Rehfuss, J. A. (1993). *Designing an Effective Bidding and Monitoring System to Minimize Problems in Competitive Contracting*. Reason Foundation "How To Guide." Los Angeles, CA: Reason Foundation.

Ridley, N. (1988). *The Local Right. Enabling not Providing*. Policy Study No 92. London: Centre for Policy Studies.

Roads (1984). *ROADS Public Fleet Survey*, Roads, 22 (12).

Ross, S. A. (1973). The Economic Theory of Agency: The Principal's Problem. *American Economic Review*, *63*, 134–139.

Rothenberg Pack, J, (1989). BIDs, DIDs, SIDs, SADs: Private Government in Urban America. *Brookings Review*, *10*, Fall, 18–21.

Rural/Metro Corporation (1993). *Perspective on Progress. Scottsdale Rural/Metro Fire Department*. Scottsdale, AZ.

Rural/Metro Corporation (1994). *Annual Report July 1993—June 1994*. Scottsdale, AZ.

Sappington, D. E. M. (1991). Incentives in Principal–Agent Relationships. *Journal of Economic Perspectives*, *5* (2), 45–66.

Savas, E. S. (1979). How Much Do Government Services Really Cost? *Urban Affairs Quarterly*, *15* (1), September.

Savas, E. S. (1981). Intracity Competition Between Public and Private Service Delivery. *Public Administration Review* (January/February).

Savas, E. S. (1987). *Privatization. The Key to Better Government*. Chatham, NJ: Chatham House.

Savas, E. S. (1989–90). A Taxonomy of Privatization Strategies. *Policy Studies Journal*, *18* (2), 343–355.

Savas, E. S. (1992a). It's Time to Privatize. *Fordham Urban Law Journal*, *19* (3).

Savas, E. S. (1992b). Privatization and Productivity. In: M. Holzer (Ed.), *Public Productivity Handbook*. New York: Marcel Dekker.

Savas, E. S. (1993). Getting Around New York. *City Journal* (Summer), 57–65.

Savas, E. S., & Ginsberg, S. G. (1973). The Civil Service: A Meritless System? *The Public Interest, 32* (Summer), 70–85.

Smith, S. R., & Lisky, M. (1993). *Nonprofits for Hire: The Welfare State in the Age of Contracting*. Cambridge, MA: Harvard University Press.

Sorber Dean, K., & Straight, R. L. (1994). *Competitive Contracting Offices: Working Better, Costing Less*. Paper presented at the American Society for Public Administration's 55th National Training Conference, Kansas City, MO (23–27 July).

Stainback, J. (1993). *Designing a Comprehensive Privatization Program for Cities*. Reason Foundation "How To Guide." Los Angeles, CA: Reason Foundation.

Starr, P. (1987). *The Limits of Privatization*. Washington, DC: Economic Policy Institute.

State–City Commission on Integrity in Government (1986). *Report and Recommendations Relating to City Procurement and Contracts.* Sovern Commission (November).

Stein, R. (1990). *Urban Alternatives: Public and Private Markets in the Provision of Local Services.* Pittsburgh, PA: University of Pittsburgh Press.

Stevens, B. J. (Ed.) (1984). *Delivering Municipal Services Efficiently: A Comparison of Municipal and Private Service Delivery.* Washington, DC: HUD Office of Policy Development and Research.

Stevens, B. J., & Savas, E. S. (1977). The Cost of Residential Refuse Collection and the Effect of Service Arrangement. *Municipal Yearbook.* Washington, DC: International City Management Association.

Szymanski, S., & Jones, T. (1993). *The Cost Savings from Compulsory Competitive Tendering of Refuse Collection Services: A Statistical Analysis.* London: CD.C Publishing.

Teeples, R., & Glyer, D. (1987). Cost of Water Delivery Systems: Specification and Ownership Effects. *Review of Economics and Statistics, 69.*

Thayer, F. (1987). Privatization: Carnage, Chaos, and Corruption. In: B. J. Carroll, R. W. Conant, & T. A. Easton (Eds.), *Private Means—Public Ends.* New York: Praeger Publishing.

Thompson, F. J. (1993). *Revitalizing State and Local Public Service: Strengthening Performance, Accountability, and Citizen Confidence.* San Francisco, CA: Jossey Bass.

Todd, J. S. (1984). *A History of Lakewood 1949–1954* (unpublished in 1969; edited for the City of Lakewood's 30th Anniversary in 1984).

Touche Ross (1987). *Privatization in America.* New York: Touche Ross & Co.

University City Science Center (1989) *Fire and Emergency Medical Services Assessment, Scottsdale, Arizona* (unpublished report for the City of Scottsdale prepared by the University City Science Center, Philadelphia).

Walsh, K. (1991). *Competitive Tendering for Local Authority Services. Initial Experiences.* London: HMSO.

Walsh, K., & Davis, H. (1993). *Competition and Service: The Impact of the Local Government Act 1988.* London: HMSO.

Williamson, O. (1975). *Markets and Hierarchies.* New York: Free Press.

Williamson, O. (1981). The Economics of Organization: The Transaction Cost Approach. *American Journal of Sociology, 87* (3), 548–577.

Williamson, O., & Ouchi, W. (1981). The Markets and Hierarchies Program of Research: Origins, Implications, Prospects. In: A. Van de Ven & W. Joyce (Eds.), *Perspectives on Organization Design and Behavior.* New York: Wiley.

Wilson, J. Q. (1989). *Bureaucracy: What Government Agencies Do and Why They Do It.* New York: Basic Books.

Index

ABOUT THE AUTHOR

Kevin Lavery is currently the chief executive of the City of Newcastle upon Tyne in Great Britain. While doing research for this book, he was on a Harkness Fellowship at the School of Public Administration at the University of California in Los Angeles.

ISBN 0-275-96428-0

90000>

EAN

9 780275 964283

HARDCOVER BAR CODE